beast   that wicked   mystery of iniquity

THE SPIRIT
OF THE
ANTI-CHRIST

Little horn   peace & safety

man of sin   mystery babylon   son of perdition

king of fierce countenance

MINISTER ROBERT JOHNSON

ISBN 978-1-64258-881-1 (paperback)
ISBN 978-1-64258-896-5 (hardcover)
ISBN 978-1-64258-882-8 (digital)

Copyright © 2018 by Minister Robert Johnson

All rights reserved. No part of this publication may be reproduced, distributed, or transmitted in any form or by any means, including photocopying, recording, or other electronic or mechanical methods without the prior written permission of the publisher. For permission requests, solicit the publisher via the address below.

Christian Faith Publishing, Inc.
832 Park Avenue
Meadville, PA 16335
www.christianfaithpublishing.com

Printed in the United States of America

CONTENTS

Introduction 5

1. The dreams of King Nebuchadnezzar, Daniel and the Rise of the Mountains of the Babylonian, Medes/Persian, Greek, and Roman Empire 17

2. The Falling Away, He, The Rapture, The Man of Sin, and The Mystery of Iniquity 48

3. Strong Delusion, The Spirit of the A-C, and The Mystery of Iniquity 113

4. Prelude to the A-C, The two Witnesses, The Birth of Jesus, Israel, and War in Heaven 126

5. The A-C, Satan, and the False Prophet 151

6. Mystery Babylon 166

7. The return of Jesus Christ, the Kingdom of Jesus, and the Final Test 185

8. The Great White Throne Judgment 202

Glossary 221

INTRODUCTION

This is a scholarly work by a non-scholar written for those non-scholars interested in end-time events. I have studied The Word of The Most High for more than thirty years. I have made the following verse my life verse—"Study to show thyself approved unto God, a workman that needeth not to be ashamed, rightly dividing the word of truth" (2 Timothy 2:15). This is an accumulation of years of reading, studying, rereading and restudying The Word of my Father. This is not a rehash of other end times books.

I love history, with an interest in WWI, WWII, and the Cold War. I firmly believe scripture gives us spiritual insight into some historical facts. In high school, I studied the history of Alexander the Great and his four top generals who took over his empire after his death. Upon my salvation, I really started studying the Bible. I read about the leopard with four wings in Daniel 7:6 and the he-goat in Daniel 8:22. I saw this as a representation of Alexander the Great and his Grecian empire, and its division upon his death. We will discuss this in detail later.

The purpose of this book is first, to give full assurance to all saints that we can trust our Father's word: "I will worship toward thy holy temple, and praise thy name for thy loving-kindness and for thy truth: for thou hast magnified thy word above all thy name" (Psalm 138:2). Thus, The Most High God protects His word more than His name. His word, the Bible, is all we have. If we can't put absolute trust in every word contained in it, what, or who then can we trust? The second purpose is, to put the end times in a concise understandable format. A degree of higher learning is not needed to understand end times events. Third, I believe this is a prophetic warning to the saints to get ready, "Your redemption draws near."

"Surely the Lord God will do nothing but, he revealeth his secret unto his servants the prophets" (Amos 3:7). This is a warning from The Most High.

INTRODUCTION

"The secret things belong unto the Lord our God: but those things which are revealed belong unto us and to our children forever, that we may do all the words of this law" (Deuteronomy 29:29).

"Behold, the former things are come to pass, and new things do I declare: before they spring forth I tell you of them" (Isaiah 42:9). There are things The Most High wants us to understand concerning future events. It is up to us to research and study those events in His Bible.

I believe The Most High has given me the following: "That the God of our Lord Jesus Christ, the Father of glory, may give unto you the spirit of wisdom and revelation in the knowledge of him; The eyes of your understanding being enlightened; that ye may know what is the hope of his calling, and what the riches of the glory of his inheritance in the saints" (Ephesians 1:17-18). I am not a prophet nor am I the son of a prophet. "Then answered Amos, and said to am-a-zi-ah, I was no prophet neither was I a prophet's son; but I was a herdman, and a gatherer of sycamore fruit (wild figs): And the Lord took me as I followed the flock, and the Lord said unto me, Go, prophesy unto my people Israel" (Amos 7:14–15).

I was in the middle of writing another book and The Most High stopped me and told me to write this book. This was not on my agenda. But it is now. Many Christians believe prophecy is no more than mere fairy tales and wishful thinking. Noah was the only person who believed The Father was going to send a flood: "By faith Noah, being warned of God of things not seen as yet, moved with fear, prepared an ark to the saving of his house; by the which he condemned the world, and became heir of the righteousness which is by faith" (Hebrews 11:7). Don't put your faith in the number of others that believe, put it in The Most High.

We are going to look at the rise of a man who will be the personification of evil and diabolical wickedness. You will find this to be the most comprehensive, compelling and informative study of the end time ruler called the anti-christ (here after referred to as the a-c), his relationship to the Mystery of Iniquity, the spirit of the a-c, Mystery Babylon, and satan. We will look at the end-time events, which will bring him to power. We will also study the spiritual condition of the Church and how it relates to his infusion.

Anti means opposite of the real. The a-c will be the opposite of Christ. The title a-c is only mentioned four times in the Bible. All four references are found in the books of 1 and 2 John. The a-c is also referred to as; the little horn, the king of fierce countenance, the beast, and the king, these are in the book of Daniel. In 2 Thessalonians (Thess.) he is referred to as man of sin, son of perdition, and that Wicked. And in Revelations (Rev.), he is referred to as simply "the beast."

The mystery of iniquity and the spirit of the a-c and mystery Babylon are all evil forces that cannot be stopped by man. They now have full control of the unsaved world as decreed by The Most High God. They are using wicked devices and gimmicks to deceive the saints into joining this wickedness, thus naturalizing the saints into ineffectiveness. Prayer will hinder but will not stop them. More on this will be presented later, so don't label me a heretic yet.

Knowing who the a-c will be and how he comes to power does nothing for your salvation or going to heaven. However, knowing he will come to power, how he comes to power, and where he may come from should give greater confidence in The Word of our Father. It shows The Father's Bible is not a book of fables put here too confuse or entertain us: "We have also a more sure word of prophecy; whereunto ye do well that ye take heed, as unto a light that shineth in a dark place, until the day dawn, and the day star arise in your hearts" (2 Peter 1:19).

I do not know who the a-c is, nor exactly where he comes from, or when he comes to power. Jesus said; "And he said unto them, It is not for you to know the times or the seasons which the Father hath put in his own power"(Acts 1:7). Then Paul wrote; "But of the times and seasons, brethren, ye have no need that I write unto you" (1 Thess. 5:1). Jesus said; "An evil and adulterous generation seeketh after a sign: and there shall no sign be given to it, but the sign of the prophet Jonah" (Matthew (Matt.) 12:39). It is not our job to worry about the time or the season of our Savior's return. Our job is to watch, pray,

INTRODUCTION

share the gospel, and be ready by keeping ourselves un-spotted from the world.

This is not a work of fiction, nor is it speculation and conjecture. But biblical facts of things to come. There is logic to the working of our Father and we must study His word to find it. We cannot put Him in a box and say He will always work the same way, or in the same manner. He is sovereign and does not have to reveal anything to us. But, He has chosen to reveal many truths concerning the end time. It is our job to search the scriptures, pray, and let His Word and Spirit speak to us.

There is considerable speculation on the identity of the a-c. A well-known radio preacher said it will be Judas Iscariot, the betrayer of our Savior. But this cannot be, since Judas hung himself, died, and was buried (Matt. 27:3–5, Acts 1:16–19). The devil can't restore life to Judas's body, because satan is a created being; he is an imitator, and manipulator, but he is not a creator. Only The Creator with life giving force can give life to non-life: "And after three days and a half the spirit of life from God entered into them, and they stood upon their feet" (Rev. 11:11). The Father is the only one with life giving power. Judas (John 17:12) and the a-c (2 Thess. 2:3), both are referred to as "son of perdition" but this does not imply it will be Judas. Son of perdition is a state of ruin which they both will share.

As a created being, satan cannot read minds, be in more than one place at a time, nor can he know the future. If satan had the ability to know the future, he would have known Job would stand and not turn his back on The Most High. You can find this in the book of Job, chapters one, two and forty-two. satan does have fallen angels who report to him events in the world. More on this later.

Let me repeat; this book is not speculation on the a-c's identity. No one knows his identity except The Most High God. The a-c himself will not know what he will become until the right time for his infusion. But this one thing I do know: he will be the right man, for the right time, and the right people. Many men throughout history could have become the a-c, but it was not The Father's time. And for this reason, satan will not know who the a-c will be until the right time.

The a-c will rise in a manner as Hitler did. If you study the events leading to WW II, Hitler was the right man, for the right time, and the right people. Hitler was not a very smart individual, but he was cunning, charismatic, and smooth-talking. He was a terrible military/civilian leader and tactician. He mishandled the war as well as Germany's economy. He did have some capable men, but he refused to use or did not know how to use them.

The a-c will be the exact opposite. Why? Because the a-c will have access to satan's accumulated, wicked spiritual knowledge in dealing with mankind, starting from Adam. There will be no human secrets the a-c will not have access too. When something is spoken in secret the demonic forces hear, then report it to satan, who in turn will give the a-c the information he needs.

The following are questions I hope to answer in this book;

1. What is the spirit of the a-c and its relationship to the mystery of iniquity?
2. Is the a-c alive today?
3. Who controls him?
4. When will he come to power?
5. How will he rise to power?
6. Where does he get his power?
7. Will he control the whole earth?
8. What does the term "Falling away" means?
9. Will any oppose him?
10. Will he have a united kingdom?
11. What is the abomination of desolation?
12. What is the nature of his kingdom?
13. How will he interact with the Jews?
14. What is the Mystery of Iniquity?
15. Who or what is the great whore Mystery Babylon?
16. Who controls this world's system?
17. Will the world get any better?
18. What is the a-c's end?

INTRODUCTION

It is my intentions to only deal with the prophecies concerning and related to the a-c and satan. Many scholars have dealt with those prophecies concerning the return of our Savior, as well as many other prophetic scriptures. I will only deal with them as needed to explain or give clear understanding of the a-c. And since this is a scholarly book, by a non-scholar I might get confused with too much information.

We will primarily use the books of Daniel and Rev. as we reveal the a-c and his works. Many biblical scholars and preachers believe the books of Daniel and Rev. are allegorical books, with a bunch of symbolic material which may or may not mean anything. Not me; I know both books are the work of Jesus Christ revealing the future to those who want to know. "The Revelation of Jesus Christ, which God gave unto him, to show unto his servants things which must shortly come to pass; and he sent and signified it by his angel unto his servant John" (Rev. 1:1). Notice He said, "Which must shortly come to pass," this is on God's time table, and it must come to pass.

"Remember the former things of old: for I am God, and there is none else; I am God, and there is none like me. Declaring the end from the beginning, and from ancient times the things that are not yet done, saying, My counsel shall stand, and I will do all my pleasure" (Isaiah 46:9–10). He knows the end from the beginning, and what must come to pass.

In my studies, I have heard and read a lot of foolish babble concerning Rev. I heard a lady speak on the radio. She said; "we are already in the tribulation, and President Obama is the a-c." The hosts of the program asked her how she knew we are in the tribulation. She replied; "I am a heavenly watcher sent to the earth to prepare the world for Christ's return." Pure foolishness. We must be careful who we listen to, and what we read. Many people speak on Rev. with no idea what they are really saying, or the condemnation they are bringing on themselves.

Read the following: "For I testify unto every man that heareth the words of the prophecy of this book, If any man shall add unto these things, God shall add unto him the plagues that are written in the book: And if any man shall take way from the words of the book of this prophecy, God shall take away his part out of the book of life, and out of the holy city, and from the things which are written in the book" (Rev. 22:18-19). So whatever title he or she has; reverend doctor, pastor, priest, teacher, prophet or prophetess. Beware, don't play with Rev. This is a serious charge by The Most High God. Anyone not sure of Rev. or want to make the whole book symbolic or metaphorical; better leave Rev. alone. Instead preach on the three Hebrew boys in the fire, or king David.

Many of the symbols used in Rev. are tools our Father uses to fool those who think they are wise, or full of earthly wisdom, and are seeking signs (1 Cor. 1:20–28). Most of the symbols used in the Bible represent people, nations, kingdoms and spirits. The Bible will interpret 99 percent of the symbols represented within its pages. There are some symbols The Father has not given us to understand. But, when it says there will be a great dictator in the last days called the a-c/beast, this must happen.

Don't be afraid to study Rev. It is a wonderful book, full of great wisdom from The Most High, plus it lets us know we win in the end. Rev. is a final call to the saints of The Most High God to live separate and holy lives, and come out from among the evil of this world's system.

In writing this book, I have intentionally broken some grammatical rules. For example, I refuse to capitalize the following; a-c, satan, and devil. So please bear with me. Also, whenever I refer to God or Jesus I will capitalize certain words e.g. Him, He, Almighty, The Most High, as well as others. I ask you to look over this. I believe The Most High deserves all the power, honor, respect, and glory we can give Him.

You will read many hard saying in this book. I might as well start now. The Bible is not a book for scholarly disputation or dialectic reasoning between two opposing camps. It is a book built on the unity of one idea sent from our Father. Dictated to His holy men for us to read and obey. It is not a word, but The Word of The Most High God to a rebellious and gainsaying people. He does not try to prove His existence, nor explain why He does some of the things He brings forth. He did not send it to us to reason over nor use as a hot

INTRODUCTION

debate topic. It is given to us to believe and be saved. None of its trues rely on our feelings. The Father did not write this for us to create reverends, doctors of divinity, or any other position of learning. You do not need a degree to understand it nor do you need to be a learn doctor to teach it. The first and only requirement is you must be saved to even begin to comprehend it.

We will not change or gloss over sections of the Bible; when this is done you have convoluted and nonsensical teaching. When I do not understand a section, I will tell you so. Heed the following warning; Do not take prophecy and try to morph it into your way of thinking, or try to make it fit your denominational beliefs. To do so will destine you to failure: time will show, you are wrong, and The Father is right. "Add thou not unto his words, lest he reprove thee, and thou be found a liar" (Proverbs 30:6).

I have not added nor taken away from the scripture. I have written on some things which the Bible teaches will take place, but I cannot say everything must happen just as I have written. I believe I have been inspired by the Holy Spirit to write this. But my writing is not infallible, nor do I believe I am the fourth person of The Trinity. I pray I have written what He has directed and have not added fillers to make it sensational or profitable. I do not think I am "holier than thou." I battle the same sins you do. I stand on the word of my Father: "Being confident of this very thing, that he which hath begun a good work in you will perform it until the day of Jesus Christ" (Philippians 1:6). I am not perfect, just forgiven.

I have tried to ensure I follow. "The prophet that hath a dream, let him tell a dream; and he that hath my word, let him speak my word faithfully" (Jeremiah 23:28). I do not consider myself a prophet. Just a lowly minister of the gospel.

The Most High God says, "Now we have received, not the spirit of the world, but the spirit which is of God: that we might know the things that are freely given to us of God. Which things also we speak, not in the words which man's wisdom teacheth, but which the Holy Ghost teacheth: comparing spiritual things with spiritual. But the natural man receiveth not the things of the Spirit of God: for they are foolishness unto him: neither can he know them, because they are spiritually discerned" (1 Cor. 2:12-14).

The above verses are not religious double talk. It is not me saying, "If you don't understand what I have written, you are not spiritual." No. There are some things which are only spiritually discerned. For example; Jesus said, "Jesus answered, My kingdom is not of this world: if my kingdom were of this world, then would my servants fight, that I should not be delivered to the Jews: but now is my kingdom not from hence" (John 18:36). Jesus was giving Pilate a spiritual application but Pilate missed it since Pilate was not a spiritual person. The Kingdom of heaven at this moment is a spiritual state. It is within you, and you must truly believe in God to receive from Him. "But without faith it is impossible to please him: for he that cometh to God must believe that he is, and that he is a rewarder of them that diligently seek him" (Hebrews 11:6). The Father will reward those who really want the truth with the truth. Pray concerning what you are about to read.

I have used a large amount of scripture. Without scripture I can prove nothing, but within its pages we find hope. And I believe the greater the repository of scripture, the greater the filter for recognizing and avoiding sin. I firmly believe the Bible is not a word, but the definitive, inspired, and Holy Spirit breathed Word of The Most High God. The Bible is the ultimate authority. There are no new revelations being received. The Bible is it, "Let God be true, but every man a liar" (Romans 3:4). Anyone who says the Bible is passé or outdated is of the devil, pure and simple: "All scripture is given by inspiration of God, and is profitable for doctrine, for reproof, for correction, for instruction in righteousness: That the man of God may be perfect, thoroughly furnished unto all good works" (2 Timothy 3:16-17). The Bible is the only book which can keep mankind on the straight and narrow road.

Those who seek heaven must become scholars of the Bible: "Then said he (Jesus) unto them, Therefore every scribe which is instructed unto the kingdom of heaven is like unto a man that is a householder, which bringeth forth out of his treasure things new and

INTRODUCTION

old" (Matt. 13:52). Without the Bible, all we have is teaching from unstable people.

I have used the following to help me in my studies. "Whom shall he teach knowledge? And whom shall he make to understand doctrine? Them that are weaned from the milk and drawn from the breasts. For percept must be upon precept, precept upon precept; line upon line, line upon line; here a little, and there a little" (Isaiah 28:9-10). It takes serious study to understand prophecy. Just as it also takes serious study to become a mature Christian.

As we study prophecy, remember it is not fanciful tales of Christian folklore. Rather, it is the true telling of events to come. We must be like the Bereans. "And the brethren immediately sent away Paul and Silas by night unto Berea: who coming thither went into the synagogue of the Jews. These were more noble than those in Thess-a-lo-ni-ca, in that they received the word with all readiness of mind, and searched the scriptures daily, whether those thing were so" (Acts 17:10–11). You must search the scriptures for yourself to see if what I have written is true.

Many Christians are looking for signs of The coming of Jesus Christ. Well, Jesus was the definitive sign of the end of the age. "This is an evil generation: they seek a sign; and there shall no sign be given it, but the sign of Jonah the prophet. For as Jonah was a sign unto the Ninevites, so shall also the Son of man (Jesus) be to this generation" (Luke 11:29-30).

"God, who at sundry times and in divers manners spake in time past unto the fathers by the prophets, Hath in these last days spoken unto us by his Son" (Hebrews 1:1–2). We have been in the last days since the resurrection of Christ Jesus. He could return any day.

Read this: "And when he (a-c) shall have accomplished to scatter the power of the holy people (Jews), all these things shall be finish. And he said, Go thy way, Daniel: for the words are closed up and sealed till the time of the end" (Daniel 12:7, 9). Daniel wanted to know when would all the events we are going to discuss happen. Instead he was told to seal his book until the end of time. "And he (angel) saith unto me, Seal not the saying of the prophecy of this book: for the time is at hand" (Rev. 22:10). However, John was told not to seal the book of Rev., "for the time is at hand." Think about that for a minute.

Allow me to inject something here. America is not specifically mention by name in the Bible. The sins of America are, but not the country. America may be great in our eyes, but it is not on The Father's short list.

The Authorized King James Bible (KJV), is the only Bible I use. I do not trust the many translations and interpretations now on the scene. These other works give the idea that man can change the words of The Most High. They remove the holiness, sacredness, and infallibility of His book. They bring in uncertainty and place too much emphasis on man's idea of what man thinks The Most High really means. I have found those other translations do not lend themselves to scripture memorization. I firmly believe The Most High protected the KJV Bible, and kept out false and manmade ideas.

This book is for Christians who are interested in the last days. If you are not a Christian, this book will offend you. If you are not a strong Christian, this book will offend you. If you do not believe the Bible is the infallible word of The Most High God, this book will offend you. If you are a follower of the broad-way, this book will offend you. If you are a strong denominational person, this book will offend you. If you are looking for political correctness, this book will offend you. And for the few who are left, it is my hope you enjoy reading this labor of love, learn some beneficial truths, and are encourage by its teaching. This may be the most serious book; other than the Bible you have read in a long time.

If the rapture has taken place (Christians have vanished) and you found this book, get prepared for a few rough years ahead. Do not take the mark, name, or number of the beast (a-c). There will be great pressure to take it. You will not be able to buy or sell without one of them. To take either of them will destine you to the lake of fire forever. Finish reading this book and do what it says in the last chapter. If you are a Christian, buy copies of this book and stash them somewhere for those who may remain on the earth.

In closing this introduction, I want to thank my wife Mary for her encouragement, her hard questions, and for giving me the

INTRODUCTION

space to carry out this project. I thank all my adult children; Kim, Dwayne, and John for saying "dad, you can do this". I thank my cousin Minister John Hepburn for listening to my ideas and giving frank advice. I thank my friend Minister Michael Walker for not saying "man, are you out of your mind." I thank my fishing buddy Minister Lavern Epps for getting me out of the house and away from the computer when I needed it. I want to thank my Air Force buddies; Pastor Clifford Little and Elder Robert Carter for giving me their frank and valuable inputs, Pastor Verlin Samples for the Bible studies he sent me, and Anthony Kelly for showing me what dedication to a cause really means. I would also like to thank my mentor Peg Bell for her encouragement and input. I thank my mother Vera Johnson for telling me "your abilities are just as good as anyone else."

Finally, I wish to dedicate this book in memory of my daughter Kimberly who passed and went to be with The Lord before I could finish writing this book. She would always say "daddy, I can't wait to read your book."

All righty then (I like that phase), let's get to work. All scripture references will be taken from The Authorized King James Version Bible, copyright 1975, by Thomas Nelson Publishers. The main scripture verses I use will be in block paragraphs. And any explanatory scripture will be identified with parentheses.

THE DREAMS OF NEBUCHADNEZZAR AND DANIEL THE RISE OF THE MOUNTAINS OF BABYLOIAN, MEDES/PERSIAN, GREECE, AND ROMAN

We are starting in the book of Daniel. Daniel tells how The Father will deal with Israel as well as the rest of the world during these end times. Daniel saw things which made his mind spin (Daniel 7:15). Many of you know the story of King Nebuchadnezzar's golden image. We pick up where Daniel stands before King Nebuchadnezzar to give the dream and its interpretation. Since you paid good money for this book, I am going to do most of the work: I will write the text, then give comment on each verse or group of verses, and then let The Spirit of The Most High do the rest.

"But there is a God in heaven that revealeth secrets, and maketh known to the king Nebuchadnezzar what shall be in the latter days. Thy dream and visions of thy head upon thy bed are these; As for thee, O king, thy thoughts came into thy mind upon thy bed, what should come to pass hereafter: and he that revealeth secrets maketh known to thee what shall come to pass" (Daniel 2:28-29).

Daniel has been called to tell king Nebuchadnezzar his own dream and its interpretation. The King had forgotten his dream, but he knew it was very important. King Nebuchadnezzar was ready to kill all his so-called mystics, because they could not tell the king his dream, much less give the interpretation. But Daniel came forth and told king Nebuchadnezzar his dream, its interpretation and that it was sent from The Most High God, who "maketh known to thee what shall come to pass."

"Thou, O king, sawest, and behold a great image. This great image, whose brightness was excellent, stood before thee, and the form thereof was terrible. This image's head was of fine gold, his breast and his arms of silver, his belly and his thighs of brass, His legs of iron, his feet part of iron and part of clay. Thou sawest till that a stone was cut out without hands, which smote the image upon his feet that were of iron and clay, and brake them to pieces. Then was the iron, the clay, the brass, the silver, and the gold, broken to pieces together, and became like the chaff of the summer threshing floors; and the wind carried them away, that no place was found for them: and the stone that smote the image became a great mountain, and filled the whole earth" (Dan. 2:31–35).

The interpretation given to Daniel concerns the end days, and the return of our Savior Jesus Christ. King Nebuchadnezzar was shown a magnificent and powerful statue of a man. The head of the statue may have resembled King Nebuchadnezzar. The dream deals with five kingdoms which will rule parts of the earth. These kingdoms are represented by five elements: fine gold, silver, brass, iron, and clay. This statue stands tall and magnificent. Until a Supernatural Stone, cut from a Supernatural Mountain without help from any earthy being, hits the statue, breaking it into chaff which the wind will blow away. The Stone then becomes a great mountain which will rule the whole earth.

Here is one key to biblical interpretation: in certain scriptural texts when the Bible mentions mountains, horns, and beasts, it is speaking of human government. You must look at the context of the verse and it will give you the meaning. For example, "And I will render unto Babylon and to all the inhabitants of Chal-de-a all their evil that they have done in Zion in your sight, saith the Lord. Behold, I am against thee, O destroying mountain, saith the Lord" (Jeremiah 51:24-25). In this verse, mountain represents the nation Babylon.

The mountain Daniel saw represents The Most High God, and The Stone is Jesus Christ: "The word that Isaiah the son of Amoz saw concerning Judah and Jerusalem. And it shall come to pass in the last days, that the mountain of the Lord's house shall be established in the top to the mountains, and shall be exalted above the hills; and all nations shall flow unto it" (Isaiah 2:1–2). Jesus will come as the final world leader forever more.

"This is the dream; and we will tell the interpretation thereof before the king. Thou, O king, art a king of kings: for the God of heaven hath given thee a kingdom, power, and strength, and glory. And wheresoever the children of men dwell, the beasts of the field and the fowls of the heaven hath he given into thine hand, and hath made thee ruler over them all. Thou art this head of gold" (Daniel 2:36–38).

Daniel tells Nebuchadnezzar, The God of heaven has given him his kingdom. And made him a king above other earthly kings. Nebuchadnezzar is the head of gold. For His own reasons, The Father has chosen Nebuchadnezzar to start this segment of His prophetic clock. King Nebuchadnezzar was a merciless ruler. He ruled with an iron fist. This is the same King Nebuchadnezzar who did the following: "And the army of the Chaldees pursued after the king (King Zedekiah), and overtook him in the plains of Jericho: and all his army were scattered from him. So they took the King, and brought him up to the King of Babylon (Nebuchadnezzar) to Rib–lah and they gave judgment upon him. And they slew the sons of Zed-e-ki-ah before his eyes, and put out the eyes of Zed-e-ki-ah, and bound him with fetters of brass, and carried him to Babylon" (2 Kings 25:5–7). The last image Zedekiah saw was the murder of his sons.

This same King Nebuchadnezzar was called "my servant," by The Most High: "Behold I will send and take all the families of the north, saith the Lord, and Neb-u-chad-rez-zar the king of Babylon, my servant, and will bring them against this land" (Jeremiah 25:9). Our Father has given or allowed all leaders to govern. All kings, queens, presidents, prime ministers, dictators, whatever you want to call the leader of that land, he or she is there by God's providence. They rule because The Most High God allows them to rule, whether they are good or sadistic. Psalm 75:4–7, Acts 17:26. Let us know The Most High places those He wants in leadership positions. "To the intent that the living may know that the most High ruleth in the kingdom

THE DREAMS OF KING NEBUCHADNEZZAR

of men, and giveth it to whomsoever he will, and setteth up over it the basest (crude) of men" (Dan. 4:17). It is then up to that leader to do right, but in most case, they do wrong. Notice Daniel 2:38: "beasts of the field" means normal animals; cow, horses, sheep, etc.

"And after thee shall arise another kingdom inferior to thee, and another third kingdom of brass, which shall bear rule over all the earth. And the fourth kingdom shall be strong as iron: forasmuch as iron breaketh in pieces and subdueth all things: and as iron that breaketh all these, shall it break in pieces and bruise. And whereas thou sawest the feet and toes, part of potters' clay, and part of iron, the kingdom shall be divided; but there shall be in it of the strength of the iron, forasmuch as thou sawest the iron mixed with miry clay. And as the toes of the feet were part of iron, and part of clay, so the kingdom shall be partly strong, and partly broken. And whereas thou sawest iron mixed with miry clay, they shall mingle themselves with the seed of men: but they shall not cleave one to another, even as iron is not mixed with clay." (Daniel 2:39–43).

Nebuchadnezzar is the head of fine gold. But as we descend from the head, the other parts of the body are represented by inferior and less precious material silver, brass, iron, and clay/iron. This means each succeeding kingdom will be politically and morally more corrupt than the preceding kingdom. Notice, that the metal is stronger as you move down the body, until we get to the feet and toes. This means each seceding nation will be more powerful than the nation before it. Let's see who each of the four other kingdoms are.

Silver represents the Medes/Persian kingdom. Notice it is given a very non-descriptive sentence. "And after thee shall arise another kingdom inferior to thee." Notice: "Make bright the arrows; gather the shields: the Lord hath raised up the spirit of the Kings of the Medes: for his device is against Babylon, to destroy it; because it is the vengeance of the Lord, the vengeance of his temple" (Jeremiah 51:11). Jeremiah prophesied the destruction of Babylon by the Medes.

The brass represents the Grecian kingdom of Alexander the great. Iron represents the empire of Rome. The iron/clay feet mixture will be the last human kingdom to rule this earth. This represents the kingdom of the a-c. The a-c will arise from some part of the nations conquered by Babylon, Mede/Persian, Greece, and Roman. There is no way to know which part of this vast empire the a-c will come from. In verse 41, "strength of iron," the a-c's kingdom will be very strong and will not allow rebellion, but it will also have a weakness; clay.

"But now, O lord, thou art our father; we are the clay, and thou our potter; and we all are the work of thy hand" (Isaiah 64:8). Clay denotes the inherent weakness of man. No matter how strong the a-c's kingdom will become, the a-c is still a man. Fully under the control of The Most High God. The a-c will do wickedly, but he can do no more than allowed by The Most High God.

Notice verse 43, "They shall mingle themselves with the seed of men: but they shall not cleave one to another, even as iron is not mixed with clay." These elements represent human government and man's futile attempt at governance such as The League of Nation, United Nations, European Union, USSR (now called The Commonwealth of Independent States), Arab League, African Union and others. They have either failed, or are struggling not to fail. Notice all ten toes of the statue are shown. They represent smaller nations made of the same iron/clay mixture; the identity of these ten nations are not revealed. There was a Bible scholar who said these were the first ten nations of the European Union, however, the union now has over twenty-five members. The best answer is; we do not yet know who these ten nations are.

For eons, mankind has tried to unite under one banner or another. It started in Genesis 11, with the tower of Babel. But these unions always fall apart, either through Godly intervention or man's hatred and distrust of each other. The league of Nations was so bad it had to be disbanded. And out of its ashes rose the United Nations, but they can't get united on anything. We have the European Union, but one or more of its member nations is always threatening to go on strike, such as England. The USSR went bankrupt. It is now called the commonwealth of Independent States. But Russia is the only independent state among them. The African and Asian nations will start something but it degenerates into a mess. The Arab league barely speak to each other. Iron and miry (common) clay is a very fragile mixture and impossible to work with. Clay is porous and iron is solid, they will not create a strong stable structure no matter how long you work with it. Clay, when dry, becomes brittle shattering easily.

In these last days, there will be one last supernatural attempt to unite all people in one cause and a one world government under the leadership of satan and the a-c. The world will think the a-c is the man, for the right time and the right people, to create a united, and stable whole government. Worship is satan's real reason for backing the a-c. We will develop this idea more in a later chapter. Once this one world government is established it will only work for a short time as declared by our Father.

"And in the days of these kings shall the God of heaven set up a kingdom, which shall never be destroyed: and the kingdom shall not be left to other people, but it shall break in pieces and consume all these kingdoms, and it shall stand forever. Forasmuch as thou sawest that the stone was cut out of the mountain without hands, and that it brake in pieces the iron, the brass, the clay, the silver, and the gold; the great God hath made known to the king what shall come to pass hereafter: and the dream is certain, and the interpretation thereof sure" (Daniel 2:44–45).

The Most High God will set up His kingdom without the help of man and there will be no heir. It will last forever with Jesus Christ, The Stone, whom the Jews and others rejected, ruling forever. His kingdom will consume, devour, gut, incinerate, break, and destroy all human government to the point they will be forgotten forever. "Thou sawest till that a stone was cut out without hands which smote the image upon his feet that were of iron and clay, and brake them to pieces. Then was the iron, the clay, the brass, the silver, and the gold broken to pieces together, and became like the chaff of the summer threshing floors; and the wind carried them away, that no place was found for them (Daniel 2:34-35)."

Notice the destruction starts with the iron/clay mixture and goes up the statue. You might be able to duck a stone aimed at your head, and you may be able to catch a stone thrown at your chest, but you can't stand when your feet get knocked out from under you. Notice He says, "What shall come to pass." This must and will happen. (Hallelujah)

Daniel's Dreams

Daniel is now given dreams and visions directly from The Most High. These dreams and visions are built on King Nebuchadnezzar's dream of chapter two, but with a few more details.

"In the first year of Belshazzar King of Babylon, Daniel had a dream and visions of his head upon his bed: then he wrote the dream, and told the sum of the matters. Daniel spake and said, I saw in my vision by night, and, behold, the four winds of the heaven strove upon the great sea. And four great beasts came up from the sea, diverse one from another" (Daniel 7:1–3).

In verse 2, Daniel tells of a great supernatural event. The four winds are stirring up the great sea of humanity. The Bible uses the term "beasts" as one description of the kingdoms. Why? Mankind has been wicked and downright mean to each other. In the animal kingdom, a lion will only attack when it is hungry, feels threaten, or unless there is something mentally or physically wrong with it. Animals are animals. They don't hate or dislike you, it is only being an animal.

Mankind, on the other hand, has a long history of meanness. From Cain to the present day. People kill for the thrill, or simply because they can. Men rape and kill women because they want to. Paul wrote the following: "If after the manner of men I fought with beasts at Ephesus" (1 Cor. 15:32). Paul didn't fight with animals but called wicked men "beasts." It started with Adam's disobedience (Roman 5:12–21). This meanness is getting worse.

The "winds" represents a supernatural influence on mankind. Supernatural forces brought to power these four leaders and their nations. There will be a supernatural event that will cause mankind to reach out to each other in a way as never before, more on this later. Out of this sea of humanity came four great kingdoms, each different from the other. Just as animals have different characteristics, so will these nations. When the Bible uses the word seas, waters, and sand, this sometimes means people and nations. The context of the verse will tell you if it is referring to a real body of water or a body of people. Here it means the sea of humanity.

Daniels tells us in verse 3, these were powerful nations. And they were different from each other as we will see. Remember, in Daniel chapter 2, Nebuchadnezzar saw a statue made of the following elements gold, silver, brass, iron and iron /clay. Now Daniel sees four great beasts and he is given specific characteristics of each nation.

"The first was like a lion, and had eagle's wings; I beheld till the eagle's wings thereof were plucked, and it was lifted up from the earth, and made stand upon the feet as a man, and a man's heart was given to it" (Daniel 7:4).

This verse refers to Nebuchadnezzar and his Babylonian kingdom. In Daniel chapter 4, Nebuchadnezzar had his wings (power and sanity) plucked by The Most High God and Nebuchadnezzar behaved like an animal for seven years. His hair grew until it resembled the feathers of an eagle and his nails like bird's claws. Nebuchadnezzar was absent for seven years, but his kingdom stayed intact. Why? The Most High rules in the affairs of man, this was His will. And it is highly probable God used Daniel as a safe keeper of the nation of Babylon for king Nebuchadnezzar those seven years. "Nevertheless leave the stump of his roots in the earth, even with a band of iron and brass" (Daniel 4:15). The Most High allowed no usurpers or a palace coup.

After seven years he Nebuchadnezzar (lion) stood up like a man and his understanding returned unto him after he recognize The Most High controls everything: "And at the end of the days I Neb-u-chad-nezzar lifted up mine eyes unto heaven, and mine understanding returned unto me, and I blessed the most High, and I praised and honored him that liveth forever, whose dominion is an everlasting dominion, and his kingdom is from generation to generation: And all the inhabitants of the earth are reputed as nothing: and he doeth according to his will in the army of heaven, and among the inhabitants of the earth: and none can stay his hand, or say unto him, What doest thou?" (Daniel 4:34–35).

"And behold another beast, a second, like to a bear, and it raised up itself on one side, and it had three ribs in the mouth of it between the teeth of it: and they said thus unto it, Arise, devour much flesh" (Daniel 7:5).

We now come to the Medes/Persian Empire represented by a bear. But not just any old bear, but a bear with one side of its body lifted higher than the other side. This is symbolic of two nations, with one stronger than the other. There is speculation on which nation was stronger Media or Persia? I am not going to add to this, so I will only say one of them was stronger than the other. King Cyrus (Persia) or King Darius (Medes); take your pick. The one side lifted, also shows a weakness. It is difficult for a bear to walk or run with one side of its body lifted higher than the other. So, there was an inherent weakness in this union. Those three ribs in its mouth may represent Babylon, Egypt, and Lydia, three nations conquered by them. "Arise devour much flesh." The spiritual world is being manifested to the physical world "devour much flesh" means to conquer many nations.

Let me show you something written about one hundred-fifty years before the Medes/Persian came to power. "Thus saith the Lord to his anointed, to Cyrus, whose right hand I have holden, to subdue nations before him; and I will loose the loins of kings, to open before him the leaved gates; and the gates shall not be shut; I will go before thee, and make the crooked places straight: I will break in pieces the gates of brass, and cut in sunder the bars of iron: And I will give thee the treasure of darkness, and hidden riches of secret places, that thou mayest know that I, the Lord, which call thee by thy name, am the God of Israel. For Jacob my servant's sake, and Israel mine elect, I have even called thee by thy name: I have surnamed thee, though thou hast not known me" (Isaiah 45:1–4). Please reread verse 4. Before King Cyrus was born he was destined to rule by order of The Most High God. The Most High even gave him the name Cyrus. Why? The Most High is showing He rules and He had a purpose for King Cyrus.

"After this I beheld, and lo another, like a leopard, which had upon the back of it four wings of a fowl; the beast had also four heads; and dominion was given to it" (Daniel 7:6).

This is Alexander the Great, ruler of the Grecian empire. Alexander was quick and stealthy, like a leopard. But notice he had four wings and four heads. The wings represent speed as does the leopard. Alexander conquered a lot of territory quickly. And upon the death of Alexander, four of his most powerful generals took over most of the Grecian empire, thus the four wings and heads.

Daniel may have written this between 609 BC and 538 BC. Alexander died sometime around 323 BC. Roughly several hundred years after Daniel wrote this. There is no way, anyhow, Daniel could have known Alexander was coming, or of Alexander's generals taking over his kingdom, except, it was revealed to him by the power of The Most High. Now look at the last statement in verse 6 "and dominion was given to it." Alexander did not get great on his own talents. Power and dominion was given to him by The Most High God (Daniel 4:35). Alexander had to succeed, it was so ordained.

"After this I saw in the night vision and behold a fourth beast, dreadful and terrible, and strong exceedingly; and it had great iron teeth: it devoured and brake in pieces, and stamped the residue with the feet of it: and it was diverse from all the beasts that were before it: and it had ten horns" (Daniel 7:7).

This wild beast was "dreadful, and terrible, and strong exceedingly." There was no known animal which could fit the description of this beast. The beast Daniel saw represents Rome and its empire. Its "great iron teeth" represents Rome's power and ruthlessness. Rome devoured any nation that did not surrender to its power. When Rome conquered a nation, and they did not resist and went along with Rome's programs. It would be left alone and allowed to continue under Rome's guidance, as well as Rome's taxes. If the nation resisted, then Rome would; "devour and brake in pieces, and stamped the residue with the feet of it."

Rome was not conquered by a stronger nation, but instead decayed from within due to the wickedness of its people. Rome was full of idolatry, adultery, fornication, lasciviousness (indecent dress and actions), full gratification of the flesh and a general rebellion against God. Sounds like any America you know? Weaker nation states were then able to conquer Rome. Those ten horns represent ten nations that will rise out of Rome's conquered empire. "And the ten horns which thou sawest are ten kings, which have received no kingdom as yet; but receive power as kings one hour with the beast" (Rev. 17:12). I do not have a clue as to their identity so I will leave that alone, but be assured they will come to power with the a-c.

"I considered the horns, and behold there came up among them another little horn, before whom there were three of the first horns plucked up by the roots and behold, in this horn were eyes like the eyes of man, and a mouth speaking great things. I beheld till the thrones were cast down, and the Ancient of days did sit, whose garment was white as snow, and the hair of his head like the pure wool: his throne was like the fiery flame, and his wheels as burning fire. A fiery stream issued and came forth from before him: thousand thousands ministered unto him, and ten thousand times ten thousand stood before him: the judgment was set, and the books were opened. I beheld then because of the voice of the great words which the horn spake: I beheld even till the beast was slain, and his body destroyed, and given to the burning flame. As concerning the rest of the beasts, they had their dominion taken away: yet their lives were prolonged for a season and time. I saw in the night vision, and, behold, one like the Son of man come with the clouds of heaven, and came to the Ancients of days, and they brought him near before him. And there was given him dominion, and glory, and a kingdom, that all people, nations and languages, should serve him: his dominion is an everlasting dominion, which shall not pass away, and his kingdom that which shall not be destroyed" (Daniel 7:8–14).

Daniel is now given a snapshot of the a-c, the great white throne judgment, and the beginning of the reign of Jesus Christ. We will deal with these near the end of our journey. We must now deal with those "horns."

"I said unto the fools, Deal not foolishly: and to the wicked, lift not up the horn: Lift not up your horn on high: speak not with a stiff neck. All the horns of the wicked also will I cut off; but the horns of the righteous shall be exalted" (Psalm 75:4–5, 10). The term horn as it is used here can mean one man or nation and it denotes self-pride. Notice the little horn has eyes and a mouth like a man. This lets us know this horn represents an individual man rather than a nation.

He will be a citizen from part of the old Roman Empire, which includes all those other nations spoken of by Daniel. He comes to power before, after, or with those ten nations. He will destroy or subdue three of the ten nations, just as the bear did in Daniel 7:5. We still are not told who those ten nations are. The a-c will speak words never heard on this earth and he will do it with great authority. Daniel is captivated by the boisterous words spoken by the a-c. It is obvious the words are against The Most High. Verse 11 tells the end of the a-c; he will be given to the burning flame. This means the lake of fire. We will discuss this later. Verse 12; lets us know that once Christ returns the ten-nation confederacy will lose their power, but the nations themselves will be prolonged.

Each of the Nations we have studied thus far had some unique trait: Babylon, the mind of an animal, but restored to power. Medes/Persia, a lopsided bear, one nation stronger than the other. Greece, four wings, the four division of the empire. Rome, ruthlessness. The a-c will have the strength of all the afore mention nations with the addition of a powerful mouth and the full help of satan. I firmly believe most people do not grasp a full understanding of how terrible this man's reign will be upon the earth and it occupants. Read the following.

"I Daniel was grieved in my spirit in the midst of my body, and the vision of my head troubled me. I came near unto one of them that stood by, and asked him the truth of all this. So he told me, and made me know the interpretation of the things. These great beasts, which are four are four kings, which shall arise out of the earth. But the saints of the most High shall take the kingdom, and possess the kingdom forever, even for ever and ever. Then I would know the truth of the fourth beast, which was diverse from all the others, exceeding dreadful, whose teeth were of iron and his nails of brass; which devoured, brake in pieces, and stamped the residue with his feet; And of the ten horns that were in his head, and of the other which came up, and before whom three fell; even of that horn that had eyes, and a mouth that spake very great things, whose look was more stout than his fellows. I beheld, and the same horn made war against the saints, and prevailed against them" (Daniel 7:15-21).

Daniel's head is spinning. He is an eye witness to what will become history. These visions and dreams were too much for him to comprehend. So Daniel wanted to know; is all this true? What does it mean? Daniel is given the interpretation of the dream by the angel Gabriel. The Bible only gives the names of three angels. They are Michael, Gabriel, and Lucifer. We need only use these names and stop making up names for other supposed angels such as Raphael; this name is not in the Bible, but is a manmade tradition.

Let's get back to our text in Daniel. This is a recap of what Daniel saw in prior visions and dreams. Babylon, Media/Persia, Greece, Roman, and the a-c's kingdom shall rise out of the earth (people) and become great kingdoms. However, this will only be for a short time, until The Most High takes the kingdoms of this earth by force and gives them to His saints. Verse 19, lets us know that Rome will be the most powerful of the first four kingdoms. Notice it has properties of brass in its body (Alexander the great) because Greece became part of Rome. Sometime soon, ten unknown nations shall arise from the ashes of the Roman Empire, in conjunction with the fifth most powerful ruler of all, the a-c.

The a-c will subdue, attack, or conquer three of the ten nations, sometime during his reign. The a-c's kingdom will be like no other kingdom this earth has seen. It will be huge, domineering, and exceedingly wicked. The a-c will speak like no other man in history. Hitler's rhetoric will be nothing compared to the great oratorical power of the a-c. The a-c shall deceive, then declare war and attempt to destroy the Jews and those who have gotten saved. (Get right, or get left).

"Until the Ancient of days came, and judgment was given to the saints of the most High; and the time came the saints possessed the kingdom. Thus he said, the fourth beast shall be the fourth kingdom upon earth, which shall be diverse from all kingdoms and shall devour the whole earth, and shall tread it down, and break it in pieces. And the ten horns out of this kingdom are ten kings that shall arise: and another shall rise after them; and he shall be diverse from the first, and he shall subdue three kings. And he shall speak great words against the most High, and shall wear out the saints of the most High, and think to change times and laws: and they shall be given into his hand until a time and times and the dividing of time. But the judgment shall sit, and they shall take away his dominion, to consume and to destroy it unto the end. And the kingdom and dominion, and the greatness of the kingdom under the whole heaven, shall be given to the people of the saints of the most High, whose kingdom is an everlasting kingdom, and all dominions shall serve and obey him" (Daniel 7:22–27).

Daniel is once again told of Rome's empire which includes the conquered nations of Babylon, Media/Persia, and Greece. The dreams are being doubled, even tripled. Notice: "And for that the dream was double unto Pharaoh twice; it is because the thing is established by God, and God will shortly bring it to pass" (Genesis 41:32). When Joseph told Pharaoh the interpretation of his dreams, Joseph informed Pharaoh The Most High God means what He says and it must come to pass.

The same "God will shortly bring it to pass" is implied with each of Daniel's dreams these events must come to pass. From somewhere out of Rome's vast empire, the ten nations and the a-c will rise. The a-c's kingdom will be very different from any kingdom this world has seen. Notice the phrase "speak great words against The Most High." This man will speak blasphemously against The Father. This gives us insight into the absolute hatred satan and the a-c will have against The Most High.

He will try to change natural times and laws, he may even try to remove the "BC and AD" from our dates. His goal; to remove anything that points to our Father. Notice our world's currents events, mankind is now striving to remove anything that points to The Father. Whether it is creation, traditional marriage, the Bible, true Christians, or the Jews. In the minds of sinful man, all of it must go. Hitler hated the Jews with a passion. The a-c will hate them with a satanic passion. The a-c will initiate the greatest effort this world has ever seen to remove the imprint of The Father from this earth. But it will fail.

The a-c will enthrone satan and himself as supreme. King Herod, Nero, Genghis Khan, Pol Pot, Stalin, Hitler, Mussolini, even ISIS will not compare to the sinister cruelty and absolute depravity of the a-c's kingdom. We are told in other verses the a-c's time is limited, and he will come to an end. Some may think this is but a fairy tale slipped into the Bible, but it is not! Daniel was told once the a-c comes to power he will rule until the "Ancient of days" returns, defeats, and passes judgment on the a-c. The saints will then possess the kingdom. This must take place one day in the future. The wrath of God, the wrath of satan, and the wrath of man all coming to an earth near you.

"Hitherto is the end of the matter. As for me Daniel, my cogitations much troubled me, and my countenance changed in me: but I kept the matter in my heart" (Daniel 7:28).

All though we are not yet to the end of our look at future history. Your thoughts should be like Daniel's, troubled and pondering this matter. Remember, this was not written just for someone like me to write about, but rather to let the world know, pay day is coming. So, who will be paying your wages?

Let us now go to Daniel chapter 8.

"In the third year of the reign of King Belshazzar a vision appeared unto me, even unto me Daniel, after that which appeared unto me at the first. And I saw in a vision; and it came to pass, when I saw, that I was at Shu-shan in the palace, which is in the province of Elam; and I saw in a vision, and I was by the river U-lai. Then I lifted up mine eyes, and saw, and, behold, there stood before the river a ram which had two horns: and the two horns were high: but one was higher than the other, and the higher came up last. I saw the ram pushing westward, and northward, and southward; so that no beasts might stand before him, neither was there any that could deliver out of his hand; but he did according to his will, and became great" (Daniel 8:1–4).

Daniel tells us this vision was like the first vision. Daniel is shown the end of Babylon's reign. It was conquered by the Medes/

Persians. In this vision, Daniel tells us he was wide awake in the palace in Babylon. He saw himself in his vision by the river Ulai. And he was amazed at what he saw. Daniel sees a ram. The ram represents the same kingdom as the lopsided bear in Chapter 7, Medes/Persia. One horn is shorter than the other. This symbolizes one was stronger than the other. The ram was very powerful and no other nation (beasts) could stand before him, nor conquer him. Imagine in your mind this great ram pushing north, south, and west. Moving against all opposition. If any nation stood in its way, one head butt and they were down and out. This combined kingdom did whatever it wanted without fear of reprisal or rebellion, until it meets the goat. Oh, what a goat it is.

"And as I was considering, behold, a he goat came from the west on the face of the whole earth, and touched not the ground: and the goat had a notable horn between his eyes. And he came to the ram that had two horns, which I had seen standing before the river, and ran unto him in the fury of his power. And I saw him come close unto the ram, and he was moved with choler against him, and smote the ram, and brake his two horns: and there was no power in the ram to stand before him, but he cast him down to the ground, and stamped upon him: and there was none that could deliver the ram out of his hand. Therefore the he goat waxed very great; and when he was strong, the great horn was broken; and for it came up four notable ones toward the four winds of heaven" (Daniel 8:5–8).

Daniel stands there contemplating this ram when suddenly, he is a witness to a great spiritual battle manifested in the physical world between the evil angels of Medes/Persian (Ram) and those of Alexander the great of the Grecian empire (goat). "For we wrestle not against flesh and blood, but against principalities, against powers, against the rulers of the darkness of this world, against spiritual wickedness in high places" (Ephesians 6:12).

Notice in verse 8, the goat has "a notable horn between its eyes." This is a direct indication of Alexander the great. Most goats have two horns, not one. Usually a ram is stronger and bigger than a goat. But Alexander was not just any old goat; he had supernatural powerful forces behind him. Notice Alexander is full of choler (anger). He moves with such fury and speed, the Ram (Medes/Persian) did not have a chance. The goat rams the ram, then wipes his hoof's on the ram in victory. No other nation was willing to step in and help the Medes/Persians. The goat just knocked him to the ground in defeat. Alexander became very strong (powerful) and ruled at a very young age. No nation could stand before him. But "one day," as all great men shall have, "the great horn was broken", which means Alexander the great, who was full of pride, died. Alexander died a slow painful death somewhere around the age of thirty-three after a night of riotous drinking. His kingdom was then divided by four of his top generals.

Some of you may think this a tall tale but Alexander the great did not think so. Allow me to relate the following; "When Alexander came to the entrance of Jerusalem Well aware of the danger, Jaddua asked the people to pray to God for His mercy and protection. Then, says Josephus, Jaddus had a dream as to how to entreat the Macedonian king. He and the other priests dressed in their robes and, accompanied by others dressed in white garments, formed a pro-cession that went out of the city to a carefully chosen place to meet the king. Alexander then did the unexpected.

Alone, he approached the high priest and members of the procession and greeted them. When asked by one of his generals why he welcomed this group, Alexander replied: "I did not adore him, but that God who hath honored him with his high priesthood; for I saw this very person in a dream, in this very habit, when I was at Dios in Macedonia, who, when I was considering with myself how I might obtain the dominion of Asia, exhorted me to make no delay, but boldly to pass over the sea hither, for that he would conduct my army, and give me the dominion over the Persians; whence it is, that having seen no other in that habit, and now seeing this person in it, and remembering that vision, and exhortation which I had in my dream, I believe that I bring this army under the divine conduct, and shall therewith conquer Darius, and destroy the power of the Persians. Alexander's visit was capped by a briefing from the book of Daniel, written several centuries earlier, which fore told the rise and conquests of Alexander. And when the book of Daniel was shewed him, wherein Daniel declared that one of the Greeks should destroy the empire of the Persians, he supposed that himself was the person intended." (Josephus, Antiquities of the Jews, Book 11, chap. 8, sec 5, William Whiston translation, 1981)

The Most High works in the affairs of men. Back to Daniel.

"And out of one of them came forth a little horn, which waxed exceeding great, toward the south, and toward the east, and toward the pleasant land. And it waxed great, even to the host of heaven; and it cast down some of the host and of the stars to the ground, and stamped upon them. Yea, he magnified himself even to the prince of the host, and by him the daily sacrifice was taken away, and the place of his sanctuary was cast down. And a host was, given him against the daily sacrifice by reason of transgression, and it cast down the truth to the ground; and it practiced, and prospered" (Daniel 8:9–12).

All territories ruled by Alexander's four generals were consumed by Rome, and from the ashes of the Roman Empire, the a-c will rise to power. He will become exceedingly powerful over the earth, to include Israel (the pleasant land.) In verse 10, we are told that the a-c will wage war against the saints of The Most High, which includes the Jews and those who became Christians after the rapture. We will discuss the rapture later in Rev.

The a-c magnifies and elevate his authority over everything. He will have a super egotistical, megalomaniacal mind (Psalm 75:5, thinks he is all that and more). Nothing is sacred but himself and satan. Truth means nothing to him; he will practice and prosper in whatever he does. he has no respect for anyone. We will talk about the "daily sacrifice" later.

In verses 11 and 12, the term "host" is used. Host may refer to Israel, its leaders or it may mean angels. I lean toward the nation Israel or its leaders. But it could refer to angels. Since I cannot find a good explanation for this word, I will leave it alone.

"Then I heard one saint speaking, and another saint said unto that certain saint which spake, How long shall be the vision concerning the daily sacrifice, and the transgression of desolation, to give both the sanctuary and the host to be trodden under foot? And he said unto me, unto two thousand and three hundred days; then shall the sanctuary be cleansed" (Daniel 8:13–14).

We are now given a time frame, "two thousand and three hundred days." This equals to roughly six years and three months, there about. We will talk about these time frames later in Rev. The a-c fights and destroys anyone he considers a threat to his rule. And he may even sacrifice saints on the altar. Gabriel now gives Daniel the meaning of this dream. Notice verse 13; "host" is used again. From this verse, I would say "host" is talking about the nation Israel.

"And it came to pass, when I, even I Daniel, had seen the vision, and sought for the meaning, then, behold, there stood before me as the appearance of a man. And I heard a man's voice between the banks of U-lai, which called, and said, Gabriel, make this man to understand the vision. So he came near where I stood: and when he came, I was afraid, and fell upon my face: but he said unto me, Understand, O son of man: for at the time of the end shall be the vision. And he said, behold, I will make thee know what shall be in the last end of the indignation: for at the time appointed the end shall be. The ram which thou sawest having two horns are the kings of Media and Persia. And the rough goat is the king of Grecia: and the great horn that is between his eyes is the first king. Now that being broken, whereas four stood up for it, four kingdoms shall stand up out of the nation, but not in his power. And in the latter time of their kingdom, when the transgressors are come to full, a king of fierce countenance, and understanding dark sentences, shall stand up. And his power shall be mighty, but not by his own power: and he shall destroy wonderfully, and shall prosper, and practice, and shall destroy the mighty and the holy people. And through his policy also he shall cause craft to prosper in his hand; and he shall magnify himself in his heart, and by peace shall destroy many: he shall also stand up against the Prince of princes; but he shall be broken without hand" (Daniel 8:15–25).

Boy, did I nail it or what? The angel Gabriel told Daniel the interpretation of the vision. "The last end of the indignation" in verse 19, represents man's full history of rebellion against The Most High God. I believe we are in the later stages of this "last end of indignation." Notice verse 23, "when the transgressors are come to full." Mankind will get what they deserved a man of sin, for a people of sin. Unsaved mankind is in full rebellion and running towards a day of reckoning with The Most High. And it shall, and must, come to an end, because it is appointed. The ram is Media/Persia. The rough goat is the kingdom of Greece and the horn between its eyes is Alexander the great who conquers the ram. Alexander suddenly dies and his four generals each take a part of his kingdom, "but not in his power," means with no help from Alexander since he is dead.

The Bible tells us what happens when The Most High God has had enough of certain nations' or groups' sins. In Genesis 15:16, the Amorites; Genesis 18:20, Sodom/Gomorrah; Jonah 1:1, Nineveh; 2 Chronicles 36:15–21, even Israel. Each of these nation's sins were allowed to come to a certain point and then the wrath of The Most High hit. The sins of the whole world are being stored in the bank of heaven accruing interest and then dividends will be paid by The Father. "But after thy hardness and impenitent heart treasurest up unto thyself wrath against the day of wrath and revelation of the righteous judgement of God" (Romans 2:5). Will your dividend distribution come from grace or justice?

Now notice what happens to Daniel when he meets a true angel from The Most High God in verses 15–18. Daniel Falls in fear, it was not an enjoyable experience. The same thing happened in Daniel 10. Let's look at it.

"Then I lifted up mine eyes, and looked, and behold a certain man clothed in linen, whose loins were girded with fine gold of U-phaz: His body also was like the beryl and his face as the appearance of lightning, and his eyes as lamps of fire, and his arms and his feet like in color to polished brass, and the voice of his words like the voice of a multitude. And I Daniel alone saw the vision the men that were with me saw not the vision; but a great quaking fell upon them, so that they fled to hide themselves. Therefore I was left alone, and saw this great vision, and there remained no strength in me: for my comeliness was turned in me into corruption, and I retained no strength" (Daniel 10:5–8).

Daniel's companions did not see the vision, but they felt the supernatural power of the angel near them. They wanted no part of it, they fled the scene, leaving Daniel to deal with this great angel by himself. Just being in his presence took Daniel's strength away. Those who want to see angels, beware it may not be an enjoyable experience. This angel was not Jesus Christ, but only an angel. The angel had to have help in fighting evil angels. "But the prince of the kingdom of Persia withstood me one and twenty days: but. Lo, Michael, one of the chief princes, came to help me; and I remained there with the kings of Persia" (Daniel 10:13). Notice Michael is called "one of the chief princes." Be assured, Jesus Christ needs no help in fighting evil angels.

Back to Daniel 8:23–25. The last great human king shall arise from the sea of humanity. He will be a fierce and powerful person endowed with the full power of satan and using all manner of witchcraft. After a catastrophic event which will impact the whole world, he will come in peacefully as the great savior of mankind. "For yourselves know perfectly that the day of the Lord so cometh as a thief in the night. For when they shall say, peace and safety: then sudden destruction cometh upon them, as travail upon a woman with child; and they shall not escape" (1 Thess. 5: 2–3).

After gaining almost total world-wide control, he will reveal his total satanic infused nature. But it will be too late for mankind to try and stop him. He will have full control and will even believe his own press reports. Notice Daniel 8:25, "He shall also stand up against the Prince of princes; but he shall be broken without hand." The way this is written, the a-c will challenge Jesus Christ to a battle, one on one. What a fool, he does not realize he has no chance. satan tried the same thing, leading one third of the angel in rebellion against The Most High. And just like satan, the a-c will be broken (defeated) without any man laying a hand on him.

Notice Daniel 8:27, "And I Daniel fainted, and was sick certain days; afterward I rose up, and did the king's business; and I was astonished at the vision, but none understood it." The time of the a-c will be a terrible time for both the Jews and the world. The events Daniel saw cause such emotional turmoil in his body he fainted and was sick for a few days. He was astonished at what he saw and heard. Those who joke about the tribulation do not understand what is coming. Nothing can compare to it. It will be as if every flood, earthquake, plague, and war throughout history, is happening at the same time repeatedly. The thought of so much happening in such a short time span is mind numbing. Some of you are doubting this could happen. But happen it will. We are going to skip most of chapter 9. It is Daniel's prayer for his people. We will take up with 9:20.

"And while I was speaking, and praying, and confessing my sin and the sin of my people Israel, and presenting my supplication before the Lord my God for the holy mountain of my God. Yea, while I was speaking in prayer, even the man Gabriel, whom I had seen in the vision at the beginning, being caused to fly swiftly, touched me about the time of the evening oblation. And he informed me, and talked with me, and said, O Daniel, I am now come forth to give thee skill and understanding. At the beginning of thy supplications the commandment came forth, and I am come to show thee; for thou art greatly beloved: therefore understand the matter, and consider the vision" (Daniel 9:20-23).

Notice Daniel was praying "thy kingdom come," in verse 20, He said, "presenting my supplication before the Lord my God for the holy mountain of God." Even then the Old Testament saints were praying for the kingdom of The Most High to come.

The angel Gabriel was sent by commandment, to inform and give Daniel skill and understanding in visions. This enabled Daniel to write what he saw, so that we might learn the plan of The Most High God. Read on and get what I think is one of the most important answers to prayer ever given.

"Seventy weeks are determined upon thy people and upon thy holy city, to finish the transgression, and to make an end of sins, and to make reconciliation for iniquity, and to bring in everlasting righteousness, and to seal up the vision and prophecy, and to anoint the most Holy. Know therefore and understand, that from the going forth of the commandment to restore and to build Jerusalem unto the Messiah the prince shall be seven weeks, and threescore and two weeks: the street shall be built again, and the wall, even in troublous times. And after threescore and two weeks shall Messiah be cut off, but not for himself: and the people of the prince that shall come shall destroy the city and the sanctuary; and the end thereof shall be with a flood, and unto the end of the war desolation are determined. And he shall confirm the covenant with many for one week: and in the midst of the week he shall cause the sacrifice and the oblation to cease, and for the overspreading of abominations he shall make it desolate, even until the consummation, and that determined shall be poured upon the desolate" (Daniel 9:24–27).

We now get a rough time table for the return of our Savior. I am not going to deal with the "Seventy weeks," I will leave that to the scholars. Notice verse 24; this is saying to us that the prophetic clock is ticking toward the end of time. The Father's agenda is as follows: First; to finish the transgression. Mankind has been given a certain time to finish what Adam started. Second; To make an end of sin. When this happens, sin will be no more. Third; To make reconciliation (salvation) for sin (iniquity.) Jesus Christ has already done this. Fourth; To bring in everlasting righteousness. This is on the way. Fifth; To seal or end the vision and prophecy. We have been given all we need to know. The end is racing toward us. And sixth; to anoint The Most Holy. This will happen upon the return of Jesus Christ or it may have happened in Heaven when He returned there.

Of those six, only one has been fulfilled, which is number three: Jesus has made reconciliation for our sins. "And all things are of God, who hath reconciled us to himself by Jesus Christ, and hath given to us the ministry of reconciliation" (2 Cor. 5:18). The rest will be taken care of upon Jesus Christ's return to rule this earth. This is the plan of The Most High. He has revealed it to us though Daniel. Take heed, and study these six.

Now back to the a-c.

When the a-c comes to power, he will enter into an agreement with Israel to bring the Jews peace and world-wide acceptance. More importantly, he will gain control of the temple mount where the dome of the Rock mosque is now located. The a-c's gaining control of the temple mount will allow the Jews either to rebuild or erect a temple. This will be a great accomplishment because the Muslims do not now allow the Jews to even pray on the temple mount.

Remember, the first temple was housed in a tent, so a great building project may not be required. The a-c will come in with pleasing words. And once he gets the confidence of the Jews and the rest of the world, in steps his true master; satan. Then the a-c will attack the Jews and Christians and ruin the city of Jerusalem. Why? What is so special about Jerusalem? "The city of God, the holy place of the tabernacles of the Most High" (Psalm 46:4).

"I have set watchmen upon thy walls, O Jerusalem, which shall never hold their peace day not night: ye that make mention of the Lord, keep not silence. And give him no rest, till he establish, and till he make Jerusalem a praise in the earth" (Isaiah 62:6–7).

"And I John saw the holy city, New Jerusalem, coming down from God out of heaven, prepared as a bride adorned for her husband" (Rev. 21:2).

Also read this: "Thus saith the Lord God; This is Jerusalem: I have set it in the midst of the nations and countries that are round about her" (Ezekiel 5:5). The word "midst" means center. In the eyes of The Most High, Jerusalem is the center of the earth. When reading the Bible notice it states; when going to Jerusalem they go up and when going away from Jerusalem you are going down. Zechariah 14:16–19; Matt. 20:17–18; Mark 3:22; John 7:10; Acts 8:5, 13:19, 15:1, these are just a few of many scriptures which state this. Jerusalem is the only city on earth with a heavenly counterpart. Jerusalem is mention over 800 times in the Bible. Much more than any other earthly city. It is important in the eyes of our Father.

Allow me a little space to say something about the Muslims and the a-c. The Muslim world is looking for the return or the revealing of the twelfth Imam or Mahdi. The twelfth Imam is some type of Muslim super-savior. And according to the Muslims' tradition, he may be hiding somewhere on the earth now or he will come from their heaven. When he is revealed or returned, he will establish a world-wide Muslim caliphate with "sharia" as law, and destroy Israel. Under Islam's teaching, everyone must become a Muslim, or their servants and pay taxes or die. The a-c must gain control of the temple mount, and somehow placate the muslims into allowing the Jews to place a temple there. The Muslims have a deep guttural hatred for the Jews. It is difficult to think the Muslims would give this kind of power to a non-Muslim.

The Arabs and the Jews are descendants of Abraham. So, will the a-c enter as a combine twelfth Imam for the Muslims as well as the messiah for the Jews? Much of the Muslim world now occupies land that once was controlled by Babylon, Mede/Persia, Greece and Rome. Think on this, should Islam take control of the world there would be nothing but chaos and war. Remember, the devil is a great deceiver. I do not know if the a-c will be muslim, Jew, or European. I do know he will be full of the devil.

We will look at parts of chapter 10 later.

"And arms shall stand on his part, and they shall pollute the sanctuary of strength, and shall take away the daily sacrifice, and they shall place the abomination that maketh desolate. And such as do wickedly against the covenant shall he corrupt by flatteries; but the people that do know their God shall be strong, and do exploits. And they that understand among the people shall instruct many: yet they shall fall by the sword, and by flame, by captivity, and by spoil, many days. Now when they shall fall, they shall be hoplen with a little help: but many shall cleave to them with flatteries. And some of them of understanding shall fall, to try them, and to purge, and to make them white, even to the time of the end: because it is yet for a time appointed" Daniel 11:31–35).

This is a two-fold prophecy. It tells of a historic fact and at the same time tells of a future event. An example of this is in Isaiah 14:9–18. This tells of the fall of the king of Babylon, but it also gives us the fall of satan within the same verses. We will focus on the future event. Daniel is told the a-c will use flattering speech and clever tricks (twelfth imam?) to fool both the Jews and the Muslims.

Remember, the Muslims not only have their Dome of the Rock mosque on the temple mount, but they have another smaller mosque, and plans for a third. Why a third mosque? The Jews have got to have some type of temple (sanctuary of strength) for the a-c to make desolate or unholy. The Jews will not put their holy temple near a pagan shrine. Thus, with the third mosque, there will be no room for a Jewish temple. If Muslims did not believe the Bible, why go to such great lengths to deny the Jews a space for a temple? Remember, the a-c will not be an obviously wicked man but will come in as the great peacemaker.

The people in Daniel 11, in verses 33, 35 and 34, may refer to some, if not all of the one hundred and forty-four thousand men of Israel. They will be missionaries to the Jews and the world during the tribulation time. "And I heard the number of them which were sealed: and there were sealed a hundred and forty and four thousand of all the tribes of the children of Israel" (Rev. 7:4). There will be twelve thousand from each tribe.

"And I looked, and, lo, a lamb (Jesus Christ) stood on the mount Zi-on, and with him a hundred forty and four thousand, having his Father's name written in their foreheads. And I heard a voice from heaven, as the voice of many waters, and as the voice of a great thunder: and I heard the voice of harpers harping with their harps: And they sung as it were a new song before the throne, and before the four beasts, and the elders: and no man could learn that song but the hundred and forty and four thousand, which were redeemed from the earth. These are they which were not defiled with women; for they are virgins. These are they which follow the Lamb whithersoever he goeth. These were redeemed from among men, being the first fruits unto God and to the Lamb" (Rev. 14:1–4). They are not "Jehovah's Witnesses" as taught by the "Watch Tower." There are no women in this group. They are all Jewish, males, and virgins (never had sex).

This shows Devine intervention and human devotion to Jesus. These men made themselves eunuchs for Jesus. They are Jewish men, who have accepted Jesus as their Savior, they have no guile or evil, are virgins, and are without fault. Sorry, Watch Tower; you lie. These true witnesses will preach the true gospel to parts or most of the world. This will help fulfill the prophecy of Matt. 24:14: "And this gospel of the kingdom shall be preached in all the world for a witness unto all nations; and then shall the end come." They will preach the true word of The Most High without any denominational contamination.

These one hundred and forty-four thousand will witness under great persecution. All of them will die at the hands of the a-c, as will many of their converts. They will be killed in the most horrific ways; fire, beheading, shooting, impaling, and ripping bodies apart. Saints will be skinned alive, impaled on poles and left to die a painful death. These are acts already conducted by mankind on their fellow man. So, imagine what a satan inspired man will come up with.

ISIS will be nothing compared to the a-c. In Daniel 11:35, those who have become saints will have great testing. They will be fooled by others who are not saints, then betrayed to the a-c. When the verse says, "shall take away the daily sacrifice," it means the a-c will stop the Jews from conducting their daily offerings to The Most High God. And place an image (idol) of himself in the temple. This is called "the abomination that maketh desolate," we will discuss this later.

This will be a time of great testing and purging for both Jews and Christians alike. All throughout the ages, mankind has been tested. The angels were tested when satan rebelled, Adam was tested, Noah was tested, Abraham, Isaac, and Jacob, were all tested. On and on, people and nations have been tested. What is the nature of our testing? Will you neglect so great salvation (Hebrews 2:3)? What is your grade?

"And the king shall do according to his will; and he shall exalt himself, and magnify himself above every god, and shall speak marvelous things against the God of gods, and shall prosper till the indignation be accomplished: for that that is determined shall be done. Neither shall he regard the God of his fathers, nor the desire of women, nor any god: for he shall magnify himself above all. But in his estate shall he honor the god of forces; and a god whom his father knew not shall he honor with gold, and sliver, and with precious stones, and pleasant things. Thus shall he do in the most strongholds with a strange god, whom he shall acknowledge and increase with glory: and he shall cause them to rule over many, and shall divide the land for gain" (Daniel 11:36–39).

The a-c will do as he and satan sees fit. He will honor satan as his god. The a-c will call himself "god," forcing earth's population to worship him and satan. Emphasis is again placed on the a-c's speech. Words no one has heard, or dared to say against The Most High God, will come out of the a-c's blasphemous mouth. Notice verse 37, he will not care about any god his fathers worshiped. Nor will he have a "desire for women." This can mean one of three things either; the a-c will be a homosexual, the twelfth Imam, or make himself a eunuch for satan, or all three. What better way to represent satan than to go completely against the system which our Father has sanctified? The homosexual cannot procreate as ordained by The Most High. So what better way for satan to mock and refute God, than by having a sodomite gain control of the earth. You may think this is far-fetched, but Ireland has elected Leo Varadkar an openly LBGT (Lesbian, bi-sexual, gay, and transgendered) as prime minister.

The homosexual lifestyle has gotten great acceptance in America and the world. Many Americans, including a large number in the church, believe the homosexual life style is normal. The media now celebrates all things LBGT. The pro-LBGT group has made this a civil rights issue, instead of what it really is; sexual perversion. The U.S. Supreme Court has given this group all the rights hetero-sexual couples have. Those who want to practice polygamy (more than one spouse at the same time), are not far behind.

Read this indictment from The Most High God; "Who changed the truth of God into a lie and worshiped and served the creature more than the Creator, who is blessed forever. Amen. For this cause God gave them up unto vile affections: for even their women did change the natural use into that which is against nature: And likewise also the men, leaving the natural use of the woman, burned in their lust one toward another; men with men working that which is unseemly, and receiving in themselves that recompense of their error which was meet" (Romans 1:25–27).

You can rework the above verses. Print your own Bible and take the above statements out. But, doing so will not change what The Father has said. Women having sex with each other, along with men having sex with other men, is "unseemly," "not natural," and "it is sin." Just as sex outside of the tradition (male/female) marriage is sin. Sin is sin. Let's read what The Most High said about Sodom and Gomorrah: "And the Lord said, Because the cry of Sodom and Gomorrah is great, and because their sin is very grievous" (Genesis 18:20). Since when as the homosexual teach, being "unfriendly" is a grievous sin.

Let's continue. "But before they lay down, the men of the city even the men of Sodom, compassed the house round, both old and young, all the people from every quarter: And they called unto Lot, and said unto him, Where are the men which come in to thee this night? Bring them out unto us, that we may know them" (Genesis 19:4–5). The term, "that we may know them," does not mean the men of Sodom brought cake and coffee so they all could get to know the men socially. It meant the men of Sodom wanted to have sex with the two male angels. I think I hear the politically correct people knocking.

The homophobic paint roller is rolling all over America. Once this book is published, they and their friends will be ready to roll over me, along with the anti-islam roller. But this does not bother me, because I am in good company, The Most High God. Please understand what I am saying. Homosexuality is no more of a sin than adultery, fornication, or lies. All sin is contrary to The Father's will. But this sin is total disrespect for the system our Father has ordained. Have you ever heard the term sin-phobic used? I wonder why?

If the a-c comes as a eunuch, this would be an imitation of Jesus Christ. Jesus was here to do His Father's will. He had no time for "baby mama drama," with women. "But he said unto them, All men cannot receive this saying, save they to whom it is given. For there are some eunuchs, which were so born from their mother's womb: and there are some eunuchs, which were made eunuchs of men: and there be eunuchs, which have made themselves eunuchs for the kingdom of heaven's sake, he that is able to receive it, let him receive it" (Matt. 19:11–12). The a-c knows he is on a mission and he does not need to be encumbered with females.

If he comes as the twelfth imam, he will not be married nor have a desire to have a wife or girlfriend, because he will be too busy with his father's (satan) business. This would also fit in Daniel 11:37:

he will turn from the Muslim worship of allah and instead worship satan. If he is Jewish he will turn from The Father, to satan.

Notice Daniel 11:38: "But in his estate shall he honor the god of forces." The a-c will be a man of war and great evil. He will honor and hold the military in great esteem. Look at Habakkuk 1:11: "Then shall his mind change, and he shall pass over, and offend, imputing this his power unto his god." The Babylonian Army so trusted in their combined strength, they made their strength a god. The a-c will do the same. He will invent new techniques for warfare. He will be very materialistic and greedy. None will be able to defeat him and those ten nations; only The Most High can win.

Daniel wrote of events and nations he knew nothing about. Daniel talked to King Nebuchadnezzar, of the Babylonian empire. Daniel talked with King Darius and may have talked with King Cyrus of the Medes/Persians Empire. But Daniel was not around when Alexander the great, of the Grecian empire took over. Yet Daniel foretold of Alexander's coming, and how Alexander's kingdom would be divide between his top four generals. Daniel was not around when Rome conquered all. Yet Daniel foretold of Rome's coming to power, just as he was told by The Most High.

If Daniel was right on those four, he will be correct on the coming of the a-c. But remember, Daniel did not see these events by looking at tea leaves, or peeping into a calf's liver, or some crystal ball. Daniel received these truths from The Most High God: "Hearken unto me, O Jacob and Israel, my called; I am he; I am the first, I also am the last. Mine hand also hath laid the foundation of the earth, and my right hand hath spanned the heavens: when I call unto them, they stand up together" (Isaiah 48:12–13). Daniel received his information from The Source.

Please allow me to show something from the book of Zechariah;

"Then I lifted up mine eyes, and saw, and behold four horns. And I said unto the angel that talked with me, What be these? And he answered me, These are the horns which have scattered Judah, Israel and Jerusalem. And the Lord showed me four carpenters. Then said I, What come these to do? And he spake, saying These are the horns which have scattered Judah, so that no man did lift up his head: but these are come to fray them, to cast out the horns of the Gentiles, which lifted up their horn over the land of Judah to scatter it" (Zechariah 1:18–21).

Zechariah saw the four main nations that destroyed Israel. Which were Babylon, Medes/Persians, Greece, and Rome. He was also shown four carpenters which would fray (destroy), those four nations. The four carpenters represented spiritual powers of four physical nations in the future that would destroyed the first four horns/nations.

In the next chapter, we will move into the New Testament for more insights into these last day events.

THE FALLING AWAY, HE, THE RAPTURE, THE MAN OF SIN, AND THE MYSTERY OF INIQUITY

We now go to Paul's teaching on the a-c and the Mystery of Iniquity. First, let's establish Paul's authority to speak concerning end-times events.

"It is not expedient for me doubtless to glory. I will come to visions and revelations of the Lord. I knew a man in Christ above fourteen years ago, (whether in the body, I cannot tell; or whether out of the body, I cannot tell: God knoweth;) And I knew such a man, (whether in the body, or out of the body, I cannot tell: God knoweth;) How that he was caught up into paradise, and heard unspeakable words, which it is not lawful for a man to utter. Of such a one will I glory: yet of myself I will not glory, but in mine infirmities. For though I would desire to glory, I shall not be a fool; for I will say the truth: and now I forbear, lest any man should think of me above that which he seeth me to be, or that he heareth of me. And lest I should be exalted above measure through the abundance of the revelations, there was given to me a thorn in the flesh, the messenger of Satan to buffet me, lest I should be exalted above measure" (2 Cor. 12:1–7).

"How that by revelation he made known unto me the mystery: (as I wrote afore in few words, whereby, when ye read, ye may understand my knowledge in the mystery of Christ)" (Ephesians 3:3-4).

"And account that the long-suffering of our Lord is salvation; even as our beloved brother Paul also according to the wisdom given unto him hath written unto you; As also in all his epistles, speaking in them of these things; in which are somethings hard to be understood, which they that are unlearned and unstable wrest, as they do also the other scriptures, unto their own destruction" (2 Peter 3:15–16).

Paul was given either a vision or taken to heaven and shown things concerning the last days and other revelations. Notice 2 Cor. 12:1: "Revelations of the Lord." Almost the exact wording used in Rev. 1:1: "The Revelation of Jesus Christ." Therefore, we can rest assured of the prophecies and teachings of Paul.

Heed the following warning. Do not take prophecy and try to morph it into your way of thinking, or try to make it fit your denominational beliefs. To do so will destine you to failure: time will show, you are wrong, and the Bible is right; "which they that are unlearned and unstable wrest, as they do also the other scriptures, unto their own destruction" (2 Peter 3:16).

"Now we beseech you, brethren, by the coming of our Lord Jesus Christ, and by our gathering together unto him, That ye be not soon shaken in mind, or be troubled, neither by spirit, nor by word, nor by letter as from us, as that the day of Christ is at hand. Let no man deceive you by any means: for that day shall not come, except there come a falling away first, and the man of sin be revealed, the son of perdition; Who opposeth and exalteth himself above all that is called God, or that is worshiped; so that he as God sitteth in the temple of God, showing himself that he is God. Remember ye not, that, when I was yet with you, I told you these things? And now ye know what withholdeth that he might be revealed in his time. For the mystery of iniquity doth already work: only he who now letteth will let until he be taken out of the way. And then shall that Wicked be revealed, whom the Lord shall consume with the spirit of his mouth, and shall destroy with the brightness of his coming" (2 Thess. 2:1–8).

We are getting heavenly revelations from The Father. Remember, Paul was either shown a vision or taken to heaven and taught many wonderful things. One of them concerns the a-c and the end times. First, he tells them do not be deceived by any one event, or what people say. We have people saying, "Christ is soon to come; the signs of the times are all around." And on the same token we have people saying, "Knowing this first, that there shall come in the last days scoffers, walking after their own lusts, And saying Where is the promise of his coming? For since the fathers fell asleep all things continue as they were from the beginning of the creation" (2 Peter 3:3–4).

Paul and Peter are saying to us do not listen to any of this. Yes, Jesus can come any day, tomorrow or twenty years from now, but no man knows when that day will be. Read this: "But, beloved, be not ignorant of this one thing, that one day is with the Lord as a thousand years, and a thousand years as one day" (2 Peter 3:8). This is not a secret message about creation taking six thousand years. This verse means The Lord is not conscious of time as we know it. He is on His time schedule. When you live in eternity as Our Father, time does not matter, unless He needs it to matter.

We do know that before Christ returns to set up His kingdom the following must happen; A falling away from the truth, and the He (church) must be remove, and then the revealing of the man of sin, the a-c. We will study them in that order, plus the Mystery of Iniquity.

THE FALLING AWAY

There is a major sign before the revealing of the a-c. What is it? "A Falling away." The Most High said, "Let no man deceive you by any means: for that day shall not come, except there come, a falling away first" (2 Thess. 2:3). What does The Father mean "falling away?" Is He saying people will fall away from the church in the last days? No. Even though church attendance is certainly down, this is not what he means. This "falling away," refers to a falling away from the truth of His word: "Now the Spirit speaketh expressly, that in the latter times some shall depart from the faith, giving heed to seducing spirits, and doctrines of devils; Speaking lies in hypocrisy; having their conscience seared with a hot iron" (1 Timothy 4:1–2). As you can see this falling away has been happening since the days of Paul. And it is on course to get worse.

Paul said, "the Spirit speaketh expressly." The Holy Father is letting us know this is going to happen. We have pastors teaching on every subject but sin. Psychology, physiology, interpersonal relationships, positive confession, name it and claim it, money cometh, walking in divine health, fuzzy logic, and other non-sense, but hardly anything on sin or holy living. Over fifty percent of church leaders don't believe there is a devil or personal sin. Others believe it is a wide open broad way to heaven. I had one high ranking preacher admit to me he chose to become a preacher because he felt it was easy work.

Paul also said, "some shall depart from the faith, giving heed to seducing spirits, and doctrines of devils." Senior pastor Stan Mitchell, of GracePointe Church in Franklin, Tenn. Said in a sermon he preached on Jan. 11, 2015; "Thus, he began to read the statement he'd written early that morning, after a scant few hours of sleep. Gracepointe Church, he told the assembly, would thereafter welcome LBGT members, not just as observers, not just at a remove. They would be full participants in church life-leadership positions, marriage child dedication."(WWW.nashvillescene.com/nashville/embracing-lbgt-members) This support for the LBGT life-style, by so-called Christian churches is part of the "falling away from the truth."

"A deceived heart hath turned him aside, that he cannot deliver his soul, nor say, is there not a lie in my right hand" (Isaiah 44:20).

If you go to the above-mentioned web site and read his statement, pastor Mitchell says nothing about The Father telling him to change the Bible. Pastor Mitchell and others have been deceived by their own minds and satan; "Thus saith the Lord of hosts, hearken not unto the words of the prophets that prophesy unto you: they make you vain: they speak a vision of their own heart, and not out of the mouth of the Lord. They say still (don't change) unto them that despise me, The Lord hath said, ye shall have peace; that they say unto every one that walketh after the imagination of his own heart, no evil shall come upon you" (Jer. 23:16-17).

Pastor Mitchell and others have; "And they shall turn away their ears from the truth, and shall be turned unto fables" (2 Timothy 4:4). Many pastors are encouraging evil doers to continue in their evil ways, no repentance needed, they say, "God is love and can't wait to get you into his heaven." Lest you think this is an isolated incident go to the web site of The United Church of Canada (UCC). This is the largest protestant organization in Canada. The UCC has no problem with same-sex marriage or other LBGT issues. The UCC has been selectively cutting out parts of the Bible they do not like. This has lead them down a slippery slope. Now they have entered a crisis of faith. They have pastors who have thrown out the whole Bible and are openly saying they are atheists and the Bible is a book of metaphorical saying. Which means only a figure of speech such as "his head is hard as a rock." When a church no longer stands for The True Word of The Most High, they will fall for anything that creeps in.

In the Religion News Service issue of May 19, 2016 (http://religionnews.com/2016/05/19united-methodists-create-lbgt-commission/) The following was written; "As the united Methodist church (UME) open their quadrennial General Conference in May of 2016. One-hundred and eleven UME clergy came out as LBGT, and additional 1,500 clergy expressed support for their colleagues." The UME has talk within its ranks of a major spilt concerning the issues of ordaining LBGT members. The African body of the UME church refused to go along with the more liberal American church. Once the UME started tampering with Scriptures it opened the door to full fledge rebellion. The Most High has not convened a heavenly conference and sent us an addendum to the Bible. Christ Jesus died for our sins to be forgiven, not overlooked. LBGT is a sin issue just like adultery or fornication.

Bishop Carlton Pearson also believes The Most High gave a new addendum to the Bible. Pearson believes LBGT is now fine in The Father's eyes and the only hell you face is here on the earth. Go to YouTube and listen to some of the perverted things he now teaches.

In Smithfield, North Carolina. The Jackson County Observer reported on May 12, 2017; "The Islamic Center of Smithfield took over a four-acre former Pentecostal church and turned it into a mosque. On hand to help them open were Christian Clergy. Pastor Jim Mclnyk, who leads ST. Paul's Episcopal Church in Smithfield, took part in Saturday's ceremony. He said, "Christianity and Islam share common origins and scriptures and that he felt it was important to participate in the mosque opening."

"I have seen also in the prophets of Jerusalem a horrible thing: they commit adultery, and walk in lies: they strengthen also the hands of the evildoers, that none doth return from his wickedness: they are all of them unto me as Sodom, and the inhabitants thereof as Gomorrah" (Jer. 23:14).

"And they bend their tongues like bows for lies: but they are not valiant for the truth upon the earth; for they proceed from evil to evil, and they know not me, saith the Lord" (Jer. 9:3). When we use earthly wisdom to discern The Father's truth we end up with.

"This wisdom descendeth not from above, but is earthly, sensual, devilish" (James 3:15). I wonder what these pastors will do when an adulterer or a pedophile attends their church, and refused to repent and give up their sins and say, "the Lord made me this way." Once you stop preaching on one sin, you must stop preaching on all sins. "Cease, my son, to hear the instructions that causeth to err from the words of knowledge" (Proverbs 19:27). If you listen to the words of this world, you will cease to follow The Word of Knowledge.

Much of what is called worship in today's modern church is really nothing but pleasing the flesh. Many churches have allowed the "visual arts," to take center stage. This includes ballet or praise dancing, which usually consists of females in body hugging clothes, rap music and other visual stuff. They say it is vital to the ministry of the church. This does not promote worship but is pleasing to the flesh. The following statement is used "we need this to bring in and keep the young people." The early church did not use gimmicks or tricks to get people saved, instead they: "But we preach Christ crucified, unto the Jews a stumbling block, and unto the Greeks foolishness" (1 Cor. 1:23). Entertainment does not convict nor does it promote conviction of sin. That is the job of The Holy Spirit. The same techniques that work then works now; "Jesus Christ the same yesterday, today and forever" (Hebrews 13:8).

We have more how-to books than ever before, with more coming out every day. And still the church is a mess. The Bible has become a resource book for self-help topics, and Christian entrepreneurs. Yet there is more adultery, fornication, backbiting, and pleasing the flesh than ever before.

THE FALLING AWAY

In many saints, their conscience has been seared with the hot iron of sin, and there is no attempt to live a holy and sanctified life. This is part of the "falling away." It is a setup to believe anything satan sends our way. There is no anticipation of the return of Christ Jesus. "Therefore be ye also ready: for in such an hour as ye think not the Son of man cometh" (Matt. 24:44). I have talked to many saints who really don't want Jesus to come anytime soon. They love this life, but The Father says: "Love not the world, neither the things that are in the world, if any man love the world, the love of the Father is not in him. For all that is in the world. The lust of the flesh, and lust of the eyes, and the pride of life, is not of the Father, but is of the world. And the world passeth away, and the lust thereof: but he that doeth the will of God abideth forever" (1 John 2:15–17).

We have saints chasing miracles, and doing everything they can think of to speak in tongues. King Herod wanted to see Jesus do a trick. "And when Herod saw Jesus, he was exceeding glad: for he was desirous to see him of a long season, because he had heard many things of him and he hope to have seen some miracle done by him" (Luke 23:8).

The scripture says the signs should follow us: "And these signs shall follow them that believe" (Mark 16:17). We have so-called saints trying to see and hear from angels, but they really are listening to seducing spirits and doctrines of devils. These spirits say pleasing things, but this is not an indication they are sent by The Most High. This is another sign of the falling away: "now the Spirit speaketh expressly, that in the latter times some shall depart from the faith, giving heed to seducing spirits, and doctrines of devils" (1 Timothy 4:1).

True discernment among the saints is at an all-time low and getting worse. We have churches now ordaining homosexuals as pastors and bishops. Pastors indulging in fornication, adultery, or worse pedophilia. But the church says nothing. This is a total repudiation of The Word of The Most High. It leads people away from the truth, The Holy Spirit is telling us this has and is happening.

We have gone through; name it and claim it, did the seeker friendly stuff, positive confession, revivals from all over the globe, the holy laugh. We have done the jabez hoop, seen the passion, went hip-hop, read the A-Z Bibles, worn the what would bracelet, been to Narnia. Everyone has been loosed. We dumped Hollywood, and are now reviving it. Done the destiny, destiny thing and the duck swamp thing whatever that was? The re-birthing of America is now making its way around the USA. These are religious gimmicks, with no redeeming value. A. W. Tozer said, "The church is limping from one gimmick to another." Think what he would say today.

The so called Christian novel section in most Christian book stores is larger than any other section. The Christian book store my wife and I used to shop at has reduced their book sections to make room for a whole foods section. There is very little food for your soul there.

In many churches, the KJV Bible is passing out of vogue. Christians churches are falling to an untold number of so called modern versions. These versions do nothing but cause doubt and questions. Such as; Can I really trust this as The Unaltered Word of God? Is this what The Father is really saying or man saying what he or she thinks it should say? These new versions do not have that inner cadence the KJV has. Which helps with memorization. I believe The Most High ensured the KJV was protected so we could rest assured that we have an accurate and definitive Bible for us to use. Many so-called great doctors and teachers of the Bible would not agree with me. I ask you to try this test. Pick a verse from one of the modern versions, then used the same verse from the KJV and see which one is easier to memorize. I would encourage you to stay with the KJV.

We have more apostles, arch-apostles, bishops, arch-bishops, doctors, elders, evangelists, teachers, prophets, prophetess, psalmists, and reverends than you can hear in ten years. And what is this reverend/doctor title? All these titles and the church is still a mess. "For the time will come when they will not endure sound doctrine; but after their own lusts shall they heap to themselves teachers, having itching ears; And they shall turn away their ears from the truth, and shall be turned unto fables" (2 Timothy 4:3-4). Sound doctrine does not matter, just sooth my itching ears.

"There are, it may be, so many kinds of voices in the world, and none of them is without signification" (1 Cor. 14:10). You must be able to discern what and from whom you are hearing. This discernment comes from studying the Bible.

"Study to show thyself approved unto God, a workman that needeth not to be ashamed, rightly dividing the word of truth" (2 Timothy 2:15).

I am amazed at how gullible and trusting saints can be. Many will follow anyone who says, "The Lord told me to tell you." This is one of the biggest lies going. "They have seen vanity and lying divination, saying, The Lord saith: and the Lord hath not sent them: and they have made others to hope that they would confirm the word. Have ye not seen a vain vision, and have ye not spoken a lying divination, whereas ye say the Lord saith it; albeit (although)I have not spoken it" (Ezekiel 13:6–7)?

We must stop looking for the next great church leader or movement and do as Jesus said in Luke 19:13, "Occupy till I come." This means getting in your Bible and study, and then carry on His work until He comes back.

"Put on the whole armor of God, that ye may be able to stand against the wiles of the devil" (Ephesians 6:11). Wiles means cunning devices and tricks. The church is being fooled by a satanic "fifth column." A fifth column works from within and behind its enemies ranks to cause confusion and to sabotage the enemy's war effort, in hope it will help defeat them. satan, has a two-prong assault; onslaughts from the world and ambushes from a fifth column within the church.

Jesus told us of this fifth column. "Another parable put he forth unto them saying, the kingdom of heaven is likened unto a man which sowed good seed in his field: But while men slept, his enemy came and sowed tares among the wheat, and went his way. When the blade was sprung up, and brought forth fruit, then appeared the tares also. So the servants of the householder came and said unto him, Sir, didst not thou sow good seed in thy field? From whence then hath it tares? He said unto them, an enemy hath done this. The servants said unto him, wilt thou then that we go and gather them up? But he said, nay; lest while ye gather up the tares, ye root up also the wheat with them. Let both grow together until the harvest and in the time

THE SPIRIT OF THE ANTI-CHRIST

of harvest I will say to the reapers, gather ye together first the tares, and blind them in bundles to burn them: but gather the wheat into my barn, . . . declare unto us the parable of the tares of the field. He (Jesus) answered and said unto them, He that soweth the good seed is the Son of man; The field is the world; the good seed are the children of the kingdom; but the tares are the children of the wicked one; The enemy that sowed them is the devil; the harvest is the end of the world; and the reapers are the angels" (Matt. 13:24–30, 36-39).

satan's fifth column looks, talk and behaves just like saints. Thus, taking an expert with a spiritual eye to differentiate between the two. This fifth column has the church reeling, due to so many pastors and other leaders bring in all manner of evil and calling it good. We are to follow Jesus Christ; not your pastor, the world's system, or the LBGT group. "Be ye followers of me, even as I also am of Christ" (1 Cor. 11:1). If your leaders are not following Christ, don't follow him or her.

"Be sober, be vigilant; because your adversary the devil. As a roaring lion, walketh about, seeking whom he may devour" (1 Peter 5:8). We must keep our discernment up and working overtime; the enemy of our soul is after us. Even as I write this book satan is working on some scholar to refute the things I am writing. I am not paranoid but I understand my enemy and some of his ways.

Look at these verses: "Wherefore, my beloved, as ye have always obeyed, not as in my presence only, but now much more in my absence, work out your own salvation with fear and trembling. For it is God which worketh in you both to will and to do of his good pleasure, Do all things without murmuring and disputings: That ye may be blameless and harmless, the sons of God, without rebuke, in the midst of a crooked and perverse nation among whom ye shine as lights in the world" (Philippians 2:12–15). We are in a crooked and perverse world and we must shine as lights, and not mirrors.

"Ye are children of light, and the children of the day: we are not of the night, nor of darkness. Therefore let us not sleep as do others; but let us watch and be sober. For they that sleep in the night; and they that be drunken are drunken in the night. But let us, who are of the day, be sober" (1 Thess. 5:5–8). There must be a difference between those of us who are of the day (saved) and those of the night (unsaved).

One more sign of this falling away from the truth: "Therefore be ye also ready: for in such an hour as ye think not the Son of man cometh" (Matt. 24:44). In most saints, there is no anticipation of The Lord's return. I hear no one pray "Maranatha" (1 Cor. 16:22), which means "The Lord is coming." Nor do I hear "Even so come, Lord Jesus" (Rev. 22:20).

Let's look as Daniel 12:10: "Many shall be purified, and made whites, and tried; but the wicked shall do wickedly: and none of the wicked shall understand; but the wise shall understand." We have entered a stage of prophecy where the wicked are doing wickedly, but don't understand why they are so wicked. They, plus many saints do not understand satan is running his events needed for his man of the hour to come forth. But we who profess salvation and having some biblical literacy, seeing and understanding that events are coalescing toward the end of the age. This knowledge of our Father's word comes from a steadfast and faithful reading and study of the Bible. "Let the word of Christ dwell in you richly in all wisdom" (Colossians 3:16).

He

"Remember ye not, that, when I was yet with you, I told you these things? And now ye know what withholdeth that <u>he</u> might be revealed in his time. For the mystery of iniquity doth already work: only <u>he</u> who now letter will let, until <u>he</u> be taken out of the way" (2 Thess. 2:5-7).

Who are these two "he," verses 6 and 7, tells us of? The first "he," in verse 6 is taking about the a-c. The "he," in verse 7, I have heard a considerable amount of teaching on this "he." Most teachers say it is The Holy Spirit of God. They teach "when The Holy Spirit of God is taken from this earth, the way for the a-c will be open." But I believe they missed key verses on this "he," and they continue to teach what they have heard or were taught by reverend doctor somebody.

THE SPIRIT OF THE ANTI-CHRIST

Let's take a thorough look at what the scripture teaches. Jesus said in John 14:16–27, "The Holy Spirit will abide with His saints forever, He will comfort us, He will bring all things to our remembrance, and He will make His abode (home) with us." In John 16:7–15, it states, "The Holy Spirit will guide the saints into all truth."

Mark 13:11 and Luke 12:12, proclaims The Holy Spirit will give the saints the right words to speak at the right time. Jesus said, "But ye shall receive power, after that the Holy Ghost is come upon you" (Acts 1:8). The Holy Spirit is the in-dwelling presence of The Father in all His saints. We are told there will be people on the earth who will get saved after the rapture (Daniel 7:21–25, Rev. 7:9–17). Those saints will need the strength and power only The Holy Spirit can give. This Holy Spirit power will enable them to stand, and die, for their testimony.

"If we live in the Spirit, let us also walk in the Spirit" (Galatians 5:25). If The Spirit is not going to be here how can they walk in the Spirit? "That the righteousness of the law might be fulfilled in us, who walk not after the flesh, but after the Spirit" (Romans 8:4).

"In whom ye also are builded together for a habitation of God through the Spirit" (Ephesians 2:22). The Holy Spirit is an absolute necessity. It is what keeps all believers. "That good thing which was committed unto thee keep by the Holy Ghost which dwelleth in us" (2 Timothy 1:14). "But ye are not in the flesh, but in the Spirit, if so be that the Spirit of God dwell in you. Now if any man have not the Spirit of Christ, he is none of his" (Romans 8:9).

"Now we have received, not the spirit of the world, but the spirit which is of God; that we might know the things that are freely given to us of God" (1 Cor. 2:12).

"But we all, with open face beholding as in a glass the glory of the Lord, are changed into the same image from glory to glory, even as by the Spirit of the Lord" (2 Cor. 3:18). Every born-again believer must have The Spirit of Christ, which is The Holy Spirit. Because, it is what changes us into the image of Christ. Those who receive salvation after the rapture will need the power of The Holy Spirit.

So, if it is not The Holy Spirit, who is this "he?" The word "He" is a male pronoun, so it must be of the male gender. So, what other male in the Bible has the hindering power to hold back the a-c? I knew you would be asking, so let me give you a few verses. "And hath put all things under his feet and gave him to be the head over all things to the church. Which is his body, the fullness of him that filleth all in all" (Ephesians 1:22-23).

"For as the body is one, and hath many members, all the members of that one body, being many, are one body: so also is Christ. For by one Spirit are we all baptized into one body, whether we be Jews or Gentiles, whether we be bond or free; and have been all made to drink into one Spirit. For the body is not one member, but many. Now ye are the body of Christ, and members in particular" (1 Cor. 12:12–14, 27).

"And he is the head of the body, the church" (Colossians 1:18).

Jesus is the head of the body (us), and as the head is male, this makes us a male body. Thus we (males and females) become "he," the entirety of the world wide true church, The Body of Christ. Our sheer numbers and prayers hinder satan and his followers from engaging in and bringing full fledge chaos upon the earth.

Once we are raptured from the earth, the a-c and satan will be free to do their evil against those left behind. Those who become saints after the rapture will go through great persecution, with many of them sealing this decision with their blood. These saints will need the strength and power only The Holy Spirit can give. Now, I do not believe I have taken the above scripture verses out of context. Please study for yourself.

You may have never heard this before. Let me give you more scriptures which should enable you to see my reasoning. Jesus said, "Ye are the salt of the earth: but if the salt have lost his savor, wherewith shall it be salted? It is thenceforth good for nothing, but to be cast out, and to be trodden under foot of men. Ye are the light of the world. A city that is set on a hill cannot be hid" (Matt. 5:13–14). Salt is a preservative and flavor enhancer, and it causes thirst.

We, the saints of The Most High, are a preservative for mankind. If we were not here, this world would be much worse than it is now.

Read the following salt story: "And God saw that the wickedness of man was great in the earth, and that every imagination of the thoughts of his heart was only evil continually. But Noah found grace in the eyes of the Lord. These are the generations of Noah: Noah was a just man and perfect in his generations, and Noah walked with God. The earth also was corrupt before God. And the earth was filled with violence. And God looked upon the earth, and, behold, it was corrupt; for all flesh had corrupted his way upon the earth. And God said unto Noah, The end of all flesh is come before me; for the earth is filled with violence through them; and, behold, I will destroy them with the earth" (Genesis 6:5, 8, 9, 11–13).

"And the Lord said unto Noah, Come thou and all thy house into the ark; for thee have I seen righteous before me in this generation" (Genesis 7:1).

Noah was salt. At least one hundred years passed between the call of Noah and the flood upon the earth. Now read what happened when the salt was secured. "By faith Noah, being warned of God of things not seen as yet, moved with fear, prepared an ark to the saving of his house; by which he condemned the world, and became heir of the righteousness which is by faith" (Hebrews 11:7). Noah may never have seen a flood, and he never saw one which could destroy all those who breathed air though their nose. But yet he moved with faith and fear at the command of The Most High, and saved his family and himself. And when did the flood come? It came after Noah and his family, along with the animals, were safe. Noah's (salt) actions condemned the rest of the earth's occupants. And just as Noah's actions condemned the world back then. The rapture will bring in The Most High God's judgements upon the present earth.

Here is another salt story. Remember when Abraham bargained with God over Sodom and Gomorrah in Genesis 18:16–33? Abraham bargained The Most High down to ten righteous people (salt) and Sodom and Gomorrah would have been spared. Ten salt-infused people would have preserved all the cities in the plain, but ten could not be found. However, Abraham became salt for Lot. "And it came to pass, when God destroyed the cities of the plain, that God remembered Abraham, and sent Lot out of the midst of the overthrow, when he overthrew, the cities in the which Lot dwelt" (Genesis 19:29). Lot and his family was saved because of Abraham.

And since Lot and his family should have been salt for those cities, when Lot's wife looked back she became what they should have been. "But his wife looked back from behind him and she became a pillar of salt" (Genesis 19:26).

Let's look at a New Testament salt story, Paul. "And when neither sun nor stars in many days appeared, and no small tempest lay on us, all hope that we should be saved was then taken away. But after long abstinence Paul stood forth in the midst of them, and said, Sirs, ye should have hearkened unto me, and not have loosed from Crete, and to have gained this harm and loss. And now I exhort you to be of good cheer: for there shall be no loss of any man's life among you, but of the ship. For there stood by me this night the angel of God, whose I am, and whom I serve, Saying, Fear not, Paul; thou must be brought before Caesar: and, lo, God hath given thee all them that sail with thee" (Acts 27:20–24). Paul was salt for the two hundred and seventy-six people on the ship.

Read what would have happened to them, when some of the sailors tried to leave the salt (Paul) before it was time. "And as the shipmen were about to flee out of the ship, when they had let down the boat into the sea, under color as though they would have cast anchors out of the foreship, Paul said to the centurion and to the soldiers, Except these abide in the ship, ye cannot be saved. Then the soldiers cut off the ropes of the boat, and let her fall off" (Acts 27:30–32). Paul was the salt. And safety was with the salt. The centurion realized this: "And the soldiers' counsel was to kill the prisoners, lest any of them should swim out, and escape. But the centurion, willing to save Paul, kept them from their purpose; and commanded that they which could swim should cast themselves first into the sea, and get to land" (Acts 27:42–43). Safety was with the living salt. The centurion realizes this and saved Paul. You are the salt of the earth. Does the world see you and your church as salt or a salt substitute?

One more example before we continue: "To wit, that God was in Christ, reconciling the world unto himself, not imputing their trespasses unto them and hath committed unto us the word of reconciliation. Now then we are ambassadors for Christ, as though God did beseech you by us: we pray you in Christ's stead, be ye reconciled to God" (2 Cor. 5:19–20). This tells us we are ambassadors for Christ. Ambassadors seek reconciliation between their home country and the guest country they are temporarily living in. But when reconciliation does not work and that nation declares war the first thing it does is recall its ambassador home. One day we will be recalled (raptured) to heaven before the war starts.

The Rapture

The rapture (taking away) of the church (He) must happen before the a-c is revealed.

"Now we beseech you, brethren, by the coming of our Lord Jesus Christ, and by our gathering together unto him, That ye be not soon shaken in mind, or be troubled, neither by spirit, nor by word, nor by letter as from us, as that the day of Christ is at hand. Let no man deceive you by any means: for that day shall not come, except there come a falling away first, and that man of sin be revealed, the son of perdition; Who opposeth and exalteth himself above all that is called God, or that is worshiped; so that he as God sitteth in the temple of God, showing himself that he is God. Remember ye not, that, when I was yet with you, I told you these things. And now ye know what withholdeth that he might be revealed in his time. For the mystery of iniquity doth already work: only he who now letteth will let, until he be taken out of the way" (2 Thess. 2:1–7).

The word *rapture* is not found in the Bible but the concept is, "For this we say unto you by the word of the Lord, that we which are alive and remain unto the coming of the Lord shall not prevent them which are asleep. For the Lord himself shall descend from heaven with a shout, with the voice of the archangel, and with the trump of God: and the dead in Christs shall rise first: Then we which are alive and remain shall be caught up together with them in the clouds, to meet the Lord in the air: and so shall we ever be with the Lord" (1 Thess. 4:15–17).

And: "It is sown (buried at death) a natural body; it is raised a spiritual body (at the rapture). There is a natural body, and there is a spiritual body. And so it is written, The first man Adam was made a living soul; the last Adam (Jesus Christ) was made a quickening spirit. Howbeit that was not first which is spiritual, but that which is natural: and afterward that which is spiritual. The first man is of the earth, earthy: the second man is the Lord from heaven. As is the earthy, such are they also that are earthy: and as is the heavenly, such are they also that are heavenly. And as we have borne the image of the earthy, we shall also bear the image of the heavenly. Now this I say, brethren, that flesh and blood cannot inherit the kingdom of God; neither doth corruption inherit incorruption. Behold, I show you a mystery; We shall not all sleep, but we shall all be changed, In a moment, in the twinkling of an eye, at the last trump: for the trumpet shall sound, and the dead shall be raised incorruptible, and we shall be changed. For this corruptible must put on incorruption, and this mortal must put on immortality. So when this corruptible shall have put on incorruption, and this mortal shall have put on immortality, them shall be brought to pass the saying that is written, Death is swallowed up in victory" (1 Corinthians 15:44–54).

"And God hath both raised up the Lord, and will also raise up us by his own power" (1 Cor. 6:14).

This is where the concept of the word Rapture is taken from. There are no earthly signs before the rapture happens. It could happen any day or night. The timing is in the hands of The Most High. Notice Paul said, "by the word of the Lord" (1 Thess. 4:15). Paul did not eat a goat cheese pizza and dreamt this story. No! Paul received this from The Most High. Also notice: "flesh and blood cannot inherit the kingdom of God." To reside in heaven, we must have a spiritual body which does not need blood.

The rapture only involves those who died saved and those who are alive and saved at the time it occurs. Those who have died, The Lord will bring their souls back with Him from heaven. Their dead bodies will be rise from the grave or brought back from wherever it is, and changed into a glorified incorruptible (never sin or die again) body then reunited with their souls and then taken to heaven. Those who are alive at this event will also be changed in a moment and receive a glorified body and taken to heaven.

THE SPIRIT OF THE ANTI-CHRIST

The rapture is the redemption of our earthly bodies. "And not only they, but ourselves also, which have the first fruits of the Spirit, even we ourselves groan within ourselves, waiting for the adoption, to wit, the redemption of our body" (Romans 8:23). "In whom we also trusted, after that ye heard the word of truth, the gospel of your salvation: in whom also after that ye believed, ye were sealed with that holy Spirit of promise. Which is the earnest of our inheritance until the redemption of the purchased possession, unto the praise of his glory" (Ephesians 1:13–14). Your soul was redeemed when you received salvation: "Receiving the end of your faith, even the salvation of your souls" (1 Peter 1:9). "But we are not of them who draw back unto perdition; but of them that believe to the saving of the soul" (Heb. 10:39). These new bodies cannot die, nor commit sin ever again.

There may be someone reading this book and you have no concept of what the spirit, soul, and body means. These terms may be foreign to you. Let's do a little 101 Bible theology: "And the very God of peace sanctify you wholly; and I pray God your whole spirit and soul and body be preserved blameless unto the coming of our Lord Jesus Christ" (1 Thess. 5:23). This tells us we are triune or three-part beings. We have spirit, soul, and body. Each has a special function in the plan of The Most High God.

The spirit is called the breath or spirit of life from God: "And the Lord God formed man of the dust of the ground and breathed into his nostrils the breath of life; and man became a living soul" (Genesis 2:7).

"Thus saith God the Lord, he that created the heavens, and stretched them out; he that spread forth the earth, and that which cometh out of it; he that giveth breath unto the people upon it, and spirit to them that walk therein" (Isaiah 42:5).

"And after three days and a half the spirit of life from God entered into them, and they stood upon their feet" (Rev. 11:11). When the spirit of breath/life from our Father entered Adam's body, God's "spirit of breath" uniting with man's earthly body created a soulish consciousness within Adam.

Thus, Adam became a living soul with a living body: "And so it is written, the first man Adam was made a living soul; the last Adam (Jesus Christ) was made a quickening spirit" (1 Cor. 15:45). The spirit is the spark of life: "For as the body without the spirit is dead, so faith without works is dead also" (James 2:26). The spirit also calls us to The Most High God. The soul connects our earthly bodies to the spiritual world and this earthly body connects us to the physical world. At death, the spirit of all men returns to God: "Then shall the dust return to earth as it was: and the spirit shall return unto God who gave it" (Ecclesiastes 12:7). The dead body is buried, and the soul the real you (the Bible calls it the heart) is either sent to heaven or hell according to your acceptance or rejection of Jesus Christ. Cremation does not alter or hinder this process.

There is no such thing as soul sleep. Read what Jesus told the Sadducees. "And Jesus answering said unto them, do ye not therefore err because ye know not the scriptures, neither the power of God? For when they shall rise from the dead, they neither marry, nor are given in marriage; but are as the angels which are in heaven. And as touching the dead, that they rise: have ye not read in the book of Moses, how in the bush God spake unto him, saying, I am the God of Abraham, and the God of Isaac, and the God of Jacob? He is not the God of the dead, but the God of the living: ye therefore do greatly err" (Mark 12:24–27).

Let's look at Luke 9:30: "And, behold there talked with him two men, which were Moses and Elijah." Jesus was on a mountain to pray and the Bible says His appearance was change and His clothes became white and glistering. And Jesus talked to Moses and Elijah. Remember Elijah was taken to heaven in a chariot of fire read it in 2 Kings 2:11.

"And Moses died on Mt. Nebo; and was buried in a valley."

"So Moses the servant of the Lord died there in the land of Moab, according to the word of the Lord. And he (The Lord) buried him (Moses) in a valley in the land of Moab, over against Beth-pe-or: but no man knoweth of his sepulcher unto this day" (Deuteronomy 34:5–6). Moses' soulless body was buried in a valley. This shows there is no such thing as soul sleep.

THE SPIRIT OF THE ANTI-CHRIST

The following also shows your soul does not sleep in the grave. "And when he had opened the fifth seal, I saw under the altar the souls of them that were slain for the word of God, and for the testimony which they held" (Rev. 6:9). And one more: "And I saw as it were a sea of glass mingled with fire: and them that had gotten the victory over the beast, and over his image, and over his mark, and over the number of his name, stand on the sea of glass, having the harps of God" (Rev. 15:2). This is a picture of living souls in heaven, not sleeping in a grave. I hope this helps you understand the concept of the word rapture.

Allow me to show the other side, a soul in hell. Jesus told of this in Luke 16:19–31. I am only going to give you parts of this horrible experience. "And it came to pass, that the beggar died, and was carried by the angels into Abraham's bosom (heaven): the rich man also died, and was buried; And in hell he lift up his eyes, being in torments, and seeth Abraham afar off, and Laz-a-rus in his bosom. And he cried and said, Father Abraham, have mercy on me, and send Laz-a-rus, that he may dip the tip of his finger in water, and cool my tongue; for I am tormented in this flame" (Luke 16:22–24).

Notice the rich man was in a burning flame and in torment. Which means he felt pain. He still had all five senses. Sight, hearing, smell, touch and taste. Those in hell will never have a good day. This world will be the best they will ever get.

He was not in hell because he was rich. Jesus said, "But God said unto him, Thou fool, this night thy soul shall be required of thee: then whose shall those things be, which thou hast provided? So is he that layeth up treasure for himself, and is not rich toward God" (Luke 12:20–21). The rich man's god was his money. He was seeking and protecting his wealth, but, he failed to seek The Most High God. Some may think hell is just a fable for ignorant people. But I am here to tell you, If there is a heaven (which I know there is), there must be a hell. We must move on.

Let me show you what is happening in the spirit world at the time of the rapture. "And I looked, and behold a white cloud, and upon the cloud one sat like unto the Son of man, having on his head a golden crown, and in his hand a sharp sickle. And another angel came out of the temple, crying with a loud voice to him that sat on the cloud, Thrust in thy sickle, and reap: for the time is come for thee to reap; for the harvest of the earth is ripe. And he that sat on the cloud thrust in his sickle on the earth; and the earth was reaped" (Rev. 14:14–16). The "like unto the Son of man," is none other than Christ Jesus rapturing His church. The angel in verse 15, refers to: "For the Lord himself shall descend from heaven with a shout, with the voice of the archangel, and with the trump of God: and the dead in Christ shall rise first" (1 Thess. 4:16).

Why are we taken out of this world before the reveling of the a-c and the tribulation: "For God hath not appointed us to wrath, but to obtain salvation by our Lord Jesus Christ" (1 Thess. 4:9). The tribulation is God's wrath upon all who reject Jesus Christ, Jews and non-Jews. "Because thou hast kept the word of my patience, I also will keep thee from the hour of temptation, which shall come upon all the world, to try them that dwell upon the earth" (Rev. 3:10).

"For the great day of his wrath is come and who shall be able to stand?" (Rev. 6:17).

Many scholars debate about "the day of the Lord" and the rapture. I am not going to add to this debate. Whether it is the day of The Lord or the rapture, our concern should be. "Watch therefore for ye know not what hour your Lord doth come. Therefore be ye also ready: for in such an hour as ye think not the son of man cometh" (Matt. 24:42–44). This is another warning for the church today. Saints are so consumed with this world's affairs, there is no anticipation for The Lord's return. There is no cry of Maranatha (The Lord is coming). Saints love this world and all its glory.

Heed the following warning. Do not take prophecy and try to morph it into your way of thinking, or make it fit your denominational beliefs. To do so will destine you to failure: time and events will show, you are wrong, and the Bible is right.

The Man of Sin

Back to the a-c: "Who opposeth and exalteth himself above all that is called God. Or that is worshiped: so that he as God sitteth in the temple of God, showing himself that he is God. And then shall that Wicked be revealed, whom the Lord shall consume with the spirit of his mouth, and shall destroy with the brightness of his coming" (2 Thess. 2:4, 8). The "he" has been taken at the rapture. The way for the a-c is open. Once the a-c consolidates his power and authority, he will oppose anything and everything that even remotely resembles Godliness and righteousness. he will sit in the restored temple in Israel and declare himself not only a god, but The God.

Remember satan is behind the a-c. And satan wants worship more than anything. "And the devil, taking him (Jesus) up into a high mountain, showed unto him all the kingdoms of the worlds in a moment of time. And the devil said unto him, all this power will I give thee, and the glory of them: for that is delivered unto me; and to whomsoever I will I give it. If thou therefore wilt worship me, all shall be thine" (Luke 4:5-7).

"In whom the god of this world hath blinded the minds of them which believe not" (2 Cor. 4:4).

"Wherein in time pass ye walked according to the course of this world, according to the prince of the power of the air, the spirit that now worketh in the children of disobedience" (Ephesians 2:2). satan is called the prince of the power of the air, and a spirit. In John 12:31, John 14:30, and John 16:11, Jesus called satan, "the prince of this world."

As the god of this world he craves worship. It is his consuming passion. satan is full of jealousy when it comes to worship. satan will kill for worship. He wanted Jesus to worship him. Do you understand the implication of this? The devil wanted The Most High God to worship him. satan wanted The Father to abdicate His Throne by acknowledging satan as the greater. Just this one time, but one time would have been catastrophic, for us and the universe. What an ego. satan will do anything to get worship. And he will temporarily get it under the a-c, even though he knows it is only for a short time (Rev. 12:12). He will bask in this world-wide worship. This will be his time and he will glory in it. The devil knows he is doomed and there is nothing he can do to prevent it. The devil's primary goal is to get worship; a secondary goal is to get as much of mankind to accompany him to the lake of fire as possible. We will talk more of satan's origin later.

This shows satan's blind obsession, he craves worship at any cost. When people commit sin, they are giving satan worship, but it is still not enough. If you are unsaved, you are a child of satan. "The field is the world; the good seed are the children of the kingdom; but the tares are the children of the wicked one" (Matt. 13:38).

"Ye are of your father the devil" (John 8:44).

"In this the children of God are manifest, and the children of the devil" (1 John 3:10). And whether you know it or not, you are worshipping satan. But he wants full-fledged world-wide adoration. Read this carefully, satan is not waiting till the end of the age to start his program. Even as you read this he and his horde are busy working to get things in place. "For the devil is come down unto you, having great wrath because he knoweth he has but a short time" (Rev. 12:12).

The evil spiritual realm understands that Jesus is coming back anytime now, and it is ready to run its program at a moment's notice. The devil is the ultimate egoist, but he is also a great long-range planner. The Great Tribulation will not be a sudden event. But, will be the accumulation of an on-going, long-term process. Events are happening for a reason. Mankind must be prepared to eagerly accept the a-c and satan. We will talk more about the a-c later in in chapter 5, when we study Rev. 13. Who do you really worship? Who sits on the throne of your heart; you, the world, satan, or The Most High God?

The Mystery of Iniquity

Paul also tells us about the mystery of iniquity, "For the mystery of iniquity doth already work" (2 Thess. 2:7). What is this Mystery of Iniquity? Let me give you what I believe is a biblical definition of the mystery of iniquity. It is a fierce, vicious, morally evil force released upon the earth. This mystery of iniquity is comprised of principalities, evil spiritual powers, rulers of the darkness of this world, and spiritual wickedness in high places of authority, it also rules within all unsaved mankind. It is the totality of evil on the earth. It is directly opposed to The Most High and His righteousness. In man it is an uncontrollable, and ever expanding evil force within this world's system.

The mystery of iniquity began with the fall of satan. Then it snowballed at the fall of Adam. It worked its will on Cain in spite of personal counselling by The Most High: "But unto Cain and to his offering he had not respect. And Cain was very wroth, and his countenance fell. And the Lord said unto Cain, Why art thou wroth? And why is thy countenance fallen? If thou doest well, shalt thou not be accepted? And if thou doest not well, sin lieth at the door, And unto thee shall be his desire, and thou shalt rule over him" (Genesis 4:5–7). Notice The Father refers to sin as if it is a person. The pronoun "him," along with it adjective "his." Cain had the option to rule over this "him" or mystery of iniquity. Instead Cain allowed it to rule him, thus killing his brother Abel. Then when confronted with the facts, he adamantly denied knowing where or what happened to his brother Abel.

The same thing happened to his father Adam. Once Adam was confronted with his rebellion, what did he do? He blamed God by saying, "The woman whom thou gavest to be with me, she gave me of the tree, and I did eat" (Genesis 3:12). Adam was made perfect but Adam had a free will. He could obey God or not obey, to love God or not to love Him. Adam chose to show he did not love God (failed to obey), thus sin entered in and ballooned into iniquity. Jesus said, "And because iniquity shall abound, the love of many shall wax cold" (Matt. 24:12).

The mystery of iniquity was at work during Noah's time, Abraham's time, David's time, Jesus' time, Paul's time, Hitler's time, Clinton's time, Obama's time, Trump's time and on into the future. It is ready at a moment's notice to influence anyone and everyone to commit some type of wickedness against The Most High.

The mystery of iniquity also resides deep within the heart or mind of all unsaved mankind. It tries to influence those of us who are saved. It speaks to everyone's mind. It whispers; "this is the new Millennium, that was then, this is now, it don't take all that, you take this Bible stuff too far, that was their culture, go ahead it looks good, and it will feel so good. Enjoy life, no one will know. Stop fighting the feeling, embrace it and live a little. Flaunt it girl, you know you are hot, this one time won't hurt, you deserve a little fling, if you don't give it up, someone else will. You have needs too. You can't stop doing everything. There is no God. You only live once. You are only human. We aren't perfect, boys will be boys, a little fun never hurt anyone. Real love, does not have to wait. God knows your heart, God is love, He does not punish. Who will it harm? Love has no gender, stop being so narrow minded, you can ask for forgiveness later, or the most popular "they can't judge you."

Someone may get caught doing something wrong and when asked "why did you do it?" They usually say, "I don't know," and they may be telling the truth. What causes a mild-mannered person to commit a heinous act of violence? Why would a medical doctor kill another medical doctor? Or what makes little girls turn on each other and attempt to kill a playmate at the behest of some video character? Or a husband who kills his whole family and others? Or a mother to drown her precious babies? What makes a young man, strangle mother and baby with his bare hands? The Mystery of Iniquity.

A teenage girl is at a school dance. She excuses herself to go to the bathroom. And once there she delivers a baby, places the baby in a plastic bag, which suffocates the baby, she cleans herself and returns to the dance. We are all left asking, what happened? The mystery of iniquity is hard at work. It takes more than religious zeal to cut someone's head off and enjoy doing it. When someone goes into a school, church, theater, or night club, to commits mass murder, there's more to it than just saying they were depressed, or they were off their meds. The individual who drove a large truck through a crowd of people and watched numerous people die in France, was more than just dedicated to his cause. The killing of millions of innocent people during WWII transcends mere hatred.

What could cause thirty-two California police officers to seek and pay a young girl for sex. Some of the officers started raping her when she was only twelve years old? With the thought of getting caught and going to jail never entering their minds. The mystery of iniquity.

THE SPIRIT OF THE ANTI-CHRIST

The mystery of iniquity and the spirit of the a-c are not mere words used to describe evil and rebellion. They are forces beyond our imagination. And once they unite in the a-c, they will unleash a formidable evil force upon the earth with great consequences. The mystery of iniquity understands we have a short attention spans so it must keep bringing new and salacious experiences to mankind. It wants us to forget one terrible event so it can move on to the next item on its agenda. Muslims attacked a cartoon convention, shoot and blow up hundreds of people and themselves. The Vegas shooter shoots hundreds and kills 54 and we look at each other with a dumb "what can we do" look? We give a hollow sounding our thoughts and prayers are with them. Then within a week or two the press and us have moved on. The battle against the mystery of iniquity is everyone's fight. You can't win with fleshly weapons. You must fight with spiritual weapons, which are The Words of God.

The mystery of iniquity can't be profiled, nor is it predictable. It is loud and stubborn. But it can also become quiet, appealing, and harmless as a dove. If it can't get its way with one generation, it will slowly work on the next generation. By using people of prominence, entertainers, and educators to change the mindset of the youth. Who in-turn influence their parents to change their minds. And soon that which we called good becomes evil, and that which was evil is then reprocessed as good.

The mystery of iniquity patiently lurks in dark corners for the right time and right people. Defeats do not upset or hinder its workings. The mystery of iniquity will double down and vigorously work to overcome all obstacles. The mystery of iniquity works behind the scenes, getting its people in power, then spring forth with its evil agenda.

The mystery of iniquity does not like the word sin. Therefore, that word must be substituted with innocuous sounding words; adultery becomes an affair, homosexuality becomes LBGT, alcoholism now moves into the medical realm as Alcohol Disorder Disease (ADD), drug abuse becomes Substance Abuse Disorder (SAD), abortion morphs into women rights, and a baby in the womb scientifically becomes a fetus. The mystery of iniquity is covering its stink with perfume. The mystery of iniquity feels so right and very pleasing to the conscience. Its speech is flattering and peaceful but when faced with opposition it will double down, over-whelm, fast talk, out-maneuver, and crush all opponents and any objections.

Never will the mystery of iniquity talk of its dangerous ways or the results of following it. The mystery of iniquity never talks about sexually transmitted diseases, nor does it use the word addiction. Once it gains control, there is no going back. It will use The Father's name and selectively use His word the Bible to get its evil way. The mystery of iniquity never sleeps; darkness and ignorance of scripture are its main tools. The mystery of iniquity wants to keep you as far from The Light of our Father as possible.

"For though we walk in the flesh, we do not war after the flesh: For the weapons of our warfare are not carnal, but mighty through God to the pulling down of strongholds" (2 Cor. 10:3-4). The mystery of iniquity is a stronghold and it can't be defeated by the flesh. Prayer and The Power of The Most High God are our only refuge.

One of the primary goals of the mystery of iniquity is to make the true church irrelevant, symbolic, and powerless. For example; the seven churches in Rev. chapters two and three, where are they? Ephesus, Smyrna, Pergamos, Thyatira, Sardis, Philadelphia, and Laodicea; where are they? They only exist on paper. A physical congregation can't be found. Even the buildings are no longer there. What happened to the churches in Thessalonica, Crete, Colossi, Antioch, Galatia, Ephesus, Joppa, Berea and other early churches? Where are they? Answer me you great doctors of the Bible. Where are they?

In Europe, empty Protestant church buildings dot the landscape. In the Netherlands, Protestants organizations expect to close 700 churches during the next four years. One church building in the Netherlands once held one thousand members: now it is a skate park. In France, the United Church of France voted to allow same-sex couples to be married by its ministers. Ireland has now made it a national law to allow same-sex marriage. The U.S. Supreme Court has done the same thing through its judicial action.

Here in America, we have pastors trying to lead two and three churches due to a lack of pastors. Church attendance is falling and no one knows how to stop it. As the protestant churches lose their strength, muslims are throwing up mosques all over the place even in some of those empty churches. Years ago, muslim Imams (holy men) discouraged muslims from living in western countries because they were afraid Christians would convert them, but no more. Muslims now have nothing to fear from Christians. What happened? Christians have left their first love, failed to overcome, followed the lies of the mystery of iniquity, and are no longer a threat; "Be sober, be vigilant; because your adversary the devil, as a roaring lion, walketh about, seeking whom he may devour: Whom resist steadfast in the faith" (1 Peter 5:8–9). If you allow the mystery of iniquity to work within you someone may ask what happened to you?

This is not a weakness of The Father's Word, but a weakness in man. Those churches vanished because of the frailness and self-reliance of mankind, rather than God reliance. The message didn't take hold deep in the minds of the people. Jesus said, "he that has an ear to hear, let him hear." It is not enough to sit passively as you hear The Father's word. You must actively put to work what you hear and read. The Most High God gave Paul the following. "Wherefore, my beloved, as ye have always obeyed, not as in my presence only, but now much more in my absence, work out your own salvation with fear and trembling. For it is God which worketh in you both to will and to do his good pleasure" (Philippians 2:12-13). We must have active, not passive, faith. The world is now asking what happened to America's churches.

Realize this one thing: The kingdom of The Most High God is a spiritual kingdom; one day it will be physical. Read this: "Jesus answered, My kingdom is not of this world: if my kingdom were of this world then would my servants fight, that I should not be delivered, to the Jews: but now is my kingdom not from hence" (John 18:36). And this: "And when he was demanded of the Pharisees, when the kingdom of God should come, he answered them and said, The kingdom of God cometh not with observation: Neither shall they, Lo here! Or, lo there! For, behold, the kingdom of God is within you" (Luke 17:20–21).

Jesus told the woman at the well: "But the hour cometh, and now is, when the true worshipers shall worship the Father in spirit and in truth: for the Father seeketh such to worship him. God is a Spirit: and they that worship him must worship him in spirit and in truth" (John 4:23-24). This is a spiritual kingdom manifested in our physical bodies. At the return of our Savior, the spiritual will become physical: "So likewise ye, when ye see these things come to pass, know ye that the kingdom of God is nigh at hand" (Luke 21:31).

Let's move on. Here in America, we have saints worried about their 401(k) accounts and other investments with little or no concern of their church or of themselves traveling down the road to irrelevance. If we do not fight the mystery of iniquity with prayer and dedication to our Father, we will go the way of Europe's churches. Jesus asked, "Nevertheless when the Son of man cometh, shall he find faith on the earth" (Luke 18:8)? We find these words of exhortation in Colossians 3:16: "Let the word of Christ dwell in you richly in all wisdom . . ." Our Father's word must dwell deep in our minds and we must meditate on it daily.

The "mystery of iniquity" is on a mission to take mankind as far from God as possible. It will not back off, nor let up. Its goal is to take mankind to his lowest point, both spiritually and morally. Paul said in 2 Timothy 3:1-5, "This know also, that in the last days perilous times shall come. For men shall be lovers of their own selves, covetous, boasters, proud, blasphemers, disobedient to parents, unthankful, unholy, Without natural affection, trucebreakers, false accusers, incontinent, fierce, despisers of those that are good, Traitors, heady, high-minded, lover of pleasures more than lovers of God; Having a form of godliness (facade), but denying the power thereof: from such turn away." And in the same chapter verses 12–13. "Yet, and all that will live godly in Christ Jesus shall suffer persecution. But evil men and seducers shall wax worse and worse, deceiving, and being deceived."

Once Adam opened the gate there has been no slowing, stopping, controlling, returning, or hope of the mystery of iniquity getting better. It will not get better with mankind in control. The wiser man proclaims himself, the more foolish he becomes "Ever learning, and never able to come to the knowledge to the truth" (2 Timothy 3:7). Unsaved mankind is vain (worthless) in their thinking, "This I say therefore, and testify in the Lord, that ye henceforth walk not as other gentiles walk, in the vanity of their mind" (Ephesians 4:17). Unsaved mankind is worthless despite all their great innovations.

These unsaved people think they are doing The Father a favor, but their actions belie their intents. They are really disobeying His word and His intents. Their thought process is worthless, since it leaves The Father out of the equation: yet they claim they are doing it in His name. "Fools make a mock at sin: but among the righteous there is favor" (Proverbs 14:9). Those who are not saved, mock sin and its dangers. Then they ridicule the righteous who have the favor of The Most High.

Man has tried many isms; communism, socialism, Marxism, Maoism, and many others. But all these grand ideas have one flaw: Man! Anytime man is involved in something he becomes the weakest link. People will scheme or plot a revolution and once in power they become worse than what they rebelled against Look at Castro in Cuba, Hitler in Germany, Lenin and Stalin in Russia, the Khmer Rouge in Cambodia, the warlords in Somalia and the Revolutionary United Front in Sierra Leone. The so called "Arab Spring" has become the Arab chaos. All these revolutions, and others, have caused great harm to an innumerable amount of people.

The United Nations was to be a grand work of man. Yet nations are still fighting each other and themselves. Nations are rushing to get nuclear weapons because they do not trust each other. Mankind thinks he can make this world a better place though education, war, and money, all without God. But he is wrong. God has given unsaved mankind over to a reprobate (worthless) state (Romans 1:17–31). Saints of The Most High, we must ensure we do not become tainted with this mystery of iniquity: "Wherefore come out from among them and be ye separate saith the Lord, and touch not the unclean thing: and I will receive you" (2 Cor. 6:17). We must not try to get as close as we can to the fence of sin without touching it, we must stay as far away as possible. The farther man moves from the light of the scripture, the darker (sinful) he becomes.

Read this: "And this is the condemnation, that light is come into the world, and men loved darkness rather than light, because their deeds were evil. For every one that doeth evil hateth the light, neither cometh to the light, lest his deeds should be reproved. But he that doeth truth cometh to the light that his deeds may be made manifest, that they are wrought in God" (John 3:19–21). The more mankind steps away from the principals of God, the lower mankind sinks. Mankind hates The Light of The Father, but loves darkness (sin) because he thinks it is pleasurable and for a season it is, but pay day must come.

Darkness (sin) can become heavy and oppressive. Mankind thinks they can control this darkness, but the mystery of iniquity can't be controlled. You can't let a little evil in, and try to keep out the real wicked stuff; it's a package deal. Also, people who reject The Light, hate those who have come to The Light. You may be called a bigot, holy-roller, intolerant or other names, all because you have come to The Light. Most people think they do not need Jesus. Some are people of high moral character, but they think this Jesus stuff is just a crutch.

The mystery of iniquity is in a full-frontal assault against true Christians. Because of our views and our stand for The Most High, we will soon become the scum of the earth. Either you compromise with sin or suffer. Get ready for it. I am not crying wolf, but giving you reality. "Come out of her my people" says The Lord.

Robert Gates, the leader of the Boy Scouts of America (2014-2016), said the following during a speech he gave at a national meeting of Scout leaders, on the topic of allowing homosexuals to become scout masters; "We must take the world as it is, and not what we want it to be." He is saying it is time to capitulate to the mystery of iniquity. He was received with a round of applause. The Boy Scouts of America, threw in the rain-bow colored towel and surrendered to the mystery of iniquity. And now all things LBGT are accepted into full membership. True Churches are next on their agenda.

The Supreme Court has given its verdict in favor of same-sex marriages. LBGT members are gaining political might and offices. Once they get the power they need, pastors will be forced to conduct same-sex marriages and if they refuse they will be sued or jailed.

"For to be carnally minded is death; but to be spiritually minded is life and peace, Because the carnal mind is enmity against God: for it is not subject to the law of God, neither indeed can be. So then they that are in the flesh cannot please God" (Romans 8:6–8). A carnal minded person is one whose mind stays on this world's system of pleasing the flesh, rather than focusing on the spiritual things of The Most High. If your mind loves the things of this world more than the spiritual things of God, then you and The Father are enemies. Enmity means enemy of God. A mind possessed by the mystery of iniquity is not, and cannot be pleasing to The Most High God. More on this later.

"Enter ye in at the strait gate: for wide is the gate, and broad is the way, that leadeth to destruction, and many there be which go in thereat: Because strait is the gate, and narrow is the way, which leadeth unto life, and few there be that find it" (Matt. 7:13–14). Saints; we must be narrow minded, yes narrow minded. Because in this context narrow means The Father's way. The broad way is the wide eight lane road of the mystery of iniquity. Jesus said in John 14:6, "Jesus saith unto him, I am the way, the truth, and the life; no man cometh unto the Father, but by me."

Jesus was not tolerant. He knocks out every ism there is. It is Jesus' way or no way. The narrow way has no side streets, no short cuts, no 'Y' in the road, nor is it wide enough for anything other than you. It is a single one-way road. Only wide enough for singleness or traditional marriage. Shacking up, LBGT, fornication, adultery, lying, stealing and other sins won't fit. You can't drive a semi-truck on the narrow way, because the semi is too wide and full of junk. You must walk the narrow way.

I was called to speak at a correctional officer's conference in Las Vegas, NV. One morning as my wife and I were leaving the hotel to walk around and look at all the fancy hotels near our hotel. A young lady asked us if we would like a few free tokens to play the slots machines. My wife said "no, we are Christians, we don't gamble." The young lady said, "this is Vegas; we don't do that here." She was saying, we don't do Christian stuff here. This was an agent for the mystery of iniquity trying to lead us down the broad way. We also passed a six-foot TV screen with a female in sexually explicit attire, inviting all to "come play with me." I thought to myself there is the mystery of iniquity embodied.

We can pray to hinder this "mystery of iniquity" from taking over the world, but prayer will not stop it (do not label me yet, read on). As a matter of fact, we are commanded to pray for this world and its leaders: "I exhort therefore, that, first of all, supplication, prayer, intercessions and giving of thanks, be made for all men; For kings, and for all that are in authority; that we may lead a quiet and peaceable life in all godliness and honesty. For this is good and acceptable in the sight of God our Savior" (1 Timothy 2:1–3). If we did not pray it would rapidly get worse for us. But, it will not get better.

Paul wrote, "This know also, that in the last days perilous times shall come. Yea and all that will live godly in Christ Jesus shall suffer persecution. But evil men and seducers shall wax worse and worse, deceiving, and being deceived" (2 Timothy 3:1, 12-13). This is a promise from The Most High God. If you are a God honoring person you shall suffer persecution. The mystery of iniquity will see to it. You do not have to seek persecution nor hold up a sign saying, "I follow Jesus," persecution will find you.

Even if Christians win every political office in America, they will not be able to change, take, or bring us to a better state. It does not matter who gains control of the White House or congress there will be no going back and there will be no making America great again. Read what Jesus said, "And Jesus answered and said unto them, Take heed that no man deceive you. For many shall come in my name, saying, I am Christ; and shall deceive many. And ye shall hear of wars and rumors of wars: see that ye be not troubled: for all these things must come to pass, but the end is not yet. For nation shall rise against nation, and kingdom against kingdom: and there shall be famines, and pestilences, and earthquakes, in divers places" (Matt. 24:4-7).

Prayer and the Bible were taken out of schools and no one has been able to bring them back. Abortion was made the law of the land and no one has been able to overturn it. A baby in the womb is now called a fetus. Tamper with an eagle's egg you could go to jail; but kill a baby in the womb and it is called "women rights." We have great well-known preachers who have been taken in by the mystery of iniquity. These preachers want to appear intelligent, modern, and pleasing to their congregations, so they stop using the term baby and instead used the scientific term "fetus."

We have had The Moral Majority, The Christian Coalition, Promise Keepers, and others try to take America back to Christian values. But all have failed. As will any earthly organization which thinks it can stop the mystery of iniquity. There will be personal revivals. But There will be no re-birthing or taking America back to Godly values. Those days are over. We have many "pillow prophets," who falsely prophesy of a great spiritual awakening in America, it "ain't gonna happen." "But evil men and seducers shall wax worse and worse, deceiving and being deceived" (2 Timothy 3:13).

In some countries if you speak against homosexuals it is labeled hate speech. If this book was printed in any of those countries, it would be banned and labeled obscene and I would be charged with hate speech. I hate no one, but I must stand for The Most High God. Many of us have love ones deceived by this LBGT lie. We love them just as we love those family members who are adulterers, fornicators, liars or any other sin. We pray for them, but just because they are family members is not a pass to not being judged by The Most High for their rejection of Him.

We must realize there is no going back to Mayberry. The good old days are gone. There is no going back. We are in a tornadic storm. We must "be strong in the Lord, and in the power of his might. Put on the whole armor of God, that ye may be able to stand against the wiles of the devil. For we wrestle not against flesh and blood, but against principalities, against powers, against the rulers of the darkness of this world, against spiritual wickedness in high places. Wherefore take unto you the whole armor of God, that ye may be able to withstand in the evil day, and having done all, to stand" (Ephesians 6:10-13). Truly we are in an evil day. Jesus said, "See that ye be not troubled: for all these things must come to pass, but the end is not yet" (Matt. 24:6).

Many, if not most, colleges were founded on Christian values. April Shenandoah, of The Sierra Times stated in the April 2002 issue that "one hundred-six of the first one hundred-eight colleges, were started on Christian values." But they have lost their first love. The name of Jesus is not mentioned in most of these colleges, unless it is in a historical context.

Young people of all ethnic back grounds are killing each other. Both those we would consider ignorant and those we would call highly intelligent. IQ does not matter. Wickedness works with the intelligent and the dumb alike. No one has been able to stop or control it. Education, basketball games, red ribbons, anti-bullying programs, or "Just say no," nothing man-made works.

I remember back in the sixties the social scientists were saying if we could get everyone a great education, people would be better citizens and act right. But it has not happened. We have highly educated people committing mass murder. The mystery of iniquity trumps education. What would make a group of thirty-eight, highly intelligent people from the heaven-gate cult, commit suicide in anticipation of the Hale/Bopp comet zooming by to pick up their souls? Mystery of Iniquity.

Never did it enter my mind that marijuana would be legalized for recreational use in any part of these United States. Mankind can't handle liquor, so how are they going to control marijuana? Drugs are running rampant and on course to get worse. Drug gangs and their corruption have made many, if not most, Latin America nations failed states. In Columbia, South America, the governmental leaders have thrown in the towel and said cocaine has won. They have stopped all attempts to eradicate the coca plant. Why? They just can't win; the mystery of iniquity trumps. A major drug king-pin escapes from prison, for the second time, using a mile-long tunnel. What is going on? The mystery of iniquity trumps again.

In Mexico, Honduras, Guatemala, El Salvador, Panama, Nicaragua, Venezuela and other South American nations, drug gangs control many parts, if not the entire government. The gangs conduct rampant assassination of governmental leaders, police officers, lawyers, journalist and anyone that gets in their way. In Venezuela, a person is murdered every twenty-four minutes. What could influence the mayor of Iguala Guerrero, Mexico to allow his police department, plus Federal forces to work in collusion with drug gang members, enabling them to kidnap forty-three college students, kill those same students, and burn their bodies? And no one, not one person has been held accountable. NPR reported on May 10, 2017, that Mexico is now the second most dangerous country in the world. Syria is number one.

Mexican drug gangs have made their way to the USA; they sell their drugs to the Crips, Bloods and other American gangs for a cheap price, ensuring the supply chain is totally own by them. Plus, some of the Mexican gangs have taken over the direct street selling of their drugs. Leaving the Crips, Bloods and other American gangs fighting over smaller turf. I believe this is what is causing the many killing in Chicago, and other cities. The American gangs are fighting each other because they are afraid of the Mexican gangs. The Mexican gangs have a great propensity for extreme violence. These Mexicans gangs don't just kill their victims, they ensure their victims suffer in the most horrendous ways. Then decapitating their victims. ISIS is late in the game. Mexican gangs have been cutting heads off for years.

This new concept has been a boost for the Mexicans. They are using semi-tractor trailer rigs to regularly drive back and forth between Mexico and the USA, each loaded with millions of dollars in profit for the gangs and tons of drugs for the USA. Our government knows this is going on but can't stop it. And what little drugs and money The Drug Enforcement Agency (DEA) finds is less than a drop in the bucket. You would be amazed at the number of major USA banks and world-wide banking institutions that are making billions of dollars knowingly laundering dirty drug money for the drug gangs.

The Mexican drug gangs are using sophisticated methods to smuggle drugs into the USA. They have constructed small two and three-man submarines to sneak drugs into this country. On March 29, 2012, our Coast Guard caught a narco-sub capable of carrying three tons of cocaine. CBS reported; In July 2015, a USA navy pilot spotted a blue semi-submersible forty-feet long, 200 miles off the coast of Mexico. When it was stopped it contained sixteen thousand pounds of cocaine worth 181 million dollars. In November 2015, one mini-sub was found empty and abandoned on the east coast of Florida. On Friday, March 25, 2016, Texas authorities intercepted a semi-submersible on its coast loaded with $200 million dollars, worth of cocaine. June 13, 2016, Spanish authorities intercepted a ship carrying six-tons or twelve thousand pounds of high quality cocaine. This is only what has been found.

In March of 2016 a flight attendant, with a major Airlines, was caught with seventy-pounds of cocaine in her luggage as she was attempting to pass through security. This cocaine had a street value of three million dollars. I guarantee this was not her first time doing this. Twelve current and former Transportation Security Agents (TSA) and airport workers were caught running a drug smuggling ring that may have brought in over twenty tons of cocaine into the USA through the San Juan, Puerto airport during the time frame of 1998–2016. And how many more are doing the same thing at airports all over the world.

The Charleston city paper of Charleston, SC reported in its June 19, 2017 issue. Thirty-four people from GA, NC, and SC were indicted on federal charge of trafficking meth and other drugs state wide. Even ordering drugs from CA. This criminal operation was orchestrated by two locked-up SC inmates using contraband smart phones and green dot reloadable Master Cards. "This know also, in the last days perilous times shall come. But evil men and seducers shall wax worse and worse, deceiving, and being deceived" (2 Timothy 3:1, 13).

The USA has a resurgence of cheap heroin being sold. Meth has taken over and destroyed many lives. Oxycodone (oxy cotton is one of its street names) takes away more than pain. A drug called spice is running rampart over parts of the USA. It killed seven in one day in Alaska. There is a synthetic designer drug called Alpha-PVP, the street name is Flakka. This drug produces a long lasting high, which makes it highly addictive. Flakka is running amok in Florida and other places. The CDC reported Fentanyl a synthetic opioid, fifty to one hundred times more powerful than morphine is flooding the streets of the USA. The police are advised not to touch or smell any white powder found at crime scenes. One sniff is powerful enough to kill you. The first-time use is enough to hook you for life.

Evil, money-hungry men and women, sit in labs creating these devastating synthetic drugs, with no concern for the people they are hurting. These are scientists, not some run of the mill street thug. We have Doctors, Pharmacists and senior citizens selling prescriptions for powerful narcotics to drug addicts, with no concern for the people they destroy. All they see are the mighty dollars.

There are; pastors, priests, teachers, members of the military, housewives, correctional officers, politicians, judges, investment bankers, hair dressers, policemen, airline pilots, mayors, rich, poor, you name it, millions are using and dying from illicit drugs. Young people are using drugs at an earlier age. A Lt. Governor of SC was caught using cocaine, and admitted giving some to his rich friends at private parties. But the authorities did not arrest his friends for using cocaine. Why? Too many of them were from powerful and rich families. Our young people from all walks of life rich, poor, black, white, smart and dumb are dying all over this USA from drug use and suicides.

Our government leaders do not know what to do, so they try to ignore or regulate this disaster. The Colorado Department of Revenue reported it collected 69.9 million dollars in tax revenue from marijuana sales and 41.8 million dollars from alcohol sales from July 1, 2014 to June 30, 2015. California has now jumped in with both feet. Other states now have their eye on this so-called gravy train. "The soul of the wicked desireth evil" (Proverbs 21:10). A Survey released by the Associated Press and The University of Chicago said sixty-one percent of the American people they surveyed support legalization of Marijuana. The state of Oregon after legalizing Marijuana says; "Smoke Responsibly." Have you heard that before?

There is a word in Rev. 21:8, "Sorcerers." According to 'Strong's Exhaustive Concordance of The Bible. The Greek word used for sorcerers is Pharmakos. Our word Pharmacy is taken from the root word Pharmakos. Does this mean drugs and the use of drugs will increase in these last days? Think about it.

America has been battling liquor, the drug of choice (the word liquor includes beer, rum, brandy, gin, champagnes, wine, whiskey, vodka, and any other liquid intoxicants) for years with no relief in sight. The CDC says over eighty-eight thousand, people die each year in liquor related deaths. The consumption of liquor is ingrained in our society. Many believe to have fun; liquor must be involved. Each year over fifty percent of all vehicular accidents are liquor related. Isn't it strange that ADD and SAD are the only diseases you can avoid by not partaking in the evil stuff?

Liquor fuels most fights and family abuse. Unsaved mankind; will find any excuse to drink liquor; births, marriage, divorce, deaths, sports games, new job, old job, loss job, holidays, no days, happy hour, or sad hour. The liquor companies advertise "drink responsibly," but there has not been a decrease but an increase in the numbers of liquor related deaths and people getting injured.

When I was in the U.S. Air Force, no squadron or base wide event was held unless liquor was involved. The Air Force and the other military branches were and still are battling a sever alcoholism problem with an untold number of DUIs (driving under the influence) throughout the branches. The senior leadership cannot or will not connect the squadron drinking events with the DUI problem. They would just say "drink responsibly." The leadership has failed to connect the dots. Military members can buy all the discounted liquor they want, at the base liquor store (which almost every base or post has). There was an unwritten order for all senior leaders both officers and enlisted, which stated that we must be a member of our respective club, officers' or enlisted club. This is not unique to just one branch, but all the military branches. Even the Secret Service agents can't say no to liquor.

College presidents are pulling their hair out trying to stop underage drinking, binge drinking and the sexual assaults, and deaths they bring. Many women wake up after a night of drunkenness to the realization they have been raped repeatedly with no idea who or how many men raped them. How can a young woman get gang raped by five men in broad daylight on a Florida beach with hundreds of young people standing around and no one intervened? Liquor!

In January 2015, President Obama was giving his State of the union speech and a Supreme Court Justice who could not resist the lure of strong drink was caught on national TV nodding off in an alcoholic stupor. Judges, politicians, pastors, priests, house wives, policemen, leaders of the community, any job title you can think of, they can't resist the allure of liquor. Cities plan a gathering in the city square, but it is not successful unless it has liquor available.

All over this world, women and children are being raped and killed daily in liquor related events with no end in sight. Hundreds if not thousands of women have been killed because they wanted to go to a bar (lounge for those who don't go to bars) for a little moderate liquor consumption and while there they met a man or men full of the mystery of iniquity who rapes, and many times kill her.

"Who hath woe? Who hath sorrow? Who hath contentions? Who hath babbling? Who hath wounds without cause? Who hath redness of eyes? They that tarry long at the wine; they that go to seek mixed wine. Look not thou upon the wine when it is red, when it giveth his color in the cup when it moveth itself aright. At the last it biteth like a serpent, and stingeth like an adder. Thine eyes shall behold strange women, and thine heart shall utter perverse things. Yea, thou shalt be as he that lieth down in the midst of the sea, or as he that lieth upon the top of a mast. They have stricken me, shalt thou say, and I was not sick; they have beaten me, and I felt it not: when shall I awake? I will seek it yet again" (Proverbs 23:29–35).

Unsaved mankind would rather drink than think about or seek The Lord. "Woe unto them that rise up early in the morning, that they may follow strong drink; that continue until night, till wine inflame them! And the harp, and the viol (stringed instrument), the tabret, and pipe, and wine are in their feasts; but they regard not the work of the Lord, neither consider the operation of his hands" (Isaiah 5:11–12). They would rather "party hardy," than think about The Most High God.

We have Christian, who advocates moderate liquor consumption or so-called social drinking for all. And they used Christ's miracle of turning the water into wine as an example. You can find this in John 2:1–11. But if this is true, and it was wine and not some kind of fruit juice, then Christ would be a deceiver: "Wine is a mocker, strong drink is raging: and whose ever is deceived thereby is not wise" (Proverbs 20:1). Christ is not a deceiver therefore the water was turned into juice. Also; "Woe unto them that call evil good, and good evil; that put darkness for light, and light for darkness; that put bitter for sweet, and sweet for bitter! Woe unto them that are mighty to drink wine, and men of strength to mingle strong drink" (Isaiah 5:20, 22). Mingle means to make. If Jesus Christ made fermented wine, (the Bible sometimes uses the same word for fermented and unfermented wine) He would be under a curse. We know Christ is not under a curse, He is the curse breaker. Thus, it could not have been alcoholic wine.

"For my thoughts are not your thoughts, neither are your ways my ways, saith the Lord. For as the heavens are higher than the earth, so are my ways higher than your ways, and my thoughts than your thoughts" (Isaiah 55:8-9). The Father's ways are much higher than ours. All fifty states say a blood alcohol level of 0.08 percent is legally drunk. Now, this is man's thinking. When would The Most High consider you drunk? He says; "Know ye not that the unrighteous shall not inherit the kingdom of God? Be not deceived: neither fornicators, nor idolaters, nor adulterers, nor effeminate, nor abusers of themselves with mankind. Nor thieves, nor covetous, nor drunkards, nor revilers, nor extortioners, shall inherit the kingdom of God" (1 Cor. 6: 9-10). As you can see a drunkard shall not inherit The Kingdom of God. So in His standards is 0.03 percent, 0.05 percent, or 0.06 percent drunk enough not to allow you in His heaven?

And how many times must you get drunk to be considered a drunkard? Researchers at the University of California, San Diego found that drivers with a blood alcohol level of 0.01, which can register that much after consumption of one beer. Were 46 percent more likely to be responsible for a crash than completely sober drivers. Researchers are urging legislators to lower the legal limit below 0.08 (May 2014 Reader's Digest). It will never happen.

Liquor is not food. You must have food and water to live. Drinking liquor in any form is purely pleasing the flesh. See Galatians 5:16–21. And why would a saint want to indulge in activity that has no redeeming value, only hell and destruction. Try to explain to the little child or the woman beaten and sexually abuse by a drunkard, how open minded you, the moderate Christian drinker are. "For so is the will of God, that with well doing ye may put to silence the ignorance of foolish men: As free, and not using your liberty for a cloak of maliciousness (evil), but as the servants of God" (1 Peter 2:15–16). "For, brethren, ye have been called unto liberty: only use not liberty for an occasion to the flesh, but by love serve one another" (Galatians 5:13). You are using the liberty we have, as a hiding place for your evil intentions.

Let me ask you this, is it acceptable to have a moderate amount of adultery or to fornicate sociability? What about a small taste of murder? Give me chapter and verse for such a thing.

When you drink liquor around the unsaved, they do not appreciate you, nor do they believe you are a forward-thinking person. Instead they look at you as a hypocrite. Do you think it is a badge of honor or a prideful thing, because you think you have become liberated and can now drink liquor? You may have listened to so called influential Christian leaders, who taught this moderation or social drinking hog wash. I suggest you rethink and restudy your Bible, lest you become a decoy duck for satan. he is going to use you to lure others to his and your evil way of thinking. The Father tells us; "Be sober, be vigilant; because your adversary the devil, as a roaring lion, walketh about, seeking whom he may devour" (1 Peter 5:8). satan wants you in an altered state of mind. The Most High wants you to be sober not slightly inebriated. Liquor feeds the flesh, not your spirit. It opens and frees your inhibitions, making you do and say things you will regret later. And show me one incident in the Bible where the people were drinking intoxicating wine and all had a good time and The Most High got the praise and glory.

"And many that believed came, and confessed, and showed their deeds. Many of them also which used curious arts brought their books together, and burned them before all men; and they counted the price of them, and found it fifty thousand pieces of silver. So mightily grew the word of God and prevailed" (Acts 19:18-20). The word of The Most High must grow and prevail, and not compromised to please our flesh. "But ye are a chosen generation, a royal priesthood, a holy nation, a peculiar people; that ye should show forth the praises of him who hath called you out of darkness into his marvelous light" (1 Peter 2:9). We are to be a peculiar people not compromising people. We represent THE MOST HIGH GOD, and we are to do things that bring Him praise, not dishonor.

And if that is not enough, "But take heed lest by any means this liberty of yours become a stumbling block to them that are weak. For if any man see thee which hast knowledge sit at meat in the idol's temple, shall not the conscience of him which is weak be emboldened to eat those things which are offered to idols; And through thy knowledge shall the weak brother perish, for whom Christ died? But when ye sin so against the brethren, and wound their weak conscience, ye sin against Christ. Wherefore, if meat make my brother to offend, I will eat no flesh while the world standeth, lest I make my brother to offend" (1 Cor. 8:9–13). Paul is saying rather than allowing my weak brother to see me eat meat that had been offered to idols and the weak brother commits sin against his conscience, I would never eat meat again period. This same example can be applied to liquor.

If it sounds as if I have an agenda against liquor, "I do." All God-fearing saints should feel the same way. Let's cut to the chase. If you are a partaker of liquor, you are a partaker of the world. "I BESEECH you therefore, brethren, by the mercies of God, that ye present your bodies a living sacrifice, holy, acceptable unto God, which is your reasonable service. And be not conformed to this world: but be ye transformed by the renewing of your mind, that ye may prove what is that good, and acceptable, and prefect, will of God" (Romans 12:1-2). This is a command to turn away from anything which could hinder your walk with The Most High. No matter how much you think you can do something, you are to be a living sacrifice. You must be ready to sacrifice all if needed for the sake of the gospel. We must be transformed to His standard, not conformed to the world's standards.

Susanna Wesley, the mother of John Wesley said, "If you wish to determine the lawfulness of a pleasure, follow this rule; Whatever weakens your reasons, impairs the tenderness of your conscience, obscure your sense of God, or take away the relish of spiritual things; whatever increases the authority of your body over your mind that is sin." Amen.

Even after all I have given you, your flesh is telling some of you not to listen to that narrow-minded man. Don't listen to me but honestly seek The Will of The Most High God. "Whether therefore ye eat or drink, or whatsoever ye do, do all to the glory of God" (1 Cor. 10:31). Go into a bar (I mean lounge), lift your glass and say the following out loud so everyone can hear, "Jesus Christ, I glorify you with this drink of liquor."

Liquor is part of the mystery of iniquity. The Government, great academics, nor Social Scientists, none have found a way to stop "the mystery of iniquity" it is a force to be reckoned with. Mankind can't handle it.

Whenever liquor is on the scene, sex is not far behind. I was visiting Atlanta, GA and saw a panel delivery truck with liquor advertising on it. The truck had a larger than life size picture of a female robot in a seductive nude pose on both side panels of the truck inviting you to buy this brand of liquor because it helps the good times roll.

The Center for Disease Control (CDC) said the following in a press release dated Nov. 17, 2015: "Cases of Sexually Transmitted Disease (STD) are on the rise Chlamydia, Gonorrhea, Syphilis, Human Papillomavirus, Herpes Simplex, and Trichomoniasis are on the rise and are vastly under reported. CDC estimates that nearly 20 million new STDs are sexually transmitted every year in this country. Half of that 20 million is among young people aged 15-24, particularly among women. Syphilis among men who have sex with other men has been increasing since 2000. This group account for 83 percent of male cases." The CDC also reported the following for the year 2015; 24,874 cases of Syphilis and 36,589 cases of Chlamydia in people ages forty-five to sixty-four—nearly triple what the stats were in the year 2000. Seniors are hooking up too. The number of people with STDs are in the millions and growing.

Do you not see why the world looks for a cure for AIDs and other STDs? Not just because STDs are very dangerous and harmful, but they slow down the sex. For this reason, drug companies worked 24/7 to develop a treatment and cure for AIDS. But Cancer kills far more people than AIDS. In Africa, there are villages that have had their entire adult population decimated by AIDS. Due to the growing AIDS epidemic in Africa, many social services workers have become so desperate they are now giving out banana and chocolate flavored condoms. Why? The population can't say no to fornication. They treat sex as a hobby. Forget the word abstinence it is never mentioned, unless it is by a church base organization.

Think on this when was the last time you heard the word AIDS on TV or seen it in print. It is treated as if it has been eradicated and is no longer a threat. The mystery of iniquity had its people tone down the rhetoric.

Those who have studied ancient Roman history, will remember Roman's last days as a nation were devoted to sex. Any kind of sexual act that could be imagine was theirs to perform. And as always it led to the mass killing of babies. Roman became weak and anemic and was conquered by its own sin.

In the ancient world, they had temple prostitutes. The modern world has done away with the temple and introduced TV. There is a reality show which features nude dating. There is another TV show which features the exploits of open marriages. Husbands, and wives swapping with other couples for sex and sexual orgies.

There is a bus driving all over America called "Girls Gone Wild." They film videos of woman, old and young pulling their tops up or off, and pulling their pants down before the TV camera; usually in places where liquor is sold and consumed. Then the videos are shown on TV for evil, perverted men to salivate over. And they wonder why sexual assaults are on the rise. People can't stop without help from The Almighty.

According to Lavu.com Dec. 5, 2016; Cities in the following countries share a unique dining experience; Milan, Italy; Tokyo, Japan; London, England; Melbourne, Australia. Each one has a restaurant called the "Amrita," which means "Immortality." To enter these restaurants, you pay a very high entrance fee, no older than sixty-four, and no more than thirty-three lbs. over-weight. Then you must take off all your clothes and put on paper under-wear (bottoms only). Then you can sit down and enjoy your meal and watch a group of male sodomites folic on stage.

The Most High God knew once Adam fell, men could no longer handle looking upon the nakedness of females. Therefore, he put clothes on Adam and Eve. But since then, man has been doing his best to undress females. Check Leviticus chapters eighteen, and twenty when you have time. As mankind evolves in its wickedness, that which once was "deviant," becomes "wickedly evil," and soon evolves into "just evil," and then "strange." And before long it is "their choice" and in the last step it becomes, "normal." We are only years away from public nudity and the legalization of sex between adults and under-age children.

John Douglas former head of the FBI's Elite Serial Crime Unit said; "There are at any given moment somewhere between twenty-five to fifty serial killers on prowl here in America." And many of those killers usually sexually assault their victims.

We had a married USA president caught in the White House having sex with a young woman and most of America thought nothing of it. The former leader of The International Monetary Fund got caught with his hands somewhere they should not have been, but no big deal, "Boys will be boys," the world says. Even when it was revealed he and his buddies were having sex orgies with high price prostitutes, no big deal, just a little sex to unwind from a hard day of giving out money. Go to Washington, DC and visit some of our male senators and representatives and witness for yourself the many young, skimpy dressed females working in their offices. Sex and power.

Rich male muslims travel to other countries to engage in all the sex they want, without the home crowd knowing about it. This enables them to still be considered an upstanding and faithful muslim back home. Several of the upper echelon of the Saudi family of Saudi Araba have been accused of this. Some rich male muslims also have a system where they do a sham marriage to a poor but good-looking woman and after they use her, she is abandon, while he moves on to the next target. Many world class American travelers, transverse all over the globe looking for so called "good sex." We have so-called Christians who leave their home town and go to another city to do their evil. I know of a denominational college where they have a yearly retreat for pastors and ministers of a certain denomination. And once they are at the college, the liquor and sex flows freely for those who want it. The mystery of iniquity at work.

A clear majority of teenagers, college students, and adults search for a friend of the opposite sex, or same-sex for so-called casual sex. They label themselves "friends with benefits." They just want a quick "hook up," without strings. Abortions and birth control pills are so popular because they enable you to have sex with little worries of producing babies. There is a web site whose sole purpose is to enable those who want to commit adultery to do so without getting caught (or so they thought).

We live in a sex crazed world; sex, sex, sex, and more sex. Sex and the female body has become idols in America. On many TV commercials and bill boards, "hot" sexy females are used to sell everything; clothes, bottled water, liquor, rugs, cars, car parts, trucks, batteries, boats, even hamburgers. Advertisers know sex sells anything. Some so-called church groups use sex to sell Jesus to the unsaved. They send their young ladies in bikinis to the beach to witness to unsaved men. They know what they are doing because they don't send older over-weight women in bikinis to preach.

People want new and exciting thrills to quench their sexual appetite. The following excerpt was taken from 'Oct. 2010 Reader's Digest; FREEDOM FIGHTER, written by Mary A. Fischer;' "Across town, at ICE headquarters. Tracy Cormier was wrapping up another investigation. She laid out stuffed animals and coloring books for a frightened four-year old girl she'd freed from a smuggler's drop house an hour before. The little girl had been drugged at the U.S.-Mexican border and kidnapped by the smuggler, who'd held her for $11,500 in ransom and let his son sexually assault her."

All perverts are not lone-wolfs some of them work for tech companies whose goal is to perfect the most anatomically correct female sex robot for their follow sex perverts who yearn for new sex thrills. This world has a major pedophile problem. We have priests, preachers, pastors, military members, teachers, lawyers, doctors, politicians, pillars of the community, rich and poor in all walks of life, preying on our children, just to please their greedy and lustful sexual appetite. Britain and Ireland has revealed a major pedophile ring, which has been sexually abusing thousands of children for decades. Many young children are being raised in very wicked, depraved, and sinister homes. These children then become abusers themselves.

Some of you reading this book know or suspect some child is being sexually assaulted right now. But you will not turn the pervert in to the authorities. When I was a teenager we had sex perverts who preyed on many teenagers in our community. The adults did not try to stop them, so we teens took it upon ourselves to warn each other to stay away from these perverts.

I had child-hood friends who told me they had attacked and beat up some of the perverts. I am not condoning their actions, but if adults acted like adults those teens would not have felt they had to do this. If you know this is going on and fail to report it, you are just as guilty as the pervert that is assaulting the child. And if the law does not deal with you The Most High will. Jesus said, "Take heed that ye despise not one of these little ones; for I say unto you, That in heaven their angels do always behold the face of my Father which is in heaven" (Matt. 18:10).

I have noticed the media romanticizing people we once considered sexual perverts. They are now put forth as avant-garde. Be it homosexuals, movie directors, actors, actress, writers, or some other powerful professional person. They are being lifted before us, as people to admire. THEY ARE SEXUAL PERVERTS. Some of you now reading this book have yourselves been abused by a sex pervert. It was not your fault. The Most High Father will not let it go, that person who abused you will face Him at the Great White Throne Judgment.

Ladies, there is such pressure on you to look "hot and sexy." It is everywhere. People are dying, to look "young and hot." Plastic surgery is big business. Plastic surgeons have some clients who are a major part of their yearly office budget. You can have wrinkles removed from almost every part of your body. You can enhance your breast, butt, even your lips through plastic surgery. For those women who want breast enhancement surgery but can't afford to pay for it. There is a web site with a listing of evil perverts who will pay for the surgery and in return they want just a few pictures of the results. We have Christian leaders, male and female who are having plastic surgery so they can look "hot" for a little while longer. Many people both female and male, have had numerous face lifts. Some of them have had their faces tighten so many times their lips are in a perpetual smile from ear to ear. Remember this no matter how much plastic surgery you have, gravity is still working and pulling everything down.

Ladies some of you are so consumed with having Kardashian breasts and butts. You will go to great lengths to get them. Even flocking to hotel rooms were quacks inject you with non-sterile commercial grade silicone. Causing sickness and many times death. All in the name of looking "hot."

Step into a drug store and you would expect to find just drugs. Not so, most of what you find there is aisle upon aisle of products to make you look "hot." Skin creams, wrinkle removers, anti-sag cream, lipstick, skin moisturizers, paste that tightens the skin, hair dyes, face paint, stuff to remove face paint, body paint, finger/toe nail paint, deer eyelashes, something for every part of you, row upon row of stuff to make you look "hot." If your butt and breast are not big or frim enough and you are afraid to go under the knife, just buy some padded under-wear and up-lifting bras to give you that firm "hot" look. I called it "hot" in a box.

We have people who make a very good living doing finger/toe nails painting. Hey "pamper yourself" is the word for today. Even the men have hair dyes and other stuff so they can maintain that "hunk" look.

I tried to find the origin of deer (eye) lashes, but was un-successful in finding a consistence origin. But, I found a verse in the Bible. "Lust not after her beauty in thine heart; neither let her take thee with her eyelids" (Proverbs 6:25). The bigger the eyelids the bigger the attraction.

This desire to look "hot" is not something you are born with. But a learned behavior. I was in a store in the checkout line one day. And I saw a lady standing in line with her "hot" clothes on. She also had her young daughter with her. I notice the daughter watching the men watch her mother's butt in those tight leggings (yoga pants included). The little girl eyes would go to her mother's butt, then to the eyes of the men standing in line. The young girl was learning to get the looks from men you must wear the "hot" clothes. This is a learn behavior. In these last days, it will only get worst.

Most women's magazines teach women how to look, regain, or fake "hotness." These "hot" magazines are nothing more than pornography. They are full of nude "hot" females (I say nude because what they have on is no way close to semi, which means half). They encourage you to continue to be "hot" play toys for men and out strut the other "hot" women. Ladies, this puts you in such competition with other women that many times you can't get along with each other. You are trying to out "hot" each other.

I have gone into stores and observed women watching each other, and even throw their nose up in the air, because "I am hotter than you are." This has been ingrained into this world's system for a long time. Even normal men's magazines must have "hot" women in them. I will not buy certain fishing magazines because they have "hot" females in bikinis. A woman in a bikini does not help me catch fish or buy a boat?

Many women are consumed with looking young and desirable, they want no wrinkles, everything firm, nothing sagging or not in place. Some are so vain they will not give their age, as if keeping silent about your age will make you look "hot." Some of you are destroying your feet by stuffing them into four, five, six inch pointed heels, in a vain attempt to have shapely legs and a protruding butt. Your clothes are so tight you must squeeze into them. And shorts so short they look like panties with your butt cheeks protruding out for all to see and lust after.

Some of you ladies reading this book are starving yourselves into near anemic and anorexic. Because men say looking very skinny is sexy. There is also a trend to dress women in short frilly dresses to have that innocent little girl look. TV is doing this on many of its commercials, the models have the face of a young girl. This appeals to the perverted men who really desires a little girl to have sex with.

My wife and I recently went to my granddaughter's high school graduation. I have never seen so much "hotness" on parade. Little girls, preteen girls, teenage girls, young women, middle age women, even older women, fat, skinny didn't matter they were trying to out "hot" each other. One lady who sat in front of us had on such skimpy, tight and low-cut clothes her throng under-wear was showing. I started to say something to the male that was with her. But I didn't want to start a fight. So, I just kept my eyes upward.

Ladies, you become angry at men because; "they admire my body and not my mind." But if you dress to be "hot" then that is what you get. I had a female TV news reporter come to my house to conduct an interview with me. She was dressed to be "super-hot." Her dress was so short, when she sat down her underwear was showing I had to keep looking up over her head so I would not see under her dress. This was the worst interview I ever did. I will never do another interview with a female dressed like that. She wanted to be taken serious but she was not dress serious. Ladies you cannot dress to be "hot" and dress for success at the same time. If it is not for sale don't advertise.

The mystery of iniquity has cause a disconnects between illusions and reality, thus spreading a veil over sound reasoning. For example, most women will not walk around in regular bra and panties in public places. Yet those same women will prance around before the public in those same items, but now it is label as swim suits or bikinis. The mystery of iniquity has fooled most people into believing it is not the same thing. They say, "it's what you wear at the beach." Even though many bikinis/thongs have far less materiel than regular bra and panties.

Please allow me to think out loud. With the advent of the swimsuits and bikinis, mixed with the mystery of iniquity, a twisted, evil, and worldly logic has crept into the minds of most men and women; saved and unsaved. The wearing of those items deceived both males and female into the mindset that being almost naked is considered the same as being fully clothe. Now, with this logic, if females can walk around almost naked, having only their nipples and genitals areas covered, and still be consider decently dressed; why be alarm when she walks around in other public places in yoga type pants, short shorts, super-mini dresses, and micro tops if the same areas are covered? Even in church, saved and unsaved. This same logic is use

THE SPIRIT OF THE ANTI-CHRIST

for men to walk around without shirts on. This is stinking thinking of the world.

This disconnect is also present in dance, ballet, ice skating, gymnastic, soft ball, tennis, even women volley ball. What is so athletic about women in bikinis playing volley ball? The young girls and women are dressed to show off their femininity (sexual parts). Very few males will go to a men's beach volleyball competition. But they flock to the women's competition. And ladies I object to men swim suits also.

This disconnect is also in play when women are dressed in lingerie and are displayed on TV, in newspapers, magazines, and store front windows. We fail to call it what it really is, pornography. People complain about the men wearing their pants below their butts, but no one says anything about females displaying their breasts or butts in public. (I might as well jump in with both feet.) Men, should not walk around with-out a shirt on or their butts showing either. I am here to tell you, all are indecent.

At sporting events, this disconnect is also present. The male cheerleaders are fully dressed. But the female cheerleaders are dressed sexy, in all kinds of cut up, skimpy and tight uniforms. The illusion says, "encourage the fans and teams." Reality is, they are dressed to excite the males, and show off their bodies. If you think I am wrong, answer me this; when was the last time you saw an overweight female cheerleader jumping up and down leading a cheer? Mmmmmmmm. And look at their movements they don't just jump up and down, but instead their movements are sexual, sensual, and meant to arouse. This includes high school, college, and pro sports.

High schools and college bands also have their "hot" girls strutting their stuff in sexually explicit outfits. There is a case before the U.S. supreme court over who has control over those "hot," sexy, and pornographic uniforms. Let me ask you this; what is the difference between a cheerleader, band hot girl or a swim suit clad woman and a stripper kicking up their legs? None! It's all pornography.

There are women lingerie football leagues in a few places in the USA. These women are out there in lingerie and little else. The only purpose this serves is for lustful men to fantasize and salivate over.

I wonder if they have young male hunks in hot pants leading the cheers. Boy, I am going to have to leave the country when this book is published.

I read an article written about a professional football cheerleader, who was brought into a church to tell of her great love and honor for The Lord. But yet she is out there shaking her butt in her tight short, short, hot pants. I wonder how many men are thinking "what a great Christian witness," as she gives them an eye full of things bouncing and shaking. Christians support the many different "hot" women beauty pageants, by bringing these women into church to speak to the congregation of their love for The Lord. These pageants are about who is the "hottest." Or else they would not have a bikini or evening grown competitions. The men also run around in their postage stamps trunks in the Mr. hunk competition. But, have you notice the church does not bring in any of the male Mr. Hunk contestants? I wonder why?

Hollywood is another supplier of pornography. The females on soap operas, TV shows, advertisements, movies, and music videos walk in their haughtiness, with stretched forth necks, wanton eyes and seductive manners. They parade around with their breast and butts showing so everyone can get a peek. They are nothing more than pornographic depictions. Pornography is a tool of the mystery of iniquity. It is lurking, prowling, waiting to entrap its victims and make him or her a captive in a life-long, sometimes losing battle to its sinful addiction.

Parents, oh parents, you must protect your children at all costs from the hideous effect of pornography. Beware what goes on in their playmates' home. Know what they are watching on TV, internet devices, and print media. Which are three of the greatest pimps of pornography. I would caution you on letting your children watch Utube alone.

An elementary school psychologist told me she is trying to counsel seven, eight, nine years and older boys, who are already addicted to pornography. What kind of character do you think they will have as they grow into adulthood or should I say abuser/hood? Pornography is ingrained into our society and it is training the next generation of abusers/predators and most of the world are not aware of it. They have been lulled to sleep by the mystery of iniquity.

Mothers and Fathers, why do you dress your little girls in those so called "cute" short mini dresses and some of you even put make-up on them? Do you think it is cute? Well, it is not. Sin is not cute, but evil. You are setting them up for some pervert to salivate over or worse. The mystery of iniquity has told you "it is so cute." Instead, you should be training them to dress and look modest while they are young and they may continue that life style once they leave your house. Think about this; men want the older women to look younger and the younger girls to look older. This is foolishness. Parents if you do not teach them modesty, then the world will teach them to be "hot."

We have saints trying to redeem Hollywood. They are fooling themselves. Hollywood is beyond reformation. They make a few movies with some redeeming content because the producers know a dollar is a dollar whether it is from a sinner or saint. Hollywood will not allow itself to be reformed. Those "hot" female stars are consumed with being the center of attraction. Look how they prance and poise when a camera is pointed their way.

Ladies, since when are you "blessed" because you have big breasts with ample cleavage, firm buttocks, or "great legs." Your anatomy has nothing to do with blessings from The Father. When Adam and Eve sinned, one of the first thing The Father did was put clothes on them (Genesis 3:21).

This sex craze mentality has also stepped boldly into the church. The day meant for Worship of The Most High, has become fashion and Hollywood strip day as women parade up and down the church aisle in all manner of undress. They have on their contoured dresses and body hugging clothes. We have entered an age where so-called Christian woman can un-dress any way they want and still feel they can call themselves Saints of The Most High and Holy God. True worship cannot take place where the flesh and "hotness" is on the throne.

A few years ago, you could tell the prostitutes by their dress. No more. Saints are dressing like they ain'ts. Many Christian women now have the minds of prostitutes. They want to be titillating, sensuous and voluptuously "hot" temples of The Most High God. The clothes worn to church by many women are tight, short, and cut up and would fit right at home in a bar, oh excuse me I meant a lounge for those who do not go to "bars."

Christian ladies when you dressed to be "hot," you become part of. "MYSTERY, BABLYON THE GREAT, THE MOTHER OF HARLOTS AND ABOMINATIONS OF THE EARTH" (Rev. 17:5). We will talk about this later in chapter six.

Some of you would label me a "clothes line preacher." Call me what you will. But, I am in good company with the original "clothes line preacher" The Most High and Holy God: "In like manner also, that women adorn themselves in modest apparel, with shamefacedness and sobriety" (1 Timothy 2:9). Ladies; most of your clothing items would not pass the modest apparel test and forget the shamefacedness part. Where is the modesty when you have lingerie on in public? Just having a long shirt over your butt to cover the tight stretch pants or sheer leggings, or yoga pants, is not modest. Covering just the nipples of your breast and genital area is not modest. We have pastor's wives and female Christian preachers and singers showing as much breast and bare thighs as the world.

Many are not agreeing with what I am writing. Why? "Take heed, brethren, lest there be in any of you an evil heart of unbelief in departing from the living God. But exhort one another daily, while it is called Today; lest any of you be hardened through the deceitfulness of sin" (Hebrews 3:12-13). The mystery of iniquity will slowly cause you to draft away from the Truths of our Father.

Many pastors and Christian counsellors will not agree with what I am about to say. But that hasn't stopped me before. There is so much pornographic dressing by women both in church and outside church it is no wonder so many Christian men are hooked on pornography. To some men it is overwhelming. I was in a store and a woman had on a pair of tight jeans with numerous holes in them. With one of the holes right next to her genital area as if to say, "here is a hole next to the hole."

THE SPIRIT OF THE ANTI-CHRIST

In one church I visited, there was a woman wearing a see through sheer dress, with only the sexual areas covered. No, she was not a visitor, but a member of this church. Over-weight women are not letting their weight stop them from trying to be "hot" either. Some women are now wearing tight leggings with nothing covering their behinds. This is in church, not just on the streets. The dresses are so short and tight. You can tell the ones who are conscience of the shortness of the dress, because they keep trying to stretch it over their thighs but they can't due to a lack of material. But many do not care, they want it all to hang out.

This hotness craze was foretold by The Most High God. In 2 Timothy 3: 1-5 a list of sins of the last days are listed. Verse 1, "This know also that in the last days perilous times shall come." It then goes on to list signs of the last days, I am only going to give a few of them. Verse 2, "Lovers of their own selves;" this means selfish and fond of pleasure, voluptuousness, sensuous (giving sexual gratification) and wanting to be admired. Also in verse 2, "Proud;" this means haughty, feeling and acting superior. In verse 3, "Incontinent;" powerless without self-control (everyone is doing it), Also in verse 3, "Despisers;" which means hostile to virtue. These are just a few of many that tells us we are in the last days.

The saints of The Most High are not to be regarded as "hot." The Father does not need "hot" saints. Being "hot" is a work of the flesh. The inward, spiritual you should not allow the old fleshly you to continue to be "hot." You may say, "It is not my fault men can't take their eyes off me." This is partially true. The Christian man bears the sole responsibility for his thinking. But you will be held responsible for putting a stumbling block, or an occasion to fall, in your brother's way. "Let us not therefore judge one another anymore: but judge this rather, that no man put a stumbling block or an occasion to fall in his brother's way" (Romans 14:13).

Ladies whether you like it or not, the Most High has made you a sexual brake. Men operate by sight. Whereas the woman responses to the man. We are now in an age of the "hot" accelerator, forget that brake stuff. Your dress shows what is in your heart, rebellion: "For rebellion is as the sin of witchcraft, and stubbornness is as iniquity and idolatry" (1 Samuel 15:23).

Romans 1:18–25 tells us how mankind has entered a state of reprobation or worthlessness to God. Look at verse 25, "Who changed the truth of God into a lie and worshiped and served the creature more than the Creator who is blessed forever. Amen." This verse tells of a practice called creature or self-worship. This is where you want others to look at you, admire you and give you worship. Ladies, when you let dress and how "hot" you look consume your life, you are calling men to come and worship at your altar and to dine at your table which is the table of Diana the sex goddess (Acts 19:26–34). If what I am saying is bothering you, good, read on. This is the flesh working overtime and it is a hallmark of "the mystery of iniquity" fleshly lust will flourish and run amok during the a-c's kingdom.

The Bible teaches in Romans 6:23: "For the wages of sin is death; but the gift of God is eternal life through Jesus Christ our Lord." Most people think this saying is outdated and passé. "This is the new millennial let it all hang out," is the word for today. Pastors it is up to you to refuse to allow this theater to continue, unless you are also taking pleasure in the views you see.

Pastors are morally falling all over the USA. They are committing adultery and fornication, because they are lead astray by their own lust as they become overwhelmed by all this "hotness" in the aisles.

Please read the following indictment from the Most High. "Because that, when they knew God, they glorified him not as God, neither were thankful; but became vain in their imaginations, and their foolish heart was darkened. Professing themselves to be wise, they became fools, And changed the glory of the uncorruptible God into an image made like to corruptible man, and to birds, and four-footed beasts, and creeping things. Wherefore God also gave them up to uncleanness through the lusts of their own hearts, to dishonor their own bodies between themselves: Who change the truth of God into a lie and worshiped and served the creature more than the Creator, who is blessed forever, Amen. For this cause God gave

THE SPIRIT OF THE ANTI-CHRIST

them up unto vile affections: for even their women did change the natural use into that which is against nature: And likewise also the men, leaving the natural use of the woman, burned in their lust one toward another; men with men working that which is unseemly, and receiving in themselves that recompense of their error which was meet. And even as they did not like to retain God in their knowledge, God gave them over to a reprobate mind, to do those things which are not convenient. Being filled with all unrighteousness, fornication, wickedness, covetousness, maliciousness; full of envy, murder, debate, deceit, malignity; whisperers, Backbiters, haters of God, despiteful, proud, boasters, inventors of evil things, disobedient to parents, Without understanding, covenant-breakers, without natural affection, implacable, unmerciful: Who knowing the judgment of God, that they which commit such things are worthy of death, not only do the same, but have pleasure in them that do them" (Romans 1:21–32).

Paul wrote this concerning the evil in his day and time. But it is more relevant now than ever before. Verses 26 and 27, directly refers to the LBGT group. Don't add or twist the scripture. It is not open for discussion or your opinion it is a command of The Most High. It is, what it is.

Read the following: "Moreover the Lord saith, Because the daughters of Zion are haughty, and walk with stretched forth necks and wanton eyes (deer lashes), walking and mincing as they go, and making a tinkling with their feet (think Hollywood): Therefore the Lord will smite with a scab the crown of the head of the daughters of Zion, and the Lord will discover their secret parts. In that day the Lord will take away the bravery of their tinkling ornaments about their feet, and their cauls, (hair bonnets) and their round tires (ornaments around the neck) like the moon. The chains, and bracelets, and the mufflers (earrings), The bonnets, and the ornaments of the legs, and the headbands (sashes), and the tablets (perfume boxes), and the earrings. The rings, and nose jewels, The changeable suits of apparel, and the mantles, and the wimples (handbags), and the crisping pins, The glasses (mirrors), and the fine linen, and the hoods (hats), and the veils. And it shall come to pass, that instead of sweet smell there shall be stink; and instead of a girdle a rent; and instead of well-set hair (hairdo) baldness; and instead of a stomacher (pretty robe) a girding of sackcloth; and burning instead of beauty (think STDs)" (Isaiah 3:16–24).

Even in ancient times women were dressing "hot," as if they were baby dolls on display, and inviting a man to come play with them. Men and women; that which you are most proud of, The Lord will something strike it down. "The way of the wicked seduceth them" (Proverbs 12:26). And this, "As a jewel of gold in a swine's snout, so is a fair woman which is without discretion" (Proverbs 11:22).

Many of you are saying "your dress doesn't matter, it's what in your heart." If that statement is true then why did The Most High have Paul write the following: "In like manner also, that women adorn themselves in modest apparel, with shamefacedness and sobriety; not with braided hair, or gold, or pearls, or costly array; But (which becometh women professing godliness) with good works." (1 Timothy 2:9-10). Or Peter, "Whose adorning let it not be that outward adorning of plaiting the hair, and or wearing of-gold, or of putting on of apparel; But let it be the hidden man of the heart, in that which is not corruptible, even the ornament of a meek and quiet spirit, which is in the sight of God of great price" (1 Peter 3:3-4). Dressing sexual is called, "And, behold, there met him a woman with the <u>attire of a harlot,</u> and subtile of heart" (Proverbs 7:10).

Our Savior Jesus Christ said, "Ye shall know them by their fruits. Do men gather grapes of thorns, or figs of thistles? Even so every good tree bringeth forth good fruit; but a corrupt tree bringeth forth evil fruit. Wherefore by their fruits ye shall know them" (Matt. 7:16–17, 20). "But those things which proceed out of the mouth come forth from the heart; and they defile the man. For out of the heart proceed evil thoughts, murders, adulteries, fornication, thefts, false witness, blasphemies" (Matt. 15:18–19). Your dress is a fruit or produce of your heart.

Paul told Timothy to teach the preceding statement not because he didn't want women looking good, but because the Christian women felt they had to complete with the unsaved women who dressed like prostitutes. Paul had to warn Timothy about Timothy's own conduct. "Flee also youth lust: but follow righteousness, faith charity, peace, with them that call on the Lord out of a pure heart" (2 Timothy 2:22).

When the Bible says in 2 Cor. 6:17, "Wherefore come out from among them, and be ye separate." This does not mean if the world shows a lot of cleavage, the saints can show a little bit. Or if the world wears their clothes short, short and tight, tight that the saints can wear theirs slightly short and tight. It means do not follow them. The church I grew up in was very conservative when it came to dress for both males and females. They have now kick that modesty stuff to the curb, everything is on display. I have seen this shift in holiness churches also. The word now is "The Lord gave this body to me, so I will show it off." One female preacher foolishly said; "The Lord gave me lips and He gave me hips, and I am going to use all of them."

Ladies, it is not my intentions to advocate the wearing of sack cloth and ashes. If you can afford a three-hundred-dollar outfit, buy and wear it. But don't let the outfit, your gold, your hairdo, your breasts and butt, out shine The Father. "Having a form of godliness, but denying the power thereof: from such turn away" (2 Timothy 3:5). The flesh without the control of the Holy Spirit leads to death. Saved men and women are: "But ye are a chosen generation, a royal priesthood, a holy nation, a peculiar people; that ye should show forth the praises of him who hath called you out of darkness into his marvelous light (1 Peter 2:9)." There is no such thing as a "hot and holy priest."

We are to be, "And be not conformed to this world: but be ye transformed by the renewing of your mind, that ye may prove what is that good, and acceptable, and perfect, will of God" (Romans 12:2). We are to be transformed or metamorphosis. Which means to change from an immature form, to an adult form. We must go from a fleshly nature to a spiritually mature person. We must not allow the world to conform us to its ways of thinking, dressing or actions. This includes both males and females. The Most High God is giving us warning before Christ's return.

All of us must. "Examine yourselves, whether ye be in the faith; prove your own selves. Know ye not your own selves, how that Jesus

Christ is in you, except ye be reprobates?" (2 Cor. 13:5). Dressing "hot" is of the world and it shows you are listening to the world: "They are of the world: therefore speak they of the world, and the world heareth them. We are of God: he that knoweth God heareth us; he that is not of God heareth not us, Hereby know we the spirit of truth, and the spirit of error" (1 John 4:5-6).

Ladies I know it seems as if I am picking on you and you are right. Your body excites males like nothing else and you know it. It is encumbered upon you not to be a partaker in any male's sin. A male's body does not get the same reaction from females as your body gets from males. The adage says; "If it is not for sale don't advertise." Remember, whom you serve and glorify Him and not yourself. And John 6:63: "It is the spirit that quickeneth (makes alive): the flesh profiteth nothing . . ." Let the following sum it up: –"Favor is deceitful, and beauty is vain: but a woman that feareth the Lord, she shall be praised. Give her of the fruit of her hands; and let her own works praise her in the gates" (Proverbs 31:30–31). I must move on.

State sponsored gambling is also on the rise, but under a new name; Education Lottery. Saints should not gamble away the hard-earned money The Lord allowed you to earn. I have a definition for gambling I found a few years ago. I wrote it down but lost who the author was. Allow me to give his definition of gambling. "Gambling is taking an artificial risk for hope of excessive gain, far beyond what the investment of time, money or skill would or could justify. It is a transaction whereby your gain must be someone else's loss. It is a willingness to take a risk that is twisted by the desire to get something for nothing. It is parasitic, producing no personal growth, with no social good." We have saints going to Las Vegas and other places to gamble away the money they should be putting towards the spreading of the gospel. The gambling industry no longer calls it gambling. It is now "gaming." So "game responsively," they say.

Mankind professes in its wisdom: drugs, liquor, sex, gambling, and the problems they bring can be controlled without help from The Most High. But instead, a Pandora's Box of evil has been opened and the lid can't be closed. A reprobate mind will say "I have it all under control." In reality, he or she has lost all control and is in a state of denial. Sin is easy to fall into, but the results of that sin are hard to avoid. "Love not the world, neither the things that are in the world. If any man love the world, the love of the Father is in not in him. For all that is in the world, the lust of the flesh, and the lust of the eyes, and the pride of life, is not of the Father, but of the world. And the world passeth away, and the lust thereof: but he that doeth the will of God abideth forever" (1 John 2:15-17).

Some of you reading this book are ready to put it down because of the things you are reading. I know it is upsetting to many and you are not receiving it. But, I expect such a reaction. I know some of you are saying "preacher, what are you for?" I am for righteousness. "But the natural man receiveth not the things of the Spirit of God: for they are foolishness unto him: neither can he know them, because they are spiritually discerned" (1 Cor. 2:14).

Many of you are saying "preacher you are very judgmental and legalistic." But I am neither, I am only doing what the Bible says. Let me explain: the most quoted verse from the Bible is where Jesus said, "Judge not," This verse is misquoted and misunderstood. The whole verse says: "Judge not according to the appearance, but judge righteous judgment" (John 7:24). I cannot judge what is in your mind. Because I do not know what is in your mind. Knowing your mind is in the realm of The Most High God. If someone at church is singing before the congregation and I say, "they are up there for show," I am judging what I cannot see. But if I hear them say, "I am doing it for my glory." They have shown what is in their mind.

The Most High God had Paul to write the following: "It is reported commonly that there is fornication among you, and such fornication as is not so much as named among the Gentiles, that one should have his father's wife. And ye are puffed up, and have not rather mourned, that he that hath done this deed might be taken away from among you. For I verily, as absent in body, but present in spirit, have judged already, as though I were present, concerning him that hath so done this deed, In the name of our Lord Jesus Christ, when ye are gathered together, and my spirit, with the power of our Lord Jesus Christ, To deliver such a one unto Satan for the destruction of the flesh, that the spirit may be saved in the day of the Lord

Jesus. Your glorying is not good. Know ye not that a little leaven leaveneth the whole" (1 Cor. 5:1–6).

Paul was saying "even though I am not there I have am relying on good information you are allowing fornicators to attend the church." He had judged the whole church was in sin because they were allowing this man to live with his step-mother as if they were married. The church may have believed they were super-spiritual in allowing this sin to go on. They were told to get it right or not allow them to come to church. Sin is like yeast a little goes a long way.

The mystery of iniquity has used TV to help destroy mankind's relationship to The Father. TV desensitizes you to evil and its dangers. You will stop saying how evil something you saw was, and instead say "what's next?" TV will convince you everyone is doing it. It will tell you The Father is the benevolent old man upstairs, who loves everyone, despite what they do, and can't wait to get everyone into heaven. This is a lie straight from satan. Life is like football, tennis, baseball or other organized sports. It would not be very interesting to play or watch if there were no rules to govern each sport. Why? The rules prevent chaos, and opens the game. The Most High God has given us rules, not to hinder us, but to keep us safe and make life interesting.

Mankind is in a reprobate state of mind and it will only get worse; "Therefore hell hath enlarged herself, and opened her mouth without measure: and their glory, and their multitude, and their pomp, and he that rejoiceth, shall descend into it" (Isaiah 5:14). Hell is enlarging itself because mankind can't stop their love affair with "the mystery of iniquity." This world is on a slippery slope, and the only hope is Jesus Christ. Once you get saved, you get off the slope. But the world and its system is still sliding down. Many great men have tried to implement various programs and schemes to bring mankind into a better state. Have any of them worked? No! And down, down, it will continue to slide until the time of the a-c, when evil will run amok. I know some of you are thinking I have a pessimistic attitude, and I do as far as mankind making things better. Mankind has not succeeded, nor will he succeed.

As saints of The Most High, we are not to just bow down and take whatever the mystery of iniquity brings our way. Least we be called "the friends of iniquity." We are to be bold as lions and speak against these evils, but we must be prepared to suffer as we are attacked by the minions of the devil. This world will not get better with man in control. Now, I do have an extremely faithful and optimistic attitude where my Father is concerned, because in the end He wins. "Christ in you, the hope of glory" (Colossians 1:27).

"Many shall be purified, and made white, and tried; but the wicked shall do wickedly: and none of the wicked shall understand; but the wise shall understand" (Daniel 12:10).

During the tribulation, many of those who receive salvation will die for their testimony. "The wicked shall do wickedly, but will not understand." The wicked do not understand why they are pushing ideas contrary to the Father's will. The wicked think they are doing right, just pushing diversity and evolving man to the next level. But, in fact they are pushing the devil's agenda.

The Mystery of iniquity is a trap that will ensnare and take you lower than you have ever been, and keep you there longer that you ever wanted to stay. It will put you in dirt and filth in which you may never be able to wash off. It will give you a smell that perfume can't mask, put you around people you can't stand, and have you doing things you never believed you would or could do.

"The thoughts of the wicked are an abomination to the Lord . . ." (Proverbs 15:26).

"And I heard, but I understood not: then said I, O my Lord, what shall be the end of these things. And he said, Go thy way, Daniel: for the words are closed up and sealed till the time of the end. Many shall be purified, and made white, and tried; but the wicked shall do wickedly: and none of the wicked shall understand; but the wise shall understand" (Dan. 12:8–10). The words that once were closed and sealed are now opening. We are nearing the time of the end. Those of us who are saved (wise) we should understand what is happening, we are nearing the culmination of the mystery plans of The Most High God. Saints should know this because we read the Bible, and believe what it says. The wicked or unsaved can't understand the words of The Father because His words sound foolish to them. Remember, 1 Cor. 2:14.

THE FALLING AWAY

To the saints. Some of the things I have written and will write may be somewhat discouraging. Please read this: "You, have been born, for such a time as this." The Most High God wanted you to be born during these last days. Because He knows you can stand and overcome with His help. Paul was born for his time. This is your time. STAND.

Let me give you a few precious verses: "Then they that feared the Lord spake often one to another: and the Lord hearkened, and heard it, and a book of remembrance was written before him for them that feared the Lord, and that though upon his name. And they shall be mine, saith the Lord of hosts, in that day when I make up my jewels; and I will spare them, as a man spareth his own son that serveth him" (Malachi 3:16–17). This book of remembrance will be one of those books to be opened at the great white throne judgment. Either this is true or The Bible is a bunch of fables. You decide, but as for me and my house, we will serve The Lord. "Jesus Christ, The Hope of Glory."

STRONG DELUSION, THE SPIRIT OF THE A-C, AND THE MYSTERY OF INIQUITY

Strong Delusion

"And <u>then</u> shall that <u>Wicked</u> be revealed, whom the Lord shall consume with the spirit of his mouth, and shall destroy with the brightness of his coming: Even him, whose coming is after the working of Satan with all power and signs and lying wonders. And with all deceivableness of unrighteousness in them that perish; because they received not the love of the truth, that they might be saved. And for this cause God shall send them <u>strong delusion</u>, that they should believe a lie: That they all might be damned who believed not the truth, but had pleasure in unrighteousness" (2 Thess. 2:8-12).

After the body of Christ is taken out of this world, The Father unleashes His great tribulation which consist of years of judgments against His chosen nation Israel, as well as the unbelievers here on the earth. The Lord is giving us a peek through Paul's writing of the Battle of Armageddon and how the a-c will be destroyed. Notice verse 8 "Wicked" this is capitalized because it denotes a real person gaining great power on the earth. he will be a great deceiver; his power will be after the working of satan, with power signs and lying wonders. To all who love not the truth of God's word, The Most High will send you strong delusion. Delusion means a lie! If you do not want the truth, God will send you a lie.

You may be calling me a heretic about now, so allow me to explain. Look at 1 Kings 22:1–40, especially verses 21–22: "And there came forth a spirit, and stood before the Lord, and said, I will persuade him. And the Lord said unto him, Where-with? And he said, I will go forth, and I will be a lying spirit in the mouth of all his prophets. And he said, Thou shalt persuade him and prevail also: go forth, and do so." Ahab would not believe the truth so a lie was delivered by one spirit to influence almost four hundred men. They lied to Ahab in order for him to die because he refused the truth.

"And all the inhabitants of the earth are reputed as nothing: and he doeth according to his will in the army of heaven, and none can stay his hand, or say unto him, What doest thou" (Daniel 4:35)?

"I form the light and create darkness: I make peace, and create evil: I the Lord do all these things" (Isaiah 45:7). The Father is sovereign, working His will upon the earth. If you don't want to believe God's truth, He will send you a lie. The Mormons, Jehovah Witnesses, Muslims, and other cults all fell for a demonic lie hook, line, and sinker. Anyone who adds or takes away from the Words of The Most High is trusting in a lie.

If your pastor is not teaching the whole counsel of The Father, then your pastor is teaching a lie. Part truth is still a lie. If you do not want to believe the truth, you will be deceived by a lie. Only those who want to hear the Shepherd's voice will hear: "And when he putteth forth his own sheep, he goeth before them, and the sheep follow him: for they know his voice. And a stranger will they not follow, but will flee from him: for they know not the voice of strangers" (John 10:4–5). Do you know your Shepherd's voice?

Spiritual warfare is being waged in the heavens right now. In Daniel 10:11–21, we are told of a spiritual battle fought in the spiritual realm and manifested in the physical world. We cannot see these spiritual battles, but we see the physical earthly results. The angel Gabriel was sent to give Daniel the interpretation of the visions which Daniel saw. Gabriel revealed a great truth to Daniel. "Then said he unto me, Fear not, Daniel: for from the first day that thou didst set thine heart to understand, and to chasten thyself before thy God, thy words were heard, and I am come for the words. But the prince of the kingdom of Persia withstood me one and twenty days: but lo, Michael, one of the chief princes, came to help me; and I

THE SPIRIT OF THE ANTI-CHRIST

remained there with the kings of Persia" (Daniel 10:12–13). And in verse 20, the angel said, "Now will I return to fight with the prince of Persia: and when I am gone forth, lo, the prince of Grecia (Greece) shall come."

Gabriel fought with the evil angels who are described as "principalities, against powers, against the rulers of the darkness of this world, against spiritual wickedness in high places" (Ephesians 6:12). These evil angels ruled the spiritual realm over Persia and Greece. Gabriel fought the prince of Persia to a draw. Then Michael (who is an archangel, and not Jesus) came to help Gabriel so he could continue the mission to give Daniel the interpretation of the dreams. The angel Gabriel had to return and continue the fight with the ruling spirit over Persia and later the ruling prince of Greece, which came later. Alexander the great (Grecia) came after the Medes/Persia. Alexander could not be allowed to do anything to hinder or destroy the Jewish nation. Remember the story of Alexander and the high priest.

Notice Daniel 11:1: "Also I in the first year of Darius the Mede, even I, stood to confirm and to strengthen him." The same angel Gabriel is still talking to Daniel. Gabriel said he stood "to comfort and strengthen," king Darius: why? Kings Darius and Cyrus were to play an important part in allowing the Jews to return to Israel and to rebuilt the temple and the city. Please read the following on your own: Ezra 1:1–10, 4:1–5, 5:1–17, 6:1–12, and Isaiah 45:1–4. The angel of The Most High was there to ensure kings Darius and Cyrus did what was needed to support the Jews in this. The evil angel (prince of Persia and Grecia) could not be allowed to hinder or stop them.

Let me give you one more spiritual realm story. "And when the servant of the man of God (Elisha) was risen early, and gone forth, behold, a host compassed the city both with horses and chariots. And his servant said unto him, Alas, my master! How shall we do? And he (Elisha) answered, Fear not: for they that be with us are more than they that be with them. And Eli-sha prayed, and said Lord I pray thee, open his eyes, that he may see. And the Lord opened the eyes of the young man; and he saw: and, behold, the mountain was full of horses and chariots of fire round about E-li-sha" (2 Kings 6:15–17).

Elisha's servant was only seeing in the natural. Elisha prayed for his servant's eyes to see into the spiritual realm, thus enabling him to see The Host of The Lord.

Our Father is giving us a window into the spiritual world of the mystery of iniquity, and the spiritual battles being fought now on behalf of people and nations in this world. The devil did not fall alone; a third of the angels bought into his lie and got kicked out of heaven. satan and these angels did not lose all their power. Remember this, they can only do as much as The Father allows them to do.

Let's go to the book of Jude. It only has one chapter; Jude 9, "yet Michael the archangel, when contending with the devil he disputed about the body of Moses, durst not bring against him a railing accusation, but said, the Lord rebuke thee." Now I do not know what "the body of Moses" means. So, I shall leave that to your pastor. Before his fall, the devil (satan) was a higher-ranking angel than Michael. Even now he still out ranks Michael, causing Michael to call on a Higher Power, "The Lord rebuke thee."

Let's return to Ephesians 6:11–12. "Put on the whole armor of God, that ye may be able to stand against the wiles of the devil. For we wrestle not against flesh and blood, but against principalities, against powers, against the rulers of the darkness of this world, against spiritual wickedness in high places."

satan is not the only evil angel ruling, although he is the god of this world. There are other evil angels who are behind the scenes controlling, or trying to control, all earthly leaders and nations. satan is a created being; he can't be everywhere at the same time. So, he has to have help. There were and are evil angels controlling and influencing the people of Babylon, Media/Persia, Greece, Rome, Germany, England, Uganda, Russia and even America. Every nation has a lead evil angel, or angels, working on behalf of the darkness of this world. They have one goal: bring in the "mystery of iniquity." It is evident they are not buddies. Each has his own agenda. Remember, satan is a liar, destroyer, divider, and murderer so his kingdom does not operate as a well-organized system with all the evil spirits getting along. There is lot of freelancing among them.

These evil angels cause wars between nations for their own purpose, as well as to try to thwart The Father's plan. These evil angels have also been used by The Father to bring in His plan. The Most High God used WWII to get the return of part of the Jewish home land. Our Father can work miracles and get things done all by Himself. But in many instances, he uses mankind to accomplish His goals. Remember Daniel 4:35: "And all the inhabitants of the earth are reputed as nothing: and he doeth according to his will in the army of heaven, and among the inhabitants of the earth: and none can stay his hand, or say unto him, What doest thou?"

Spiritual wickedness operates in places we are not aware of. If we knew or saw it, we would be terrified and afraid to leave our homes. Read this: "When the unclean spirit is gone out of a man, he walketh through dry places, seeking rest, and findeth none. Then he saith, I will return into my house from whence I came out; and when he is come, he findeth it empty, swept, and garnished. Then goeth he and taketh with himself seven other spirits more wicked than himself, and they enter in and dwell there: and the last state of that man is worse than the first, even so shall it be also unto this wicked generation" (Matt. 12:43-45). Evil spirits desire to dwell within unsaved mankind. And if they are cast out, they keep coming back to see if their former home is occupied. If it is not occupied by the Spirit of The Father, the evil spirit moves back in and bring a few more wicked house guests with him.

The devil and his crew have absolutely no redeeming value. If they allow any good, it is only to bring in evil. Remember, man is still a free will individual. satan and his evil angels can't read your mind. However, they will can send thoughts to try and influence you to do evil. Mankind can and does rebel against satan and his angels by not following orders and following their own human minds. When we agree with The Most High and follow Him, satan then considers us as rebels on his earth. A rebel can't stand, another rebel.

Many wicked, and powerful angels are still held captive in a certain part of hell: "For if God spared not the angels that sinned, but cast them down to hell, and delivered them into chains of darkness, to be reserved unto judgment" (2 Peter 2:4). This verse tells us of evil angels held under "chains of darkness," until the great white throne judgment. This is some type of supernatural chain, which imprisons and keeps these evil angels in this jail. An evil angel will be loosed from this hell or bottomless pit to lead an attack on the a-c's kingdom and the world. Neither satan nor the a-c will be able to control him. We will talk about this later.

Evil angels are not looking forward to the lake of fire: "And when he was come to the other side into the country of the Ger-ge-senes, there met him two possessed with devils, coming out of the tombs, exceeding fierce, so that no man might pass by that way. And, behold they cried out, saying, What have we to do with thee, Jesus, thou son of God? Art thou come hither to torment us before the time" (Matt. 8:28-29). Evil spirits and satan, are in no rush to go into torment. You shouldn't either.

You have been given a lot of scripture. Why? Because scriptures are all we have. Either it is true or not, you decide for yourself. All I have told you must happen since The Father put it in His Bible, and I believe Him. We must not look for signs. However, we should see things are moving toward some kind of spiritual conclusion. Man left to himself, will destroy this world. Read this: "For yourselves know perfectly that the day of the Lord so cometh as a thief in the night. For when they shall say, Peace and safety; then sudden destruction cometh upon them, as travail upon a woman with child; and they shall not escape. But ye, brethren, are not in darkness, that that day should overtake you as a thief. Ye are all the children of light, and the children of the day: we are not of the night, nor of darkness" (1 Thess. 5:2–5).

We are not to be ignorant of the events happening around us. "Lest Satan should get an advantage of us for we are not ignorant of his devices" (2 Cor. 2: 11). We don't have to read something extra into each incident. But we need to see and understand the totality of all events are leading to some type of world-wide conclusion. We are of The Light and we should see darkness (sin) is taking over and trying to move the children of The Light out of its way. Our enemy satan will tell the world "it is not as bad as those Christians say, they are just fear mongering." Wake up, body of Christ, our redemption draws near.

THE SPIRIT OF THE a-c, AND THE MYSTERY OF iniquity

"Little children, it is the last time: and as ye have heard that anti-christ shall come, even now are there many anti-christs; whereby we know that it is the last time. They went out from us, but they were not of us; for if they had been of us, they would no doubt have continued, with us: but they went out, that they might be made manifest that they were not all of us. But ye have an unction from the Holy One and ye know all things. I have not written unto you because ye know not the truth, but because ye know it, and that no lie is of the truth. Who is a liar but he that denieth that Jesus is the Christ? He is an-ti-christ, that denieth the Father and the Son" (1 John: 2: 18-22).

"And every spirit that confesseth not that Jesus Christ is come in the flesh is not of God: and this is that spirit of an-ti-christ, where of ye have heard that it should come: and even now already is it in the world. They are of the world: therefore speak they of the world, and the world heareth them. We are of God; he that knoweth God heareth us. He that is not of God heareth not us. Hereby know we the spirit of truth, and the spirit of error" (1 John 4:3-6).

"For many deceivers are entered into the world, who confess not that Jesus Christ is come in the flesh. This is a deceiver and an anti-christ" (2 John 7).

Here is the definition of "the spirit of the a-c;" Any person or spirit living in the past, present, or coming future, who denies or refuses to confess that The Most High God sent His Only Son, Jesus Christ in the flesh, born of a virgin, to do a substitutionary, sinless, atoning work, which included His death, resurrection and ascension to heaven. And that He will return to rule and reign on this earth. whosoever rejects The Spirit of Truth and embraces a spirit of error is possessed by the spirit of the a-c and is not of our Father.

The spirit of the a-c has been around as long as the mystery of iniquity. The devil started this in heaven, when he and his angels rebelled. It is lurking around every corner waiting to deceive any who will buy into its lie. The a-c will be the full embodiment of this spirit of anti-christ. The a-c will rewrite satan's history and teach errors about The Most High God. The a-c will call satan good and The Most High evil. John says, "many deceivers" were around during his time. We have many who have this "spirit of error." Many of them sit and speak in church every Sunday. The devil and his angels or demonic spirits are the leaders of this a-c conspiracy. Their sole aim is to get as much of mankind to follow their evil way of thinking, and to draw church members away from The Truth.

Notice, "They are of the world: therefore speak they of the world, and the world heareth them" (1 John 4:5). This is a threefold test. First: they are of the world. Their concern is purely things of this world. Secondly: they speak good sound bites pushing this world's and satan's agenda, i.e., Love has no gender or don't' judge. The world loves to hear this, because it sounds so good. And that's the third test: the world hears its own.

Read, 1 John 4:6: "We are of God: he that knoweth God heareth us; he that is not of God heareth not us. Hereby know we the spirit of truth, and the spirit of error." Those of us who are of The Most High God, hear Him. No matter how difficult the saying, "The sheep hear his voice. And a stranger will they not follow, but will flee from him: for they know not the voice of strangers" (John 10:3, 5).

Let me give you an example of this. Some years ago, I was stationed in the country of Turkey. I was assigned to work in a fifty-foot tower. On a clear day, I could see for miles. On this day, I saw two large herds of sheep converging on a tree near the base perimeter fence. Now each herd had its own shepherd. There may have been a couple of hundred sheep between the two groups. I watched these two herds become one large herd. The shepherds sat down under the tree for two hours. When the shepherds got up to leave. I said to myself "how in the world will they separate those sheep?" I had a pair of binoculars, so I watched the shepherds. Each one of them said something. And the most amazing thing happened. The sheep separated themselves. The shepherds just took off and never looked back. The sheep followed their respective shepherd, and none of the sheep seemed confused as to whom to follow, "And a stranger will they not follow." I did not understand this until I became a Christian. Do you know your shepherd's voice?

Back to the a-c. There is not, nor will there be a supernatural man walking this earth waiting for a sign from satan to become the a-c. The a-c is not hiding in a cave, nor is he in suspended animation at the North Pole, and he is not hiding in a subterranean well. He will not come from outer space riding on a meteorite. The a-c is not in the deep blue sea, nor will he be created by some nuclear explosion. And he most definitely will not be the result of satan having sex with a woman. As J. Vernon Mcghee says; "These are fanciful tales conceived by psycho-ceramic minds (cracked pots)."

The a-c will not only be fully human, but also fully possessed by satan. he will be a <u>MAN</u> of great ability; able to bring order out of great chaos, diplomatic, very charismatic, able to maneuver others to his way of thinking, and get their full co-operation in conducting his (satan's) agenda. All throughout the ages, many men could have become the a-c, but the time was not right. The man who will become the a-c does not know this is his destiny. Judas did not join Jesus' group of disciples thinking, "at the right time, I will betray Jesus into the hand of the High Priest." Read the following: "And the chief priests and scribes sought how they might kill him: for they feared the people. Then entered Satan into Judas surnamed Iscariot, being of the number of the twelve. And he went his way, and communed with the chief priests and captains, how he might betray him unto them" (Luke 22:2–4). Judas was the right man, for the right time, the right people and the right circumstance.

The a-c will be fully deceived and believe his own lies. He will be totally receptive to satan and for a while he will be a secret worshipper of satan. Once he is in control, he will openly worship satan before the entire world. Remember this, our world is getting smaller. When I say "smaller," I mean technology is in an ever-evolving state and increasing man's global reach. Cell phones and computers have done more to increase man's reach in the past one-hundred years than anything else. "Many shall run to and fro, and knowledge shall be increased" (Daniel 12:4). Today's smart phone or smart device can accomplish ten times what the early computers could do. Knowledge has increased exponentially.

The Most High has given mankind great intellectual abilities in all manner of technology. Computers, cell phones, robotics, driverless cars, conducting warfare, air planes, space travel, architect, medicine, and others. Work is on-going to develop material to make soldiers invisible. If mankind can conceive it, he will try to build it. However, man cannot fix his character! No matter how good the technology, someone will find a way to corrupt it. Look at the internet. It's a good system for gathering information and sharing knowledge. But mankind has corrupted the net and turned it into a billion-dollar pornography network. Type the wrong word into your search engine, and pornography pops onto your screen.

At the tower of Babel, Genesis 11:1–9, mankind was united by one language and evil. Today mankind is uniting through technology and evil. The use of technology has enabled mankind to over-come the language barrier. My cell phone will translate my English into other languages. Some of this technology has been corrupted, and has enabled many to become billionaires. Who knows how many young children, women, and men have been killed after being used to make wicked films for the internet.

Hackers are lurking on the internet to steal your information from any source: retail stores, your home PC, your cell phone, banks, government files, and hospital records. Then this information is used to make large sums of money. I receive e-mails from Nigeria, FBI, Jan wan, and other places trying to work on greed in order to steal my information. The government can't stop this evil use of technology. Its' own computers are hacked every-day. The a-c will be a master in the use of all manner of technology in his quest for world dominance.

Have you ever wondered why the internet has not been secured from hackers? And yet it is push upon us as if it is a most secure network. Why? Advance technology will be needed to help control the a-c's kingdom. Therefore, it is promoted as such a good and beneficial system. Many people believe technology will evolve us to the next evolutionary step. All of this is in preparations for the a-c and satan's rule.

The a-c is more than just a mere man, he is the right man for the right time, right people, and right circumstances. After being

THE SPIRIT OF THE ANTI-CHRIST

fully infused with this "spirit of the a-c" he will bodily become the a-c. He will bring in great spiritual error to deceive the world. And he will be the leading force in rebelling against The Father. He will be full of deceit, evil, a full child of the devil, stiff-neck, uncircumcised in heart, ears, an enemy of all righteousness, and rejecting all things of The Most High. He will rise similar to Hitler, seemingly out of nowhere. People will look to him to restore order. And as part of this order, he will launch a pogrom to destroy both the Jews and those who have become Christians. The a-c and the mystery of iniquity will have a satanically inspired hatred for Jews and Christians. The a-c will make Hitler and his henchmen look like amateurs.

Hitler was not a highly intelligent person. He had many wickedly smart people around him but he failed to use their full abilities. Hitler had a way with words, but words by themselves will not ensure success. He had some very capable generals but he would not allow them to conduct the war as a military man would. Hitler thought he was a smart tactician. But words do not win wars. The a-c on the other hand will not only have a great mouth, speaking great things. The a-c will also have at his disposal all the accumulated human and wicked spiritual knowledge satan and his angels have gathered in their dealing with mankind over the centuries. "And the devil, taking him up into a high mountain, showed unto him all the kingdoms of the world in a moment of time. And the devil said unto him, all this power will I give thee, and the glory of them: for that is delivered unto me; and to whomsoever I will I give it" (Luke 4:5-6).

The a-c will seem to be a great benefactor to the Jewish nation, but he will hate them. The Jewish people have been made the scapegoat for many nations, both old world and new. If something bad happened, the Jews caused it. If the economy went bad, the Jews caused it. Hitler blamed the Jews for him starting WWII. The Jews are blamed for lack of peace in the Middle East, yet the real reason for lack of peace is the Arabs' hatred for each other. The Arabs hate each other with a passion. Their hated for Israel is secondary. Christians are also on their list.

The Arabs hatred for each other is ordain by The Most High: "And the angel of the lord found her by a fountain of water in the wilderness, by the fountain in the way to Shur. And he said, Hag-gar, Sar-a-i's maid, whence camest thou? And whither wilt thou go? And she said, I flee from the face of my mistress Sar-a-i. And the angel of the Lord said unto her, return to thy mistress, and submit thyself under her hands. And the angel of the Lord said unto her, I will multiply thy seed exceedingly, that it shall not be numbered for multitude. And the angel of the Lord said unto her, Behold, thou art with child, and shalt bear a son, and shalt call his name Ishma-el; because the Lord hath heard thy affliction. And he will be a wild man; his hand will be against every man, and every man's hand against him: and he shall dwell in the presence of all his brethren" (Genesis 16:7–12). Therefore, the Arabs can't get along with each other, or Israel, it is in their DNA.

The Jews are The Father's chosen people, nothing will change that. "Thus saith the Lord, which giveth the sun for a light by day, and the ordinances of the moon and of the stars for a light by night, which divideth the sea when the waves thereof roar; The Lord of hosts is his name; If those ordinances depart from before me, saith the Lord, then the seed of Israel also shall cease from being a nation before me forever. Thus saith the Lord; If heaven above can be measured, and the foundations of the earth searched out beneath, I will also cast off all the seed of Israel for all that they have done, saith the Lord" (Jeremiah 31:35–37). If you see the sun still shining and the moon and stars ruling the night, then Christians have not replaced the Jewish Nation. Christians have been grafted into the tree until the "fullness of the Gentiles come (The Father's dealing with us the non-Jews)." The tribulation will start the restoration of Israel. Read Romans 11:13–30.

Where are the Midianites? Who can say I am a Canaanite, Jebusite, Amalekite, Edomite or Hittite? Can anyone say Nimrod is in my family tree or King Nebuchadnezzar is on my Mother's side of the family? These and others have disappeared into the annals of history. The people who call themselves Palestinians are not real Palestinians. They took that name and are using it to discredit Israel. They are really Arabs. Only the Jews can trace their lineage and say "I am a Jew and I am still here."

Israel is the only democracy in the Middle East. If I sound pro-Israel; I am. Why? "Now the Lord had said unto Abram (Abraham), get thee out of thy country, and from thy kindred, and from thy father's house, unto a land that I will show thee: And I will make of thee a great nation, and I will bless thee, and make thy name great; and thou shalt be a blessing: And I will bless them that bless thee, and curse him that curseth thee: and in thee shall all families of the earth be blessed" (Genesis 12:1–3). I want the blessing of The Father, so I will bless Israel every chance I get.

Look at the nations that have turned against Israel: Egypt, Syria, Iran, Iraq, England, Germany, France, Spain, and others all of them are now "also ran" which means they didn't finish first, second, or third; they just; "also ran." If the so-called Palestinians want to stop losing to Israel, they must stop cursing the nation of Israel and bless Israel, thus ensuring a blessing for themselves. But this the Arabs will never do, because the Arabs do not want peace with Israel, instead their goal is to destroy The Most High's chosen people.

And to those saints who have a dislike toward the Jews, remember this we read a Jewish Bible, written by Jews, which tells of a Jewish Savior.

Christianity cannot be taught in most public-school systems. But the koran is allowed and even used as a text book. Children are encouraged to practice the holidays and feasts of islam. This world and its system hates The Father, His Word and His people. The Bible has been thrown out and the koran is now in.

Even now as I type this manuscript when I type in the word 'Bible' using a lower case "b," no problem. But when I type in the word koran my computer's spell checker tells me the lower case "k" should be replaced by an upper case "K." My computer is in cahoots with this rebellion. The spirit of the a-c is here now, waiting for the right time, right people, and the right man, to infuse with this satanic power. The right people are gathering now, the right man, and the right time will be here soon.

PRELUDE TO THE A-C, THE TWO WITNESSES, THE BIRTH OF JESUS, ISRAEL, AND WAR IN HEAVEN

We will now turn to the book of Rev. As we bring all this information to its conclusion.

Many so called "Christians scholars" teach Rev. is a book of allegorical illustrations, with very little if any factual information. This is not true. Just because they do not believe nor understand Rev., does not mean it is not a factual book of things to come.

Rev. is the only book in the Bible which guarantees a blessing to those who read, hear, and keep those things written within its pages: "Blessed is he that readeth, and they that hear the words of this prophecy, and keep those things which are written therein: for the time is at hand" (Rev. 1:3). And remember it is: "The Revelations of Jesus Christ, which God gave unto him, to show unto his servants things which must shortly come to pass; and he sent and signified it by his angel unto his servant John" (Rev. 1:1). And John's task: "Write the things which thou hast seen, and the things which are, and things which shall be hereafter" (Rev. 1:19). Revelation was given to John the scribe by Jesus Christ "The Revelator."

Much of Rev. is written in a chronological order, with what I call "parenthetical phases." A parenthetical phase is the author's way of giving us background information as if He is saying; "by the way this also is or will happen, and why it happened." It may or may not be in order, or related to what is now happening, but it is place there to give background information. It could be one sentence or whole chapters.

We will not do a verse by verse exposition, but only those verses needed, or are related to the a-c. In Rev. 5; we are shown a scene in heaven. The Most High Father is on His throne holding a special book with seals wrapped around it. No one is found worthy to open the book. Then suddenly "The Lamb, Jesus Christ," appears in a spiritual form. And He and only He is worthy to step forth, take the book, and open the seals. Out of these seals the a-c and other judgments come upon the earth. Let's get started.

PRELUDE TO THE a-c

The a-c comes to power after the rapture; "And I looked, and behold a white cloud, and upon the cloud one sat like unto the Son of man, having on his head a golden crown, and in his hand a sharp sickle. And another angel come out of the temple, crying with a loud voice to him that sat on the cloud thrust in thy sickle, and reap: for the time is come for thee to reap; for the harvest of the earth is ripe. And he that sat on the cloud thrust in his sickle on the earth; and the earth was reaped" (Rev. 14:14-16).

This is a parenthetical phase. Jesus Christ, "The Son of man," is told to reap the earth of His saints. We know this event by the name "Rapture." Remember the word "Rapture" is not found in the Bible but the concept of a "taking away" is. Notice verse 15, "for the time is come for thee to reap; for the harvest of the earth is ripe." There are two reaping represented here. This first one in verses 15 and 16 are a clean reaping (rapture) and it is done by Christ Jesus. Whereas the second reaping in verses 17 through 20 is bloody (war) and conducted by angel. We will read about that one later.

We are given a set time for the rapture. What time is that? When the fruit (us) is at its ripest point (the harvest is ripe). But all this is in the time frame of The Most High God. Saints, stop listening to those date setting false prophets. Who knows; you may be the one holding the rapture back. Because you refuse to allow The Most High to ripen (get right) you.

PRELUDE TO THE A-C

Let's review: "For the mystery of iniquity doth already work: only <u>he</u> who now letteth will let, until <u>he</u> be taken out of the way. And then shall that <u>Wicked</u> be revealed, whom the Lord shall consume with the spirit of his mouth, and shall destroy with the brightness of his coming" (2 Thess. 2:7-8).

The rapture of the body of Christ has taken place. Many people have disappeared; there is a vacuum of uncertainty on the earth. No one knows for sure what has happened to all those missing people. Black, white, red, brown, and yellow people from all or most nations have disappeared. Nations are distrustful of each other. Blame is hurled all over the earth as nations accuse one another over the whereabouts of their missing populace. This may result in a full or limited world war.

Nations have been bumbling into wars for a long time so it will not take much to start another one. We live in a dangerous and unstable world; USA, England, France, Israel, North Korea, Russia, Pakistan, India, and China all have approximately 16,300 nukes (Business Insider). And as you can see from this list these nukes are controlled by many ungodly, and unstable people. It would not take much for one or more of these leaders to unleash nuclear destruction upon the earth. Fear and pride are the usual cause of wars. North Korea and other nations fear the USA. And the USA fears other nuclear nations.

We have nations all over this world, who are either failed or one catastrophic event from failure: Honduras, Mexico, El Salvador, Panama, Nicaragua, Venezuela, Nigeria, Uganda, Libya, Tunisia, Sudan, South Sudan, Ethiopia, N. Korea, Somalia, Bulgaria, Greece, Turkey, Spain, Albania, Germany, Russia, Kyrgyzstan, Iraq, Afghanistan, Caribbean Island nations, even the USA, and this is just the short list.

Alright let's get back to Rev.

"And I saw when the Lamb (Jesus) opened one of the seals, and I heard, as it were the noise of thunder, one of the four beasts saying, come and see. And I saw, and behold a white horse: and he that sat on him had a bow; and a crown given unto him: and he went forth conquering, and to conquer" (Rev. 6:1–2).

THE SPIRIT OF THE ANTI-CHRIST

I heard a well-known TV preacher say the person coming out of the seal is Jesus Christ. But this is wrong. Jesus does not come out of a seal. Jesus is opening the seals. When Christ returns, He comes from Heaven, and is well armed. Who then is this pretender? None other than the a-c. The a-c is the first judgment sent upon the earth by The Father as punishment for man's sin. The a-c is given a crown vs Jesus' many crowns. "His eyes were as a flame of fire, and on his head were many crowns" (Rev. 19:12). The a-c has a bow with no arrows, because satan does his fighting and gives him his power. "And his power shall be mighty, but not by his own power" (Daniel 8:24).

"And the dragon (satan) gave him his power, and his seat and great authority" (Rev. 13:2).

The a-c comes as an imitator of Jesus Christ. The a-c will perform great wonder and kingship signs. The a-c rides a white horse, which represents power and conquest, but as we read earlier, he has no power of his own. "And his power shall be mighty, but not by his own power" (Daniel 8:24). Notice that he has a bow, but no arrows. A bow is useless without arrows. This lack of arrows also signifies deception: "For when they shall say, Peace and safety; then sudden destruction cometh upon them" (1 Thess. 5:3). The a-c will ride in as a man of peace, until he gains control and then the real power broker shows up. A crown was also given to him. This crown, and the ability to conquer, will be given to him by satan. He will fool many, even the Jews. The spirit of the a-c has now infused him and he waits for the right time to show his real intentions.

The Most High God says: "For such are false apostles, deceitful workers, transforming themselves into the apostles of Christ And no marvel; Satan himself is transformed into an angel of light. Therefore it is no great thing if his ministers also be transformed as the minsters of righteousness; whose end shall be according to their works" (2 Cor. 11:13-15).

The a-c will bring satan's teachings to the world. These teachings will sound so right and wholesome they will fool the very elect. Some of these teachings, even now, are fooling many, even Christians. Teaching like this; everyone has rights and deserves dignity to live as they want, love has no gender, we are all God's children, and this "you can't judge," sounds good, but it really means "we should be able to flaunt and break God's laws at will." The a-c will be a minister of satan and he will have the same smooth, silky-sounding voice as his father satan. But they can't fool The Almighty. He's not taken in by good sound bites. He knows what is in each of us.

satan's "minsters of righteousness" are deceiving whole churches because the saints fail to follow: "Study to show thyself approved unto God a workman that needeth not to be ashamed, rightly dividing the word of true" (2 Timothy 2:15). Saints, if you do not have a love and desire for our Father's word, there's a good chance you are not saved or you are operating in a carnal state: "As newborn babes, desire the sincere milk of the word, that ye may grow thereby: If so be ye have tasted that the Lord is gracious" (1 Peter 2:2–3). Just as babies need milk to grow. All Christians needs the Word of our Father to grow. This plainly states if you do not believe The Lord is gracious, and received salvation, you will not desire His Word. I have had heard many saints say, "I don't do no reading," as if it is a badge of honor. It is a very foolish and ignorant statement. It is vital to read your Bible; and if your reading is not up to par, then purchase a set of Bible CDs.

"And there went out another horse that was red; and power was given to him that sat thereon to take peace from the earth, and that they should kill one another: and there was given unto him a great sword. And when he had opened the third seal, I heard the third beast say, Come and see, And I beheld, and lo a black horse; and he that sat on him had a pair of balances in his hand" (Rev. 6:4–5).

The red horse and its rider brings war. Notice the rider of the red horse comes with a great sword. The adjective "great" is used. The little peace left is now taken from the earth as mankind begins a wholesale slaughter of each other. War brings the black horse of famine. The rider on this horse has a pair of balances in his hand. The balances are scales used to weigh food. Food will be hard to acquire for the common man.

"And I heard a voice in the midst of the four beasts say, A measure of wheat for a penny, and three measures of barley for a penny; and see thou hurt not the oil and the wine" (Rev. 6:6).

The oil and wine symbolize the super-rich. Their vast wealth will insulate them from some of the suffering at first. This will also cause a socio-economical class struggle between the rich and the poor, the haves and the have not's. The grain used to make bread is barley, which is cheap and coarse. It may take a day's wages just to buy cheap, hard bread. War brings famine and the two together will cause millions to die.

"And I looked, and behold a pale horse: and his name that sat on him was Death, and Hell followed with him. And power was given unto them over the fourth part of the earth, to kill with the sword, and with hunger, and with death, and with the beasts of the earth" (Rev. 6:8).

We have two riders on this pale horse. Death and Hell. Death signifies people are dying and hell accepts those who are not saved. They are not riding at a leisurely trot, but at full gallop. They have but a short time to accomplish much. Notice we have spiritual beings riding white, red, black, and pale spiritual horses. These spiritual riders symbolize natural events taking place on the earth. The spiritual realm is being manifested in the natural world. Christ has reaped the earth of His saints. The devil has infused his man of the hour with the spirit of the a-c.

People are dying all over the earth by the sword, hunger, and animals gone wild. Mankind will soon realize they cannot continue like this and must come together before they destroy each other and the earth. But how do they stop the madness?

Nations fighting nation, kingdoms against kingdoms, a limited nuclear war may have or is about to take place. Famines, and pestilences have gripped the earth, beasts of some kind are killing people. Death and Hell reigns over a fourth part of the earth. Death kills and hell receives. There is no order, only chaos. Jesus said: "And there shall be signs in the sun, and in the moon, and in the stars and upon the earth distress of nations with perplexity; the sea and the waves roaring" (Luke 21:25). Nations will be perplexed with no idea what to do.

Then, suddenly from nowhere, comes this smooth talking, charismatic man with answers for all man's problems. He has no distractions, no hidden scandals. He placates everyone, he knows how to stop the madness. The world is fooled. This is the man of peace, with great ideas. satan has now infused his man of the hour with "the mystery of iniquity" and "the spirit of the a-c." We now have satan embodied in a man. He soothes the fears of the nations; they may even give him control of their nuclear stockpiles. He starts his plan of establishing his/satan's kingdom. We now have the right man, for the right time, the right people, and the right circumstances.

Along with establishing peace and safety, he must get a location for the Jewish temple. The Jewish temple cannot reside next to what the Jews consider paganism. Either the dome of the rock mosque must go or somehow the Jews are convinced to allow it to co-exist next to the temple. This is unlikely, but possible. The Muslims will not allow a Jewish temple to be built near the dome of the rock. The a-c must either take the temple mount or convince the Arabs and Jews to co-exist on the temple mount.

Remember, the Jews do not have a way to obtain forgiveness of their sins because they have no temple or priesthood to conduct sacrifices. Once they see the great things the a-c accomplishes, such as world peace, restoration of their temple, as well as his supposed death and resurrection. The Jews will declare the a-c their long-waited messiah.

Does the temple have to be placed on Mt. Moriah? This is where Abraham was tested to see who he loved the most, Isaac or The Most High (Genesis 22:2). King David chose this site, because this is where the death angel stopped during King David's punishment. For the background on this read 1 Chronicles 21:1–21, and the following 2 Chronicles 7:12, 15, and 16. The Most High God said He has chosen the temple as a house of sacrifice. But does this mean Mt. Moriah must be the site for the temple. Yes.

There is a very serious Rabbinical organization entrusted with making everything needed in preparation for the restored temple. (www.templeinstitute.org) They do not know when. But, they know the materials must be ready. Because a temple must and will come: says The Most High. The temple does not have to be made of brick and mortar. The first temple was a tent. Robes for the high priest and the helper priests are under construction. This organization also says they have the Ark of the Covenant.

They must also have a pure red heifer. The project to breed a pure red heifer is in full swing. This red heifer must be all red with no other color. Once they obtain this heifer it must be killed and burned to ashes. Then the ashes of this pure red heifer must be mixed with water then used to sanctify, anoint, and purify the high priest and the temple (Numbers 19:1–22). The priests cannot do their priestly duties, nor can the temple be used, until it is cleansed by this process only, there can be no substitute.

Even when they succeed in breeding a pure red heifer. They still have a major obstacle. A priest who has never been near a dead body. This means he must never have attended a funeral, been in a hospital or a cemetery, because being near a dead body would defile him making him ritually unclean and unable to use the ashes of the red heifer to cleanse the other priests and the temple. (Could the a-c fulfil this requirement)? The Jews have already conducted genealogy searches and found direct descendants of Aaron, Moses' brother, the first high priest. And they have a growing number of Levites (Cohen or Kohen) to help the high priest carryout his duties. But they must have those ashes of the red heifer and a ritually clean priest.

The true orthodox Jews place more emphasis on the temple than they place on service to The Most High God. Read this: "Trust ye not in lying words, saying, The temple of the Lord, The temple of the, The temple of the Lord are these" (Jeremiah 7:4). They believed the temple was more important than The Father. Before Jesus' time and during His time great emphasis was placed on the temple by the Jews: "And as he went out of the temple, one of his disciples saith unto him, Master, see what manner of stones and building are here!" (Mark 13:1). This obsession is still there and will only increase when the a-c comes to power. The Jews will think this is their time. The Jews may also believe the a-c will restore the kingdom of David to its rightful place and glory. We need to stop here in order to get a little more back ground information (parenthetical phase) on other things happening.

During the time of the a-c, judgments from The Most High are raining on the earth: "And when he had taken the book, the four beasts and four and twenty elders fell down before the Lamb, having every one of them harps, and golden vials full of odors, which are the prayer of saints" (Rev. 5:8). Our faithful prayers are collected and then: "And another angel came and stood at the altar, having a golden censer: and there was given unto him much incense, that he should offer it with the prayers of all saints upon the golden altar which was before the throne. And the smoke of the incense, which came with the prayers of the saints, ascended up before God out of the angel's hand. And the angel took the censer, and filled it with fire of the altar, and cast it into the earth: and there were voices, and thunderings, and lightning, and an earthquake" (Rev. 8:3–5). Pray on saints, pray on, your prayers are going to cause fire, earthquakes, the sun to darkened, and great hail weighting about one-hundred pounds to falls on the earth.

Rev. chapters 6 through 8:5 gives us the seal judgments. The seven trumpet judgments are in chapters 8:6 through chapters 11. Each of these judgments get progressively worse. The vials of wrath will start in Rev. 16. There are all kind of judgements falling on the land, sea, and rivers. Great creatures, and evil angels are released from the bottomless pit (abyss). This is the full wrath of God hitting the earth without mixture. This means grace and mercy are not mixed with His wrath: "The same shall drink of the wine of the wrath of God, which is poured out without mixture into the cup of his indignation" (Rev. 14:10). The earth will stagger under all this destruction. I have heard people say the judgments sound like the results of nuclear war. But I say unto you, The Most High God does not need man's nuclear arsenal to do his bidding.

Jesus called these events: "For these be the days of vengeance, that all things which are written may be fulfilled" (Luke 21:22). The Most High God is sending His wrath on a rebellious world.

"And they had a king over them, which is the angel of the bottomless pit, whose name in the Hebrew tongue is A-bad-don, but in the Greek tongue hath his name A-pol-ly-on" (Rev. 9:11).

"And the rest of the men which were not killed by these plagues yet repented not of the works of their hands, that they should not worship devils, and idols of gold, and silver, and brass, and stone, and of wood: which neither can see, nor hear, nor walk: Neither repented

THE SPIRIT OF THE ANTI-CHRIST

they of their murders, nor of their sorceries, nor of their fornication, nor of their thefts" (Rev. 9:20–21).

Two groups of terrible, wicked, and powerful spirits are temporarily released from the bottomless pit to torment and kill. But wicked mankind will not repent. These spirits will have an evil angel as their leader, his name is Abaddon or destroyer: "For if God spared not the angels that sinned, but cast them down to hell, and delivered them unto chains of darkness, to be reserved unto judgment;" (2 Peter 2:4). As we said earlier, powerful angels who rebelled along with satan are being held in the bottomless pit with supernatural chains. The same type of chain that will hold satan in the pit for a thousand years, more on this later.

Certain of those angels will be set free to punish mankind during the tribulation. Abaddon/apollyon is not satan. Nor has satan been to hell, nor is he over hell and he does not have and never did have the keys to hell: "I am he that liveth, and was dead; and, behold, I am alive for evermore, A-men; and have the keys of hell and of death" (Rev. 1:18). Jesus has those keys.

Evils spirits care nothing for mankind or each other. They may even get joy in hurting mankind. They show no mercy. These evils spirits will torment mankind for five months with tails that sting like a scorpion's stinger. Whoever is stung by these creatures will have excruciating pain, but will not die. Will it be real tails? I do not know. But whatever it is, it will hurt. This evil angel will lead them to attack everyone left on the earth, to include the people of the a-c's kingdom. satan nor the a-c will be able to control these evil creatures. I have heard some scholars say these creatures may be helicopter gunships. I do not believe they are gunships but real creatures. I do not know if they will sting those saints who got saved after the rapture. But I do know even after all this, evil mankind will not repent of their evil deeds, nor stop the worshipping of their idols and satan.

The only ones who are not hurt are the one hundred and forty-four thousand. "Saying hurt not the earth, neither the sea, nor the trees, till we have sealed the servants of our God in their foreheads. And I heard the number of them which were sealed; and there were sealed a hundred and forty and four thousand of the tribes of the children of Israel" (Rev. 7:3-4). These men are sealed and nothing can hurt them until they have completed their mission. Those saints who have gotten saved during the tribulation may also be stung by those demonic creatures; I can't find anything saying otherwise.

THE TWO WITNESSES

"And I will give power unto my two witnesses, and they shall prophesy a thousand two hundred and threescore days, clothed in sackcloth. And if any man will hurt them, fire proceedeth out of their mouth, and devoureth their enemies: and if any man will hurt them, he must in this manner be killed. And when they shall have finished their testimony, the beast that ascendeth out of the bottomless pit shall make war against them and shall overcome them, and kill them. And their dead bodies shall lie in the street of the great city, which spiritually is called Sodom and Egypt, where also our Lord was crucified. And they of the people and kindreds and tongues and nations shall see their dead bodies three days and a half, and shall not suffer their dead bodies to be put in graves. And they that dwell upon the earth shall rejoice over them, and make merry, and shall send gifts one to another; because these two prophets tormented them that dwelt on the earth. And after three days and a half the spirit of life from God entered into them, and they stood upon their feet; and great fear fell upon them which saw them. And they heard a great voice from heaven saying unto them, Come up hither, and they ascended up to heaven in a cloud; and their enemies beheld them. And the same hour was there a great earthquake, and the tenth part of the city fell, and in the earthquake were slain of men seven thousand: and the remnant were affrighted, and gave glory to the God of heaven" (Rev. 11:3, 5, 7-13).

We do not know the exact time when these two witnesses will start preaching. However, they will preach for three plus years (1,260 days), in Jerusalem. The a-c, his police, nor his soldiers will be able to kill them until they have finished preaching in the heart of the city. When the two witnesses have finished their preaching then and only

THE SPIRIT OF THE ANTI-CHRIST

then can the evil angel from the bottomless pit in Rev. 9:11, succeed in killing them.

The accepted belief is these two witnesses are Moses and Elijah. But Moses can't be one of them because he died on Mt. Nebo, and was buried some-where in a valley in the land of Moab. Which is in present day Jordan (Deuteronomy 34:1–9). I do believe Elijah is one: "And he said (Elijah), Thou hast asked a hard thing: nevertheless, if thou see me when I am taken from thee, it shall be so unto thee: but if not, it shall not be so. And it came to pass, as they still went on, and talked, that, behold, there appeared a chariot of fire, and horses of fire, and parted them both asunder; and Eli-jah went up by a whirl-wind into heaven" (2 Kings 2:10–11).

Enoch will be the second witness. "And Enoch walked with God: and he was not; for God took him" (Genesis 5:24). "By faith E-noch was translated that he should not see death; and was not found, because God had translated him: for before his translation he had this testimony, that he pleased God" (Hebrews 11:5). Enoch was a prophet. "And E-noch also, the seventh from Adam, prophesied of these, saying Behold, the Lord cometh with ten thousands of his saints" (Jude 14). Elijah and Enoch were taken to heaven to await this mission.

These real "Jehovah witnesses," are dressed in sack cloth which is the robe of sorrow. Anyone who tries to kill them will be killed by fire which they will spew out of their mouth. You may say "no way." Remember, we are talking about the power of The Most High God; is anything too hard for Him? Enoch and Elijah do miracles such as turning water to blood and smiting the earth with plagues. Remember, they are not doing this, but The Most High God is the power source behind the plagues and the fire.

Notice Rev. 11:8, Jerusalem is called Sodom and Egypt. The Most High God, considers the Jewish nation a spiritual parallel to Sodom and Egypt, wicked and corrupt. There is an interesting fact concerning our Lord Jesus Christ and Jerusalem. After Jesus started His adult ministry, He never spent a night in the city of Jerusalem. He considered it defiled. Only after He was taken prisoner the night before He was crucified did He stay there most of the night and that was by design (Luke 21:37–38, John 8:1–2).

Look at Rev. 11:9, once Enoch and Elijah are allowed to be killed it says "all nations and kindred and tongues shall see their dead bodies left on the street for three and half days." How could this be seen all over the world? John knew nothing about cell phones, mobile devices, Skype, Facebook, internet, and twenty-four hours news channels? John didn't know of these things, but The Most High God knew we would have these capabilities. People from all over the world will see them and rejoice at their death, even sending gifts to each other. Even the sending of gifts to each other is prophetic. How could they send gifts during John's time, it would have taken too long? But now we have UPS, Fed Ex, Amazon and others, the gifts can now get there overnight. Prophecy is right on time.

For eighty-four hours, two dead bodies are left in the street. The world will be full of joy at their deaths. Sending gifts to each other, just happy, happy. Because of the torment these two brought upon the people of the earth. Then suddenly, the two witnesses stand up. A great voice cries out "Come up hither." The world will also see their resurrection and hear them called up to heaven. There is a great earthquake in Jerusalem, part of the city is destroyed, and seven thousand people are killed. Those left alive are afraid and give glory to our Father, but it is too late.

THE BIRTH OF JESUS, ISRAEL, AND WAR IN HEAVEN

I want to give you a little background information on the Jewish nation, and a one-sided war in heaven.

"And there appeared a great wonder in heaven; a woman clothed with the sun, and the moon under her feet, and upon her head a crown of twelve stars. And she being with child cried, travailing in birth, and pained to be delivered. And there appeared another wonder in heaven; and behold a great red dragon, having seven heads and ten horns and seven crowns upon his heads. And his tail drew the third part of the stars of heaven, and did cast them to the earth: and the dragon stood before the woman which was ready to be delivered, for to devour her child as soon as it was born. And she brought forth a man child, who was to rule all nations with a rod of iron: and her child was caught up unto God, and to his throne" (Rev. 12:1–5).

We are now given a concise history of the nation of Israel. The sun represents Jacob (Israel), the moon represents Rachel his wife, and the twelve stars are the twelve sons of Jacob (Genesis 37:9–11). The child is Jesus Christ, whom satan (the dragon), tried to kill after He was born by using King Herod (Matt. 2:13–16). The seven heads on the dragon are the seven nations which all have attacked and tried to destroy the nation of Israel. I believe they are Egypt, Syria, Assyria, Babylon, Mede-Persia, Greece, and Rome. When I say "destroy," I mean to assimilate its unique culture and relationship to The Father. All seven of these nations were used by God to judge Israel. I am not dogmatic about those seven nations, since many nations have tried to destroy Israel.

Remember those ten horns? They are the same ten found in the book of Daniel. We do not know who they are, but they do come somewhere out of the Babylonian, Mede-Persia, Grecian and Roman Empires. The seven heads and ten horns are attached to the body of satan which means he and his angels influence them.

Let's get a short history on the origin of satan. From what we can find in the Bible, satan was a high-ranking angel or archangel. And his original name was Lucifer which means "day star or bright one." Some of his names are; the devil, anointed cherub, tempter, ruler of demons, beelzebub, evil one, enemy, liar, father of lies, murderer, ruler of the world, god of this age, angel of light, great red dragon, and serpent.

"Son of man, take up a lamentation upon the king of Ty-rus, and say unto him, Thus saith the Lord God; Thou sealest up the sum, full of wisdom, and perfect in beauty. Thou hast been in Eden the garden of God; every precious stone was thy covering, the sardius, topaz and the diamond, the beryl, the onyx, and the jasper, the sapphire, the emerald, and the carbuncle, and gold: the workmanship of thy tabrets and of thy pipes was prepared in thee in the day that thou was created. Thou art the anointed cherub that covereth; and I have set thee so: thou wast upon the holy mountain of God; thou hast walked up and down in the midst of the stones of fire. Thou wast perfect in thy ways from the day that thou wast created, till iniquity was found in thee. By the multitude of thy merchandise they have filled the midst of thee with violence, and thou hast sinned: therefore I will cast thee as profane out of the mountain of God: and I will destroy thee, O covering cherub, from the midst of the stones of fire. Thine heart was lifted up because of thy beauty, thou hast corrupted thy wisdom by reason of thy brightness: I will cast thee to the ground, I will lay thee before Kings, that they may behold thee" (Ezekiel 28:12–17).

"How art thou fallen from heaven, O Lucifer, son of the morning! How art thou cut down to the ground, which didst weaken the nations! For thou hast said in thine heart, I will ascend into heaven, I will exalt my throne above the stars of God: I will sit also upon the mount of the congregation, in the sides of the north: I will ascend above the heights of the clouds; I will be like the most High" (Isaiah 14:12–14).

The above verses have a double meaning. It may start talking about an earthly person then switch to its real meaning a spiritual being. This is what happened here. No man has had all those stones for a covering. No earthly man other than Adam has been in the Garden of Eden. No man has been called a cherub. A cherub is a heavenly creature and not a naked human baby with wings flying around in heaven. Nor has any man walked upon the holy mountain of God; or "walked up and down in the midst of the stones of fire."

The real meaning gives the history of Lucifer. Remember, all created beings are given the ability to obey or not to obey. He started out as a created perfect archangel, obeying The Father. He may have been the greatest of the angels in power and looks. Many Bible scholars teach satan was over a heavenly choir. I find nothing in the Bible to substantiate this belief.

Somewhere along the line Lucifer allowed pride and jealousy to develop in his mind. He developed a severe case of the "I will." "Only by pride cometh contention: but with the will advised is wisdom" (Proverbs 13:10) he wanted the glory, praise, worship, and power, of

The Most High. he led a third of the angels in a futile rebellion, lost his position, got kicked out of his heavenly home, lost his name, had it changed to satan, and the lake of fire is promised to him.

"For such are false apostles, deceitful workers, transforming themselves into the apostles of Christ. And no marvel; for Satan himself is transformed into an angel of light. Therefore it is no great thing; if his ministers also be transformed as the ministers of righteousness; whose end shall be according to their works" (2 Cor. 11:13–15).

The enemy can and will fool people into believing a lie. satan and his evil angels will come to you with things that sound so right but they are against our Father's will. It is not a hard thing for them to come in as ministers of righteousness. Just as the a-c will come at the right time, and to the right people. Remember: the tares. And; "Beware of false prophets, which come to you in sheep's clothing, but inwardly they are ravening wolves" (Matt.7:15).

One more verse:

"Ye are of your father the devil, and the lust of your father ye will do. He was a murderer from the beginning, and abode not in the truth, because there is no truth in him. When he speaketh a lie, he speaketh of his own: for he is a liar, and the father of it" (John 8:44).

Once satan started formulating his plan to take over heaven and kill The Most High God, murder developed in his heart. satan lied to the other angels and convince them they could win. When we lie we are following satan. Most Holy Father in heaven have mercy on us.

Do not play around with satan. Do not make jokes about him. Do not use nick names such as; old slew foot or pointy head. satan is not wearing a red suit nor does he have horns and carry a pitch fork. And he does not, nor has he ever had the keys to or controlled hell. he is not king or prince over hell, nor does he visit there: "Be sober, be vigilant; because your adversary the devil, as a roaring lion, walketh about, seeking whom he may devour; Whom resist steadfast in the faith, knowing that the same afflictions are accomplished in your brethren that are in the world" (1 Peter 5:8–9). He goes throughout the earth seeking to steal the word of The Most High. he wants to sift, deceive, devour, and kill you (Job 1:7–12, Matt. 13:37–39, Luke 22:31).

Satan does control death to some extent. "Forasmuch then as the children are partakers of flesh and blood, he also himself likewise took part of the same; that through death he might destroy him that had the power of death, that is, the devil;" (Hebrews 2:14) How much control over death he has I do not know. I do know he can do nothing without The Most High allowing him to.

"Then Satan answer the Lord, and said, Doth Job fear God for nought (nothing)? hast not thou made a hedge about him, and about his house, and about all that he hath on every side? Thou hast blessed the work of his hands, and his substance is increased in the land. But put forth thine hand now and touch all that he hath, and he will curse thee to thy face. And the Lord said unto Satan, behold, all that he hath is in thy power: only upon himself put not forth thine hand. So Satan went forth from the presence of the Lord" (Job 1:9–12). The Most High is sovereign and nothing is done without Him allowing it to go forth.

satan is described as a roaring lion and just as you would take a roaring lion seriously, you should do the same with satan. The goal of satan is your death with your soul sent to hell and then both body and soul to the lake of fire. satan does not want you to take him seriously. To make light of him is very dangerous. To those of you who wear a cross hoping that it will keep satan and his demons away. It does not work they are not afraid of a cross on your neck, small cross or a large cross, he is not afraid of your cross, no matter what it is made of.

Do not be afraid of him. Do not become obsessed with the devil or the study of demons. They have not possessed your cat or dog. Everyone that is sick or mentally ill is not demon possess. No-where in the Bible do you find a saint, whose full time is spent casting out demons."Ye are of God, little children, and have overcome them: because greater is he that is in you, than he that is in the world" (1 John 4:4). Your only defense is He who died on the cross, Christ Jesus, "Which he wought in Christ, when he raised him from the dead, and set him at his own right hand in the heavenly places, Far above all principality, and power, and might, and dominion, and every name that is named, not only in this world, but also in that which is to come" (Ephesians 1:20-21).

Do not debate with him or his demons: "Fret not thyself in any wise to do evil" (Psalm 37:8). This lets us know we are not to debate within ourselves to commit evil. If the evil forces can get you fretting whether to commit evil, they have won the battled.

You must use scriptures, just as Jesus did in Luke 4:1–8. Please take time to read it. You must do as Michael the archangel did appeal to The Higher Power; "Yet Michael the archangel, when contending with the devil he disputed about the body of Moses, durst not bring against him a railing accusation, but said, The Lord rebuke thee" (Jude 9). Jesus Christ is The Higher Power.

Did you know angels must obey the scriptures also? "And I John saw these things, and heard them. And when I had heard and seen, I fell down to worship before the feet of the angel which showed me these things. Then saith he unto me, See thou do it not: for I am thy fellow servant, and of thy brethren the prophets, and of them which keep the saying of this book: worship God" (Rev. 22:8–9).

Remember this, satan is not all powerful. If he and his angels had the same use of their power as they did in heaven, we would all be in a terrible condition. I firmly believe their main focus is in the spiritual world and hindering the Word of The Most High from getting through to mankind, and to accuse us before our Father.

Let me give you a spiritual example of this. "And he showed me Joshua the high priest standing before the angel of the Lord, and Satan standing at his right hand to resist him. And the Lord said unto Satan, The Lord rebuke thee, O Satan; even the Lord that hath chosen Jerusalem rebuke thee: is not this a brand plucked out of the fire? Now Joshua was clothed with filthy garments, and stood before the angel. And he answered and spake unto those that stood before him, saying, Take away the filthy garments from him. And unto him he said, Behold, I have caused thine iniquity to pass from thee, and I will clothe thee with change of raiment. And I said, Let them set a fair mitre upon his head, So they set a fair mitre upon his head, and clothed him with garments. And the angel of the Lord stood by. And the angel of the Lord protested unto Joshua, saying, Thus saith the

Lord of hosts; If thou wilt walk in my ways, and if thou wilt keep my charge, then thou shalt also judge my house, and shalt also keep my courts, and I will give thee places to walk among these that stand by" (Zechariah 3:1–7).

Here is what's happening. After Israel was taken captive by the nation of Babylon and held there for the appointed time. King Cyrus of the Medes/Persian kingdom allowed those who wanted to go to Israel and rebuild Jerusalem and the temple to do so. They were led by Zerubabel, who became the governor and Joshua (Jeshua) as high priest (Ezra 1:2). Zechariah was allowed to see into the spiritual world as satan stood condemning Joshua as being unfit to be the high priest before The Most High Father. The filthy garments represented Joshua's sins. "But we are all as an unclean thing, and all our righteousness are as filthy rags; and we all do fade as a leaf; and our iniquities, like the wind, have taken us away" (Isaiah 64:6).

The Father rebuked satan, and took away the sins of Joshua. This is represented by the new garments (The righteousness of our Father). And Zechariah got so overjoyed at this sight he asked The Father to give Joshua a new hat (mitre) to go along with the new outfit. Joshua was then told to go and carry out his assignment. We have been made clean by the blood of our Lord Jesus Christ. And I want me one of those new hats. Glory!

satan's main desire is to be worshipped. "And the devil, taking him (Jesus) up into a high mountain, sowed unto him all the kingdoms of the world in a moment of time. And the devil said unto him, all this power will I give thee, and the glory of them: for that is delivered unto me; and to whomsoever I will I give it. If thou therefore wilt worship me, all shall be thine" (Luke 4:5–7). Worship is one of satan's goals.

Please forgive me there is so much information contained in the Bible I would need volumes of books to write about all of it. I am trying to keep this book short, and to inform you on very important facts. Please bear with me.

We must take a parenthetical phase and deal with Matt. 24. Most of this chapter pertains to the Jews. Very little is for the church. There are a few events that will touch the whole world such as; "And ye shall hear of wars and rumors of wars: see that ye be not troubled: for all these things must come to pass, but the end is not yet. For nation shall rise against nation, and kingdom against kingdom: and there shall be famines, and pestilences, and earthquakes, in divers places" (Matt. 24:6-7). These are happening all over the world. Nations are fighting each other, nations are fighting within nations, famines, pestilences, and earthquakes are increasing. Peace and tranquility seems to be very elusive for mankind.

Most of the other verses are for the Jewish nation. For example, "Then let them which be in Judea flee into the mountains" (Mat.24:16). Jesus said, "But pray ye that your flight be not in the winter, neither on the sabbath day" (Matt. 24:20). Judea is in Israel and the church does not have a Sabbath day. The Sabbath was made for the Jewish nation. Tell your pastor if he or she teaches on this chapter, they must point out which verse is for the Jewish nation and which is for the rest of us. Jesus said, "For then shall be great tribulation, such as was not since the beginning of the world to this time, no nor ever shall be. And except those days should be shortened, there should no flesh be saved: but for the elect's sake those days shall be shortened" (Matt. 24:21-22). Jesus is saying this will be a great and terrible time and those days must be cut short for the elect's sake.

Now back to Rev. 12. Which deals with the persecution of Israel by the devil, the world, the war in heaven, and how satan, plus the angels, who followed him were cast out of heaven. Jesus gives us a little insight into satan's fall. In Luke 10:17–18, "And the seventy returned again with joy, saying, Lord, even the devils are subject unto us through thy name. And he said unto them, I, beheld satan as lighting fall from heaven."

"And there was war in heaven: Michael and his angels fought against the dragon; and the dragon fought and his angels. And prevailed not; neither was their place found any more in heaven, And the great dragon was cast out, that old serpent, called the Devil, and Satan, which deceiveth the whole world: he was cast out into the earth, and his angels were cast out with him. And I heard a loud voice saying in heaven, Now is come salvation, and strength, and the kingdom of our God, and the power of his Christ: for the accuser of our brethren is cast down, which accused them before our God day and night. And they overcame him by the blood of the Lamb, and by the word of their testimony: and they loved not their lives unto the death. Therefore rejoice, ye heavens, and ye that dwell in them. Woe to the inhabiters of the earth and of the sea! For the devil is come down unto you, having great wrath because he knoweth that he hath but a short time. And when the dragon saw that he was cast unto the earth, he persecuted the woman which brought forth the man child. And to the woman were given two wings of a great eagle, that she might fly into the wilderness, into her place, where she is nourished for a time, and times and half time, from the face of the serpent. And the serpent cast out of his mouth water as a flood after the woman, that he might cause her to be carried away of the flood. And the earth helped the woman, and the earth opened her mouth, and swallowed up the flood which the dragon cast out of his mouth. And the dragon was wroth with the woman, and went to make war with the remnant of her seed, which keep the commandments of God, and have the testimony of Jesus Christ" (Rev. 12:7–17).

There was war in heaven. satan convince a third of all the angels, they could overthrow The Most High God. This would have given satan control over everything. Think about this phenomenon. Here is satan, a created being. Telling other created beings "let's overthrow The Creator." These angels saw The Most High create the universe, "Mine hand also hath laid the foundation of the earth, and my right hand hath spanned the heavens: when I call unto them, they stand up together" (Isaiah 48:13). And they shouted for joy (Job 38:4–7). This created being convinced the other created beings, "we can do this." satan is such a smooth talker. satan and his horde are talking right now to mankind. You must not allow yourself to get in a conversation with satan or any of his representatives. Satan fooled an untold number of angels and you are no match for him, you must have the word of The Most High God in your mind at all times. The Word acts as a filter for what you hear and think. "And take the helmet of salvation, and the sword of the Spirit, which is the word of God" (Ephesians 6:17).

THE SPIRIT OF THE ANTI-CHRIST

Rev. 12:10–12 tells us how to get the victory over satan and the world. First; you must be saved and believe in the work Christ Jesus accomplished on the cross (His Blood). Second; you must live a testimony for Him, no secret saints allowed (the word of our testimony). Third: you must be willing to die for Jesus Christ, if necessary (love not, our life). Look at 12, "Rejoice, ye heavens, ye that dwell in them." The saints are told to rejoice, why? The end is near.

Then they are told, "Woe to the inhabiters of the earth and of the sea!" Many so-called saints believe satan is only a symbol of evil and not a real being. I am here to tell you satan, is a real supernatural being and not a symbol of evil. he is evil and he can only be in one place at a time. Only The Most High is Omnipresent which means everything is in His presence; He is Omnipotent meaning nothing is as powerful as He is; and He is Omniscience which means nothing is new to Him. Those on the earth are told "Woe." Why? The devil, is superhot, because he lost in heaven and he knows he only has a short time to do his thing on the earth.

satan is a created angel and he will be either embodied (possess) in or give power to the a-c. The Most High God cannot lie. The devil tried to destroy Israel by sending masses of people (flood) to try and assimilate the Jewish nation. He used wars, inter-marriage, and attempts to get the Jewish nation to be like every other nation, thus removing its unique relationship to The Father. But instead of wiping out the Jews, the earth (by order of The Most High) ensured they remained a nation, by swallowing or stopping the flood of people from wiping out the Jewish nation. However, satan has won a partial victory since the Jews are in temporary disbelief and have lost their relationship to The Father by their sins and rejection of Jesus Christ. This does not mean they are no longer His chosen people. If as you read this, and you see the sun, moon or stars shining, then The Father has not abandon the Jewish nation.

"Two wings of a great eagle" (Rev. 12:14). Symbolizes The Devine Providence of The Most High God, He will protect His people Israel. "But they that wait upon the Lord shall renew their strength; they shall mount up with wings as eagles; they shall run, and not be weary; and they shall walk, and not faint" (Isaiah 40:31).

PRELUDE TO THE A-C

Back to Rev. 12:17: "Who is the remnant of her seed? Christians. The Jews are now in unbelief because they do not believe in Jesus Christ. Those, who now have the "testimony of Jesus Christ," and keep His word are on satan's hit list. This includes believing Jews and Christians. But remember, the church has not and will not take the place of the Israel.

Let me give another parenthetical phase.

"And I saw another angel fly in the midst of heaven, having the everlasting gospel to preach unto them that dwell on the earth, and to every nation, and kindred, and tongue, and people, Saying with a loud voice, Fear God, and give glory to him; for the hour of his judgment is come: and worship him that made heaven, and earth, and the sea, and the fountains of waters" (Rev. 14:6–7).

This angel will preach the true gospel to everyone on the earth. Every nation and tongue will hear the gospel in their native language. He will not have any denominational tint, nor will he have any ulterior motives. This angel will do what man has not been able to do, which is preach the true, uncompromising word of The Most High God. After he preaches the gospel, another angel preaches a prophetic message concerning Mystery Babylon.

"And there followed another angel, saying, Babylon is fallen, is fallen, that great city, because she made all nations drink of the wine of the wrath of her fornication" (Rev. 14:8).

We will study Babylon later. A third angel now preaches a fire and brimstone sermon;

"And the third angel followed them, saying with a loud voice, If any man worship the beast and his image, and receive his mark in his forehead, or in his hand, The same shall drink of the wine of the wrath of God, which is poured out without mixture into the cup of his indignation; and he shall be tormented with fire and brimstone in the presence of the holy angels, and in the presence of the lamb: And the smoke of their torment ascendeth up for ever and ever: and they have no rest day nor night, who worship the beast and his image, and whosoever receiveth the mark of his name (Rev. 14:9-11).

This angel preaches with a loud voice warning all mankind to stay away from the a-c. They are told; not to worship him or his image, not to receive his mark, in their forehead or hand. And if they do, the lake of fire will be their home forever. These angels will preach and mankind will not be able to stop or tune them out. If anyone worships any part of this evil coalition, salvation is out. They cannot be saved, because there is no repentance on their part and no forgiveness on The Father's part. I believe these angels will preach these great sermons before the mark of the beast is revealed. But people will not listen. Even when told to stay away from evil most people will not listen: Why? Because mankind is a rebel at heart. Jesus said; "But those things which proceed out of the mouth come forth from the heart; and they defile the man. For out of the heart proceed evil thoughts, murders, adulteries, fornications, thefts, false witness, blasphemies" (Matt. 15:18-19).

Rebellion is in the heart of man. After Adam's willful sin. his sinful and rebellious nature was passed on to all of us. It was Adam's willful sin; don't blame Eve she was tricked. "And the Lord God said unto the woman, what is this that thou hast done? And the woman said, The serpent beguiled (tricked) me, and I did eat" (Genesis 2:13). "But I fear, lest by any means, as the serpent beguiled Eve through his subtilty (trickery), so your minds should be corrupted from the simplicity that is in Christ" (2 Corinthians 11:3).

"For Adam was first formed, then Eve, And Adam was not deceived, but the woman being deceived was in the transgression" (1 Timothy 2:13-14).

Adam sinned willfully. As soon as he heard and gave credence to the lies of satan, the mystery of iniquity and rebellion formed in his heart. He may have felt The Most High was holding something good from him. Adam did not just fell into sin as Eve did. Adam's sin was purposeful, deliberate, and presumptuous. Please read Romans 5:12–21 and Job 31:33. Adam was not off in the back forty weeding. He was right there as Eve was being tricked. Adam was listening to every word satan and Eve said. satan's lie was meant for Adam to hear, and hear he did. Adam ears itched when he heard the part about being gods. Please reread Genesis 3:1–7.

I am so weary of the following statement; "Adam saw all that woman and could not bear to be without her." Adam was not looking and lusting after Eve's body nor was he afraid of not having her any more. Adam wanted to be like The Most High God. Adam failed his test of obedience. "For as by one man's (Adam) disobedience (willful) many were made sinners (us), so by the obedience (willful) of one (Jesus) shall many be made righteous (us)" (Romans 5:19). If Adam had not eaten of the tree nothing would have happened. Just as Jesus came willfully, Adam sinned willfully. Notice Eve is not mention at all in that verse. A sacrifice could have been made for Eve. She would have been forgiven and case closed. Adam failed both God and Eve. The only hope is the nature which is in Christ Jesus.

Notice; Rev. 14: 11, "And the smoke of their torment ascendeth up for ever and ever: and they have no rest day nor night." If the angels had only said "And the smoke of their torment ascendeth up for ever and ever." I would have to give credence to those who teach that you burn up in a fire that never goes out. But the Bible does not stop there. The angels said; "and they have no rest day nor night." This means they are physically in torment day time, night time, all the time, and never burn up. They have supernatural bodies for a supernatural fire.

THE A-C, SATAN, AND THE FALSE PROPHET

We will now study the a-c and his buddies. Notice something The Almighty told Paul to write, "Now we beseech you, brethren, by the coming of our Lord Jesus Christ, and by our gathering together unto him. And now ye know what witholdeth that <u>he</u> might be revealed in his time. For the mystery of iniquity doth already work: only he who now letteth will let, until <u>he</u> be taken out of the way. And then shall that <u>Wicked</u> be revealed, whom the Lord shall consume with the spirit of his mouth, and shall destroy with the brightness of his coming: Even him, whose coming is after the working of Satan with all power and signs and lying wonders, And with all deceivableness of unrighteousness in them that perish; because they received not the love of the truth, that they might be saved" (2 Thess. 2:1, 6–10). The saved church (he) must be out of here before the revealing of the a-c, the rapture will usher in the a-c and his kingdom.

These things seem beyond our comprehension. But we must remember the following; just because we do not understand all the works of our Father does not mean it will not happen. Let's read on.

"And I stood upon the sand of the sea and saw a beast rise up out of the sea, having seven heads and ten horns, and upon his horns ten crowns, and upon his heads the name of blasphemy" (Rev. 13:1).

John stands on the shore of humanity. And from this sea of people, the beast (a-c) rises to power, and not from some supernatural event. John sees those same seven heads and ten horns satan had in Rev. 12:3. This informs us beyond a shadow of a doubt, satan is the driving force behind the a-c. Those seven heads each had a blasphemous name written on it.

"And the beast which I saw was like unto a leopard, and his feet were as the feet of a bear, and his mouth as the mouth of a lion: and the dragon gave him his power, and his seat, and great authority" (Rev. 13:2).

John sees the spirit of the beast (a-c.) The descriptions are taken from Daniel 7:1–7. The leopard represents Greece, the bear paws represent Medes/Persia, and the lion's mouth represents Babylon. From somewhere within what was the former empires of those nations, the beast comes to power. "After this I saw in the night visions and behold a fourth beast, dreadful and terrible, and strong exceedingly; and it had great iron teeth; and it brake in pieces, and stamped the residue with the feet of it: and it was diverse from all the beasts that were before it: and it had ten horns. I considered the horns and, behold, there came up among them another little horn, before whom there were three of the first horns plucked up by the roots: and behold, in this horn were eyes like the eyes of man, and a mouth speaking great words" (Daniel 7:7-8).

The description of this fourth beast in Daniel describes the Great Roman Empire. The description given for Rome is "dreadful, terrible, and strong exceeding." This beast is beyond description, it was a powerful and destructive creature, no nation stood against it, just as no nation will stand against the a-c, he will be dreadful, terrible, and powerful just like Rome. But he will be a man, and not a nation. I do not have adequate words to describe how wicked and dreadful the a-c will be. No other human being will be able to stop him.

John was given this description to convey to us the origin of the a-c and how ferocious he will be. This description seems to transcend a human being, but it will be a man. The most dangerous creature in the jungle is not the rogue bull elephant, hungry lion, angry hippo, running rhino, or the vicious viper, but evil man. Only man will kill for the fun and sport of watching another creature or human die. Only man kills simply because he can. The a-c will be like no other human being. Think of all the evil dictators who have ever existed on the earth. Combine their characteristics into one person, and you may begin to get a glimpse of the a-c.

Notice Daniel 7:8; the little horn has eyes; the other ten horns do not. The eyes represent a man; the ten regular horns represent nations. This horn speaks great words, or may I say he roars like only a man can. The a-c will get everyone's attention and devour many nations. Remember; Daniel 7:4: "The first was like a lion." This represented Nebuchadnezzar and his Babylonian Kingdom. The a-c will come from somewhere within what is left of the Babylonian, Medes/Persia, Greece, and the Roman Empire. And it plainly says satan (dragon) gives this beast (a-c) his power, seat, and great authority. Remember Luke 4:6, "And the devil said unto him, All this power will I give thee, and the glory of them: for that is delivered unto me; and to whomsoever I will I give it."

The first man Adam, conceded this power to satan. I believe Adam had many spiritual powers. But once he sinned, he lost access to those powers. satan, will be able to give certain spiritual powers to the a-c. If satan jumped from behind a bush and revealed himself, and said "worship me," most people would not do it. Yet people will follow a great human leader in worshipping his power source. In the Old Testament, if the Jews had a leader that worshiped God, most of the people followed him or her in worshipping God. If the leader was evil and worshipped idols, most of the people would also follow him or her in worshipping idols. A sheep will follow a leader to its death. Who is your shepherd?

How will satan give these powers to the a-c? I do not know. Will satan actually possess the body of the a-c? I do not know. Will satan stand beside the a-c and execute whatever 'wonder signs' needed? I do not know. But this I do know: the a-c will have powers like no other man on this earth. Will the a-c have powers as Jesus had? No, Jesus is God, so the a-c cannot have as much power as Jesus has. However, the a-c will have some powers, how much can only be speculative. I do know it will be power no other human, (except Adam), has ever had. The Most High will allow the a-c to have this power because the a-c is a judgement from The Most High. The phrase; "All this power will I give thee, and the glory of them" in Luke 4:6. Is the subject of another book maybe one of you may write it.

"And I saw one of his heads as it were wounded to death; and his deadly wound was healed: and all the world wondered after the beast. And they worshiped the dragon which gave power unto the beast: and they worshiped the beast, saying, Who is like unto the beast? Who is able to make war with him" (Rev. 13:3–4)?

The a-c is somehow hurt; he may even appear to be dead. He then appears to be resurrected. When the world's population see this. They are highly impressed. The death and resurrection of the a-c will be shown on TV, cell phones, IPads, note books, and computers. The a-c may be declared dead by a doctor. The wound or wounds, may be shown, so there will be no doubt he is dead. And at the right moment, he will appear to resurrect himself.

I have heard some Bible teachers say this verse is talking about the Roman empire being destroyed and resurrected. But this is not so. All the other verses in this chapter are talking about a man, so why should this one verse talk about a nation.

Remember, the a-c and satan are deceivers and imitators; he is imitating Jesus Christ with this supposed healing and resurrection. I say "supposed" because satan cannot give life. He can manipulate things, but he has no life-giving powers since he is a created being. The world is taken in by this trick and think they have witness a miracle. All who believe in, or were close to believing in the a-c, now openly worships the a-c and satan. At last, satan has what he has always wanted; open adoration. The people of the world will say "the a-c has reached self-realization, and has obtained godhood."

"And there was given unto him a *mouth speaking great things* and blasphemies; and power was given unto him to continue forty and two months. And he opened his mouth in blasphemy against God, to blaspheme his name, and his tabernacle, and them that dwell in heaven. And it was given unto him to make war with the saints, and to overcome them: and power was given him over all kindreds, and tongues, and nations" (Rev. 13:5–7).

The a-c has now shown his true loyalties, and turns on the Jewish nation and they realize they made a tragic mistake, the a-c is not their Messiah. They may remember: "If there arise among you a prophet, or a dreamer of dreams, and giveth thee a sign or a wonder, And the sign or the wonder come to pass, whereof he spake unto thee, saying, Let us go after other gods which thou hast not known, and let us serve them; Thou shalt not hearken unto the words of that prophet, or that dreamer of dreams for the Lord your God proveth you, to know whether ye love the Lord your God with all your heart and with all your soul" (Deuteronomy 13:1-3).

But it is too late. The a-c is using his boisterous mouth to speak blasphemy against all The Righteousness of The Most High God. Remember Daniel 7:8, "In this horn were eyes like the eyes of man, and a *mouth speaking great things.*" Also Daniel 7:25, "And he shall speak great words against the most High, and shall wear out the saints of the most High, and think to change times and laws: and they shall be given into his hand." The word "mouth" is used once again. This man will have a vocabulary like no other. The a-c blasphemes The Father, Jesus Christ, His Name, His tabernacle, and everyone in heaven. Notice the word "tabernacle" in Rev. 13:6. The a-c has made a way for a Jewish tabernacle and then he desecrates it with his words and actions.

We are given a few time periods concerning the length of the tribulation period; Daniel 7:25: time and times and the dividing of time, Daniel 8:14, 2,300 days; Daniel 9:27, one week, which means seven years; Daniel 12:11, 1,290 days; Daniel 12:12, 1,335 days; Rev. 11:,2, forty-two months, Rev. 11:3, 1,260 days; Rev. 12:6, 1,260 days; Rev. 12:14, time, and times, and half a time, and Rev. 13:5, forty-two months. Now exactly when the a-c's kingdom will start is unknown. It would be hard, if not impossible to tell exactly how long the tribulation will last. Seven years has been the accepted length most people quote. But if you do the math, most of these times given do not equal exactly seven years.

Notice where it says time, and times, and half a time, this means three and one-half years. Since there are two of these lengths given, they equal seven. And this is where the term "seven years of tribulation" is taken. Plus, the number seven is the number for perfection. Many use Dan. 9:25–27 to say seven years. But with us not knowing when certain things start or end, seven is the best I can come up with. Jesus used the term "great tribulation," but He never said it would be seven years. I am not saying it won't be seven years long, but it will be pure terror, whatever the time length.

The a-c will start his pogrom to eliminate both Jews and Christians. This will be worse than the holocaust. The a-c declares total war on all saints. The Nazis did terrible things to the Jews, as well as others it considered less than human. They Conducted unimaginable, and torturous experiments, which caused slow, agonizing, and painful deaths. They burned and gassed millions of people. But those atrocities will be minor compared to what the a-c will do with his satanic-controlled mind. he will care nothing about fairness, right, wrong or the rule of law. The laws of all nations under his control will be abolished. It will be his way, his laws, and his thoughts only. Bibles will be banned, churches, if there are any, will be closed. There will be no democrats, republicans, independent, socialist, communist, or any other party affiliation. It will be his ideology or death.

"And all that dwell upon the earth shall worship him. Whose names are not written in the book of life of the Lamb slain from the foundation of the world. If any man have an ear, let him hear. He that leadeth into captivity shall go into captivity: he that killeth with the sword must be killed with the sword. Here is the patience and faith of the saints" (Rev. 13:8–10).

Verse 8, shows everyone will not serve the a-c. Those who have gotten saved since the rapture will not bow and worship him or satan. Their names are in "The Book of Life." Notice Rev. 13:9: "If any man have an ear, let him hear." Jesus, our savior used this phase over twenty-eight times (before I stopped counting) in Matthew, Mark, Luke, John, and Rev. You better be hearing, if you can hear? You better pay attention to what and who you hear. "And he (Jesus) said unto them, Take heed what ye hear . . ." (Mark 4:24). You are reading this book, but the words are mentally being spoken in your mind. Take heed.

In Rev. 13:10, Jesus gives a reassuring voice to His saints. Those who are about to be killed need not be afraid. Read the following: "And I saw as it were a sea of glass mingled with fire: and them that had gotten the victory over the beast, and over his image, and over his mark, and over the number of his name, stand on the sea of glass having the harps of God" (Rev. 15:2). These saints have their names written in "the book of life of the Lamb slain from the foundation of the world." This is the patience and faith of the saints; "Heaven awaits."

Notice in Rev. 15:2, the word "victory" is used. These people were killed, how is that victory? They will refuse to go along with the plans of the a-c and satan, and will pay for that rebellion with their lives. But, how can death be equated with victory? When any saint is killed, or suffer for the stand they take against the devil and this world, they have obtained the victory: "As it is written, for thy sake we are killed all the day long; we are accounted as sheep for the slaughter. Nay, in all these things we are more than conquerors through him that loved us" (Romans 8:36-37).

"So when this corruptible shall have put on incorruption, this mortal shall have put on immortality, then shall be brought to pass the saying that is written, Death is swallowed up in victory O death, where is thy sting? O grave where is thy victory? The sting of death is sin; and the strength of sin is the law. Buts thanks be to God which giveth us the victory through our Lord Jesus Christ" (1 Cor. 15:54-57).

Read the following: "And to you who are troubled rest with us, when the Lord Jesus shall be revealed from heaven with his mighty angels, In flaming fire taking vengeance on them that know not God, and that obey not the gospel of our Lord Jesus Christ: Who shall be punished with everlasting destruction from the presence of the Lord, and from the glory of his power" (2 Thess. 1:7-9). Thus when a saint is killed for the testimony of Jesus Christ, he or she has gotten the victory. Also remember, "And they overcame him by the blood of the lamb, and by the word of their testimony: and they loved not their lives unto the death" (Rev. 12:11). AMEN!

Read this also: "And when he had opened the fifth seal, I saw under the altar the souls of them that were slain for the word of God, and for the testimony which they held: And they cried with a loud voice, saying, How long, O Lord, holy and true, dost thou not judge and avenge our blood on them that dwell on the earth? And white robes were given unto every one of them; and it was said unto them, that they should rest yet for a little season, until their fellow servants also and their brethren, that should be killed as they were, should be fulfilled" (Rev. 6:9-11). There is a set number of saints to be killed during the tribulation. Once this number is fulfilled the end will come. "And except those days should be shortened, there should no flesh be saved: but for the elect's sake those days shall be shortened" (Matt. 24:22).

"And I beheld another beast coming up out of the earth; and he had two horns like a lamb, and he spake as a dragon. And he exerciseth all the power of the first beast before him, and causeth the earth and them which dwell therein to worship the first beast, whose deadly wound was healed. And he doeth great wonders, so that he maketh fire come down from heaven on the earth in the sight of men" (Rev. 13:11-13).

Now the last person of this unholy trinity, the false prophet, makes his appearance. He is also a man. The false prophet comes "up out of the earth." This means from within humanity. Notice he has the appearance of a lamb, but when he speaks it sounds like satan, which means he is also demonically controlled and full of the spirt of the a-c. The false prophet "exerciseth all the power of the first beast before him." satan is the power source, the a-c is the displayer of this power. And the false prophet is the cheerleader and does "great wonders." Notice the false prophet does not mention satan's name, but only points to the a-c. This cheerleader does not promote himself. Just as The Holy Spirit does not promote Himself but promotes The Father and Jesus: "Howbeit when he, the Spirit of truth, is come, he will guide you into all truth: for he shall not speak of himself; but whatsoever he shall hear, that shall he speak: and he will show you things to come. He shall glorify me: for he shall receive of mine, and shall show it unto you. All things that the Father hath are mine: therefore said I, that he shall take of mine, and shall show it unto you" (John 16:13–15).

The false prophet encourages everyone to worship the a-c. he does not speak the truth, but will proclaim lies just like his father

THE SPIRIT OF THE ANTI-CHRIST

satan. The false prophet will push the idea that everything has been given to the a-c. The false prophet has a silky-smooth tongue and is very charismatic. I do not believe there will be a world-wide ecumenical church saying anything about The Most High God. But, there will be a world-wide a-c/satanic church, whose Pope will be the false prophet.

Remember, judgments from The Father are falling upon the earth. The false prophet attempts to cause doubt as to who is the originator of these judgments, by also calling fire down from the skies. This deception is similar to the actions of Pharaoh's magicians: Exodus 7:10–12, 20–21, 8:7, 18, 19. And just as Pharaoh's magicians could only imitate, the false prophet will only imitate. Yet it will be enough to fool most people.

"And deceiveth them that dwell on the earth by means of those miracles which he had power to do in the sight of the beast; saying to them that dwell on the earth, that they should make an image to the beast, which had the wound by a sword, and did live. And he had power to give life unto the image of the beast, that the image of the beast should both speak, and cause that as many as would not worship the image of the beast should be killed" (Rev. 13:14–15).

The false prophet is also a true child of satan. he deceives many by these so-called miracles. But he can only do them in the sight of the a-c. Also notice this in verse 14: "which had the wound by a sword, and did live." The false prophet is not talking about the nation Rome, but a man. A real walking, talking human being. The false prophet is the main instigator of the "abomination of desolation." He tells those on the earth "see the great power of this man-god; he was killed but he resurrected himself. he has to be god, and we must worship him, by making an image and place the image and him in the holy of holies and worship them." All those who believe man can become a god, this will be their hour and their man. We now have satanic, creature, and idol worship in the Holy of Holies. But fear not, The Father has not been surpassed, because He was never in this temple.

Jesus spoke of this; "When ye therefore shall see the abomination of desolation, spoken of by Daniel the prophet, stand in the holy place, (whoso readeth, let him understand)" (Matt. 24:15). This is also in Daniel 9:27. Once the Jews see this they will realize their mistake. This also shows that sometime during the tribulation the a-c has moved to Jerusalem and made it his headquarters.

Somehow the false prophet makes it appear he gave life to the image causing it to speak on its own volition. The false prophet tells everyone to worship the image or die. It is not a TV monitor, but a real statue of the a-c. It is either his entire body or a bust of his head. The purpose of this so-called miracle is to make the inhabitants of the earth think the a-c has life-giving power. This image has no soul, so is it some sort of manipulation of technology by satan? But how? I do not know; maybe through some sort of computerization by artificial intelligence. Scientists are now experimenting on how to make computers "self-aware," which means to think and make decisions without human input. We have cells phones with which you can carry on limited conversation and get limited answers to your questions. My cell phone has more power and can do more things than a room size computer from the sixties.

Let me tell you of an experience I had with my computer. I was working on another book on how and why I got shot six times by a gang member on orders from the leaders of the Crips gang in prison. (I was over the contraband section at a maximum-security state prison in SC). I went on the internet looking for a speech to-text program. I found one and was going to order it the next day. As I was leaving the web, my computer spoke the following; "I can do what you are looking for." It then told me where to look on the hard drive. I never had an experience of this nature before, nor has it spoken on its own since. I didn't know if I should look for the program, or cast the demon out of my computer.

How satan accomplishes this feat we are not told. But if you do not worship the image, you will be killed. This statement lets us know there will be people who will not take his mark, nor worship him, and many will pay with their lives. "And I saw another sign in heaven, great and marvelous, seven angels having the seven last plagues; for in them is filled up the wrath of God. And I saw as it were a sea of glass mingled with fire: and them that had gotten the victory over the beast, and over his image, and over his mark, and over the number of his name, stand on the sea of glass, having the harps of God" (Rev. 15:1–2). Notice they are not on a cloud with harps, but before The Almighty. They have paid with their lives and have gotten the victory over the a-c and satan.

"And he causedth all, both small and great, rich and poor, free and bond, to receive a mark in their right hand, or in their foreheads. And that no man might buy or sell, save he that had the mark, or the name of the beast, or the number of his name. Here is wisdom. Let him that hath understanding count the number of the beast: for it is the number of a man; and his number is Six hundred threescore and six" (666) (Rev. 13:16–18).

The a-c, the false prophet, and man now show their full rebellion. Even though an angel preached against taking the mark (Rev 14:6–11). The false prophet will demand everyone to receive and openly show either, the mark of the beast, the name of the beast, or the number of the beast's name. These will be forced upon mankind. Some will gladly take the mark others will be reluctant. But, if you want to eat, work, buy or sell, you must take at least one of them. There will be no paper/coin money.

I was in a store recently and saw a man place his smart phone near the cashier and allowed her to scan his phone to pay for the items he brought. The technology to go cashless is here, only the logistics and the fear of governmental control must be overcome. Many national governments (to include the USA) would love to get rid of paper money and coins. Tax collections would sky-rocket, loop-holes and tax havens would cease. Israel is actively exploring the technology and implication to go cashless as soon as possible. In Seattle, Washington, Amazon has open its first cashless retail store. There are no clerks to run the cash registers because there are no cash registers. All you need is your smart phone and the Amazon app. There are scanners at the front door. Scan your smart phone and the money for your purchase is deducted from the bank.

The technology to place a bar code or something similar anywhere on or in your body is here. It can store medical, financial, and other personnel information. The following excerpt was taken

THE A-C

from the July 24, 2017, USA TODAY Network written by Mary Bowerman; "A Wisconsin technology company is offering its employees microchip implants that can be used to scan into the building and purchase food at work. Three Square Market. (www.32market.com/public#about) A company that provides technology for breakroom or micro markets. Has over fifty employees who plan to the have the devices implanted. The tiny chip, which uses RFID technology or Radio-Frequency Identification, can be implanted between the thumb and forefinger within seconds. CEO Todd Westby said in a company statement "Eventually, this technology will become standardized allowing you to use this as your passport, public transit, all **purchasing opportunities** etc." (Bold letters are mine.)

Did you know many if not all new LCD TVs send out a signal which indicates which TV program you are viewing? We cannot hear it, but the newer smart phones pick up the signal and relay it to the rating agencies. You have no control over this app. This was reported by The National Public Radio network (NPR) on May 16, 2017. Your smart TV and smart phone may be listening to you and reporting what you say you may need, to advertising agencies. Which can then target you with the right ads. Technology is setting the stage for the a-c.

Most of the Economical systems of this world are in a fragile condition. A catastrophic world-wide event (rapture) could be the catalyst for a total world financial collapse and the ushering in of a one world cashless currency.

The Bible does not tell us what the mark will be, or the a-c's name. We do know 666 stands for man. Six is the number of man. Mankind was made on the six day. The number 666 has no significance now. It is not bad luck. Saints of The Most High there is no such thing as good or bad luck. Everything moves by The Power of God (Acts 17:28). The number 666 will only have significance during the time of the a-c. And then, this number 666, the mark of the a-c, or the name of the a-c, must be prominently displayed in your right hand or forehead. There will be no secret worshippers here.

Come let us look at another parenthetical phase.

THE SPIRIT OF THE ANTI-CHRIST

"And I heard a great voice out of the temple saying to the seven angels, go your ways, and pour out the vials of the wrath of God upon the earth. And the first went, and poured out his vial upon the earth; and there fell a noisome and grievous sore upon the men which had the mark of the beast, and upon them which worshiped his image. And the second angel poured out his vial upon the sea; and it became as the blood of a dead man: and every living soul died in the sea. And the third angel poured out his vial upon the rivers and fountains of waters; and they became blood. And I heard the angel of the waters say, Thou art righteous, O Lord, which art and wast, and shall be, because thou hast judged thus. For they have shed the blood of saints and prophets, and thou hast given them blood to drink; for they are worthy. And I heard another out of the altar say, Even so, Lord God Almighty, true and righteous are thy judgments. And the fourth angel poured out his vial upon the sun; and power was given unto him to scorch men with fire. And men were scorched with great heat, and blasphemed the name of God which hath power over these plagues; and they repented not to give him glory. And the fifth angel poured out his vial upon the seat of the beast; and his kingdom was full of darkness; and they gnawed their tongues for pain, And blasphemed the God of heaven because of their pains and their sores, and repented not of their deeds" (Rev. 16:1–11).

Angels are pouring judgments directly against the a-c and his subjects. Notice Rev. 16:2: "There fell a noisome and grievous sore upon the men which had the mark of the beast, and upon them which worshiped his image." This means a nasty, and painful sore attacks the subjects of the a-c's kingdom. Will it be on the a-c or the false prophet? I believe so. This is not given to us. The next judgement is against the water, it is turned into coagulated blood. They are given to drink what they have spilled, human blood. All creatures in the sea that get their air from the water will die because their gills cannot draw oxygen out of coagulated dead blood.

Notice Rev. 16:3: the word "sea" instead of "seas." Is this one body of water or all seas and oceans. we do not know. Now Rev. 16:4 says "rivers and fountains of waters." This lets us know the head or originating points of rivers and streams will be turned to blood and then flow through-out the river. We are not told how long these bloody waters will last. Our bodies can do without food for a while but we must have water in a matter of days. They may drink; "And thou hast given them blood to drink; for they are worthy (Rev. 16:6)."

The sun shines full force and mankind is scorched with fire. A fifth angel pours out darkness; not just any darkness, but darkness which causes pain. This may be similar to the darkness sent upon Egypt. "And the Lord said unto Moses, Stretch out thine hand toward heaven, that there may be darkness over the land of Egypt, even darkness which may be felt. And Moses stretched forth his hand toward heaven; and there was a thick darkness in all the land of Egypt three days: They saw not one another, neither rose any from his place for three days" (Exodus 10:21–23). This is supernatural darkness. I have been deep inside caves, and it was so dark I could not see my hand right before my eyes. But it was not painful. The darkness that was upon the Egyptians was so thick it was literally felt by them. Light could not penetrate it, candles were useless. The Egyptians could not see each other, so they just sat and were afraid to move for three days.

This time, neither light bulbs, nor super flashlights will be able to penetrate the darkness. Not only will it be dark, dark, it will also be a painful darkness. People will gnaw (bite) their tongues. But rebellious mankind will not repent of their dark evil deeds. They will continue to blaspheme The Almighty God. There are people on this earth right now, whose minds are so full of darkness (evil), that they will not allow the light of the glorious gospel to penetrate their wicked minds.

They believe beyond a shadow of doubt that if they kill themselves and other innocent people in the name of their god he will usher them into a personnel erotic heaven with seventy-two perpetual virgins. This is pure evil, with no legitimate grounds for belief, only lust: "In meekness instructing those that oppose themselves; If God peradventure will give them repentance to the acknowledging of the truth; And that they may recover themselves out of the snare of the devil, who are taken captive by him at his will" (2 Timothy 2:25–26). satan's got a noose around their necks. he is leading them around, and having them do his will. satan does not mind if they say they are doing the will of The Most High, because satan knows better; plus, it will bring more subjects into his evil noose.

It is easy to recognize a man-made religion. Because man is the center of the religion, and man gets the best part of the deal. Muslims get their forever virgins. Mormons get to become gods and have sex throughout eternity and populate their own universe. Hindus and others reach a state of perfectness. The witnesses get to spend a great time with family and friends in their new earth. All are man centered. Only Christianity is God centered. Man could not come up to the Standards of The Most High. So, The Most High became a man to pay for man's sin. It is not about man. But it is all about The Most High Father.

MYSTERY BABYLON

This is a most confusing chapter. Is this chapter telling us of an evil city, evil system, evil financial system, evil religious system and evil kingdom, all at the same time? I believe it is meant to include all five, the totality of evil in the world (mystery of iniquity). Remember this; Mystery Babylon is not a separate system, it is in cahoots with satan, the a-c, and the false prophet. Babylon is mention over three hundred times in the Bible and usually it is in an evil context. Babylon represents evil and the deifying of mankind. Let's see what we can come up with.

"And there came one of the seven angels which had the seven vials, and talked with me, saying unto me, Come hither; I will show unto thee the judgment of the great whore that sitteth upon many waters: With whom the kings of the earth have committed fornication, and the inhabitants of the earth have been made drunk with the wine of her fornication" (Rev. 17:1–2).

We start our journey toward an understanding of the great mystery of Babylon. As I stated earlier, what exactly is the great mystery Babylon no one knows for sure. I am going to give you what I received since you paid good money for this book. However, there are many things we will not know until we get to heaven.

Notice verse one, "sitteth upon many waters." We are given the interpretation of this phase, "And he saith unto me, The waters which thou sawest, where the whore sitteth, are peoples, and multitudes, and nations, and tongues" (Rev. 17:15). This lets us know great Babylon is more than a mere city, because the waters represent multitudes of people and nations, with many languages. Does this mean it is an order, place, religious system, financial system, or the totality of evil on the earth?

I have heard speculation by others saying it could be Jerusalem, Rome, even somewhere here in America. But it is more than just one place. It is more of a system of places connected by evil, the a-c, and satan. "Kings of the earth have committed fornication, and the inhabitants of the earth" (Rev. 17:2). Also, "And the woman which thou sawest is that great city, which reigneth over the kings of the earth" (Rev. 17:18). No one group of people are affiliated with mystery Babylon, but the whole earth. This is not Old Testament Babylon. "And Babylon, the glory of kingdoms the beauty of the Chaldees' excellency, shall be as when God overthrew Sodom and Go—mor'-rah. It shall never be inhabited, neither shall it be dwelt in from generation to generation: neither shall the Arabian pitch tent there; neither shall the shepherds make their fold there" (Isaiah 13:19–20).

"The word that the lord spake against Babylon and against the land of the Chal-de-ans by Jeremiah the prophet. How is the hammer of the whole earth cut asunder and broken! How is Babylon become a desolation among the nations! The Lord hath opened his armory, and hath brought forth the weapons of his indignation: for this is the work of the Lord God of hosts in the land of the Chal-de-ans. Therefore the wild beasts of the desert with the wild beasts of the island shall dwell there, and the owls shall dwell therein: and it shall be no more inhabited forever: neither shall it be dwelt in from generation to generation" (Jeremiah 50:1, 23, 25, 39).

These verses tell us that Old Testament Babylon would be destroyed and never inhabited again nor reach its former glory days. Many scholars teach Old Testament Babylon will be revived and once again reach its glory days. The Most High God says it will not be inhabited nor reach its former glory. You decide whom you will believe, as for me I believe the report of The Lord God.

Quickly, before we miss something: "Behold, the day of the Lord cometh, cruel both with wrath and fierce anger, to lay the land desolate: and he shall destroy the sinners there of out of it. For the stars of heaven and the constellations thereof shall not give their light: the sun shall be darkened in his going forth, and the moon shall not cause her light to shine. And I will punish the world for their evil, and the wicked for their iniquity; and I will cause the arrogancy of the proud to crease, and will lay low the haughtiness of the terrible" (Isaiah 13:9–11). This tells me mystery Babylon may symbolize the world's order of evil.

We need a parenthetical phase right here.

Let us go to the book of Zechariah (Zech.) He was shown many visions. These visions were spiritual events that were to be manifested in our physical word. "Then the angel that talked with me went forth, and said unto me, Lift up now thine eyes, and see what is this that goeth forth. And I said, What is it? And he said This is an e-phah that goeth forth, He saith moreover, This is their resemblance through all the earth" (Zech. 5:5–6). Zechariah was shown a bushel basket, which travels all over the earth. The angel uses the word "their" which may mean more than one.

What's in that basket, let's see? "And, behold, there was lifted up a talent of lead: and this is a woman that sitteth in the midst of the e-phah. And he said, This is wickedness. And he cast it into the midst of the e-phah; and he cast the weight of lead upon the mouth thereof" (Zech. 5:7–8). Notice the angel cast "wickedness" into the lap of the woman sitting in the basket then puts a lead weight into the mouth of the basket. Let's go on: "Then lifted I up mine eyes, and looked, and, behold, there came out two women, and the wind was in their wings; for they had wings like the wings of a stork: and they lifted up the e-phah between the earth and the heaven. Then said I to the angel that talked with me, Whither do these bear the e-phah. And he said unto me, To build it a house in the land of Shi-nar: and it shall be established, and set there upon her own base" (Zech. 5:9–11).

What is this? Is it "the mystery of iniquity," sent to Babylon? Shi-nar is another name for Babylon. Daniel 1:1–2 tell us Shi-nar is Babylon and this wickedness was taken there. Those creatures are not angels but evil creatures. nowhere in the Bible do we find female angels. But why is wickedness portrayed as women? Let's go back to Rev. 17.

THE SPIRIT OF THE ANTI-CHRIST

"So he carried me away in the spirit into the wilderness, and I saw a woman sit upon a scarlet-colored beast, full of names of blasphemy, having seven heads and ten horns. And the woman was arrayed in purple and scarlet color, and decked with gold and precious stones and pearls, having a golden cup in her hand full of abominations and filthiness of her fornication: And upon her forehead was a name written, MYSTERY, BABYLON THE GREAT, THE MOTHER OF HARLOTS AND ABOMINATIONS OF THE EARTH. And I saw the woman drunken with the blood of the saints, and with the blood of the martyrs of Jesus: and when I saw her, I wondered with great admiration" (Rev. 17:3–6).

Mystery Babylon is a system of evil portrayed as women in the book of Zech., as well as here in Rev. 17. The a-c will use this evil system to further his goals. The Father calls it, "THE MOTHER OF HARLOTS AND ABOMINATIONS OF THE EARTH." The Bible also portrays evil as a woman in Proverbs 5:1–11, 7:6–27 and 9:13-18. Wisdom is also portrayed as a woman in Proverbs 1:20–31, 2:1–22, 3:13–19, 4:1-9, 8:1–36, and 9:1–12.

Why not use a man? Because on the surface evil can be very beautiful, alluring, seductive, pleasurable and marvelous to look upon. But the hidden parts of evil are what gets you. Remember Hebrews 11:25: "Than to enjoy the pleasures of sin for a season;" Wisdom on the other hand is very beautiful, alluring, pleasurable and marvelous, but with no hidden compartments. As best as I can figure Mystery Babylon and Mystery of iniquity are one and the same, "the totality of an ever expanding, and all-consuming evil system." Ladies do not be offended at this portrayal, The Most High used this not me.

Rev. 17:1, Calls great Babylon a whore, with Rev. 17:2, and 3 saying "everyone in the world has been drunk with the wine of her fornication." This is not sexual fornication, but spiritual fornication; which is rebellion against The Almighty Father. This is the same terminology used in Rev. 2:20–22. Jesus tells us of "Jez-e-bel" another symbol of wide spread evil portrayed as a woman; "Notwithstanding I have a few things against thee, because thou sufferest that woman Jez-e-bel, which calleth herself a prophetess, to teach and to seduce my servants to commit fornication, and to eat things sacrificed unto idols. And I gave her space to repent of her fornication; and she repented not. Behold, I will cast her into a bed, and them that commit adultery with her into great tribulation, except they repent of their deeds" (Rev. 2:20-22).

One more verse; "Thou hast built thy high place at every head of the way, and hast made thy beauty to be abhorred, and has opened thy feet to everyone that passed by, and multiplied they whoredoms. Thou hast also committed fornication with the Egyptians thy neighbors, great of flesh; and hast increased thy whoredoms, to provoke me to anger" (Ezekiel 16:25-26). The Father is admonishing the unfaithfulness of His people, Israel. He is saying they have committed spiritual fornication by hooking up with the Egyptians and other nations in turning away from Him. He is calling Israel a whore. He does not mince His words. He calls it, what it is. Evil.

You may not like this explanation, but it is what it is. Mankind's downfall begun with Adam and Eve and our restoration will end with the destruction of the a-c, satan, and Mystery Babylon (worldwide evil), portrayed as a woman. But, why use the name Babylon? In the Old Testament and in ancient history Babylon was portrayed as a wickedly evil nation. They had a mountain of human skulls and they also would take some of their captives and skin them alive; then used this human skin to cover furniture. Babylon represents worldwide evil. I would encourage you to read Jeremiah chapter 51, and you will see the parallel between old Testament Babylon and Mystery Babylon. Both, wicked as can be. Mystery Babylon is part of the spiritual kingdom of satan.

There is another parallel between Old Testament Babylon and Mystery Babylon, witchcraft;, "But these two things shall come to thee in a moment on one day, the loss of children, and widowhood: they shall come upon thee in their perfection for the multitude of thy sorceries, and for the great abundance of thine enchantments. Stand now with thine enchantments, and with the multitude of they sorceries, wherein thou hast labored from thy youth; if so be thou shalt be able to profit, if so be thou mayest prevail. Thou art wearied in the multitude of thy counsels. Let now the astrologer, the stargazers, the monthly prognosticators, stand up, and save thee from these things that shall come upon thee" (Isaiah 47:9, 12-13). This was written to old testament Babylon. Both used witchcraft in accomplishing their evil goals.

Please allow me to add something here from my teenage years. The church I attended did their best to keep the teens active and engaged. Sometimes they went too far. The elders allowed a game which was nothing but witchcraft. The crowd would be told to maintain silence. Four of the smallest teenagers would be selected, then one placed at each of the four corners of a chair. Then the heaviest adult there, would sit in the chair. We would alternately place one hand over the head of the adult sitting in the chair. (I have intentionally left out vital steps). Two of us would place our forefingers under each arm pit and the others placing theirs under each knee lock. And we would then lift him over our heads with no effort.

This symbolize the teenagers becoming one with the adult, thus not feeling his weight. You may ask why place this in this book? Witchcraft and satanism are the same. It is very dangerous and should not be practice by anyone, no matter how innocent it seems. Pastors make sure your youth pastor or youth workers are not allowing any type of satanism, witchcraft, or role-playing games in your church. Not even the ones using Christian characters. It is not harmless fun and games. It is satanism pure and simple.

I am about to jump in with both feet once more. The church has been duped by so called white magic. This happens when the church allows magic to come into and among its members just because it may teach some good values or good may defeat evil. It is not harmless teaching, but witchcraft. The Harry Potter's series is very dangerous. In that it teaches good witchcraft overcoming evil witchcraft. There is no such thing, witchcraft is witchcraft and all of it is evil. The Chronicles of Narnia by C. S. Lewis are in the same evil group with Harry Potter. It uses one of satan's favorite tricks. Drop a few Christian themes here and there and the church will love it. It is witchcraft pure and sample. I have even heard pastors preaching on J. R. R. Tolkien's fantasy books. All of them are full of witchcraft. Pastors I ask you to seek honest guidance from The Father on what I have told you.

As we move toward the end days. Expect more manifestations of the supernatural both within and outside the church. Many church members will be fooled by these evil signs, because they are seeking power signs, instead of walking by faith. There will be so-called great healing ministries and schools teaching healing and prophetic operations. But it will not be of The Father: "Not everyone that saith unto me, Lord, Lord, shall enter into the kingdom of heaven; but he that doeth the will of my Father which is in heaven. Many will say to me in that day, Lord, Lord, have we not prophesied in thy name? And in thy name have cast out devils? And in thy name done many wonderful works? And then will I profess unto them, I never knew you: depart from me, ye that work iniquity" (Matt. 7:21-23). This shows us there will be great satanic deception in the church.

If these people have such great power, they should go into hospitals and just their shadow passing over those sick patients should heal them. On your own read Acts 5:12–16, Acts 8:5–8, Acts 14:3, Acts 19:11–12. Please do not think I do not believe in divine healing, I do. I once worked for the S.C. Department of Corrections. A contract hit was placed on my life by Inmates. On March 5, 2010, I was shot six times in the abdomen and chest area with a .38 revolver during a home invasion. I bled out three times and was given sixty-three units of blood. My doctor said it is a miracle I am still alive and able to function, because they gave up on me. I know I received a miracle. My next book will be on this miracle and what led up to it.

Back to mystery Babylon. "I saw a woman sit upon a scarlet-color beast, full of names of blasphemy, having seven heads and ten horns" (Rev. 17:3). The a-c is now covered in scarlet, which is a bright red color. Why red? In the animal kingdom, bright color sometimes indicates an animal is poisonous and is a warning to other creatures, "I am dangerous, don't mess with me." The devil and the a-c are very dangerous and not to be trifled with. Some animals such as the peacock and male Cardinals use its color to attract mates. The a-c and mystery Babylon will attract people.

Notice Rev. 17:4, Mystery Babylon is gloriously arrayed in the finest and costliest apparel. She is; adorned, bedizened, dolled up, dressed to the nines, tricked out, or whatever you want to call it, with gold, precious stones, pearls, and with a golden cup full of sin. Sin is beautiful at first glance; the cup seems so harmless and inviting, until you take a drink.

"Than to enjoy the pleasures of sin for a season" (Hebrews 11:25).

"Babylon hath been a golden cup in the Lord's hand, that made all the earth drunken: the nations have drunken of her wine; therefore the nations are mad" (Jer. 51:7). It is ordained by The Most High.

"She has her name written on her forehead "MYSTERY, BABYLON THE GREAT, THE MOTHER OF HARLOTS AND ABOMINATIONS OF THE EARTH" (Rev. 17:5). She is called "THE GREAT." Our Father is giving us a warning concerning evil. It is bold, great, and overwhelmingly attractive. I am reminded of the following;, "And, behold, there met him a woman with the attire of harlot, and subtile of heart. (She is loud and stubborn; her feet abide not in her house: Now is she without, now in the streets, and lieth in wait at every corner)" (Proverbs 7:10-12). This is a composite of evil. It is everywhere, waiting for unsuspecting and careless victims. I hope you have read Jer. 51, if not please read it.

Notice how this evil system loves to kill those who follow Jesus; she can't get enough of the saints' blood; "And I saw the women drunken with the blood of the saints and with the blood of the martyrs of Jesus" Rev. 17:6. I believe this is not just during the tribulation time but throughout the ages, evil has had a blood lust for the followers of The Most High. Let me say something here. This Mystery Babylon is not the Roman Catholic Church. The bright colors are not an indication of the pope. I know this is against what many have been taught by great Bible scholars but this is not so. This is much bigger than the church of Roman. It may become part of the evil system but will not have a controlling part. The a-c will allow no one to upstage him.

"And the angel said unto me, Wherefore didst thou marvel? I will tell thee the mystery of the woman, and of the beast that carrieth her, which hath the seven heads and ten horns. The beast that thou sawest was, and is not, and shall ascend out of the bottomless pit, and go into perdition: and they that dwell on the earth shall wonder, whose names were not written in the book of life from the foundation of the world, when they behold the beast that was, and is not, and yet is. And here is the mind which hath wisdom. The seven heads are seven mountains, on which the woman sitteth. And there are seven kings: five are fallen, and one is, and the other is not yet come; and when he cometh, he must continue a short space. And the beast that was, and is not, even he is the eighth, and is of the seven, and goeth into perdition" (Rev. 17:7-11).

We are not to marvel or admire evil. Eyeball evil too long and you will become part of it.

Rev. 17:8-11, are the most difficult verses in Rev. I am going to give what I believe they mean. We know the ten horns come to power sometime during the reign of the a-c. We know mystery Babylon rides on the back of the beast. In verse 8; "was and is not and yet is, refers to the a-c, remember Rev. 13:3. The a-c (was) on the scene, then killed (is not), and somehow fakes a resurrection (yet is). And when he does this the unsaved will wonder and begin to admire the a-c. Why? Because their names are not written in "The Book of Life." v8, says the beast shall ascend out of the bottomless pit. This is not a reference to Abaddon in Rev. 9:11, but to the a-c who ascends out of the bottomless pit of people on the earth. All of v8 refers to the a-c.

"The seven heads are seven mountains, on which the woman sitteth" (Rev. 17:9). Many Bible scholars have taught that this verse describes Rome and the Roman Catholic church. Because Rome sits on seven hills or mountains. But this is not correct. Remember, sometimes when the Bible uses the term mountains it is referring to nations. This is what is being describe here: nations and not the city of Rome. "But in the last days it shall come to pass, that the mountain of the house of the Lord Shall be established in the top of the mountains, and it shall be exalted above the hills; and people shall flow unto it" (Micah 4:1). The Lord's Kingdom (mountain) will overshadow all earthly nations (hills and mountains). None of the mountains under the city of Rome has fell or not yet become mountains. The seven heads and seven mountains refer to seven nations. Also see Jer. 51:25.

Rev. 17:10, "And there are seven kings; five are fallen, and one is and the other is not yet come . . ." Those, "five are fallen, and one is," are; Egypt, Assyria, Babylon, Medes/Persia, and Greece. All five of these nations had and then lost control of the nation of Israel. Thus they "are fallen." And Rome "is." At the time John wrote Rev. Rome was in control of the nation of Israel. Now the "other is not yet come," could be any one of the following nations; Byzantine, Arabs, Mamluks, Ottoman, British, or others I am are not sure of. These nations controlled Israel after Rome. But I can't say which one The Father is referring to. Verse 11, is a reference to the a-c, because he comes out of a nation that was part of those seven. Notice it says "goeth into perdition." Nations cannot go into perdition or lake of fire, only people. Remember, 2 Thess. 2:3, calls the a-c "the son of perdition."

"And the ten horns which thou sawest are ten kings, which have received no kingdom as yet; but receive power as kings one hour with the beast" (Rev. 17:12).

We have discussed these ten kings (horns). We do not know who they are and how they come to power. The a-c and satan brings them into their circle of evil for a specific time.

"These have one mind, and shall give their power and strength unto the beast, These shall make war with the Lamb, and the Lamb shall overcome them: for he is Lord of lords, and King of kings: and they that are with him are called, and chosen, and faithful" (Rev. 17:13–14).

These two verses are parenthetical phases. They remind us the ten nations will be unified in support of the a-c for a time. It also tells us of their end, which is when they run to do battle with The Lord of lords and King of kings. We will discuss this later. If you are not saved The Father is calling you right now as you are reading this book; "For he saith, I have heard thee in a time accepted, and in the day of salvation have I succored thee: behold, now is the accepted time; behold, now is the day of salvation" (2 Cor. 6:2). If you are not save or born again from your sins, today is the day you must be saved. If you have been born again, then you have been chosen in Jesus Christ and you must be faithful.

MYSTERY BABYLON

"And he saith unto me, The waters which thou sawest, where the whore sitteth, are peoples, and multitudes, and nations and tongues. And the ten horns which thou sawest upon the beast, these shall hate the whore, and shall make her desolate and naked, and shall eat her flesh, and burn her with fire. For God hath put in their hearts to fulfill his will, and to agree, and give their kingdom unto the beast, until the words of God shall be fulfilled. And the woman which thou sawest is that great city, which reigneth over the Kings of the earth" (Rev. 17:15–18).

"Mystery Babylon" in this context is a double prophecy which refers to a system and a city. Yet it is more than a mere city but a system of evil with its tentacles encompassing the world. It also has a location or headquarters somewhere. Notice the ten horns or nations, hate the whore. They are evil so they can't just hate evil because they would hate themselves. The people of satan's kingdom can't get along with each other. Evil spirits put up with each other but they do not get along, just as evil people now put up with each other but do not get along most of the time. Look at WWII; Germany and Russia signed a non-aggression pact. Hitler knew he was going to attack Russia at the right time and he did, almost defeating Russia. Hitler fooled Stalin into trusting him. They tolerated each other, but really hated each other.

Somewhere, somehow those ten nations are going to attack something or somewhere they think represents "Mystery Babylon." This is another one of those double prophecies. It speaks of mystery Babylon and physical Jerusalem. I do know at a certain time the a-c will be in Jerusalem. The Father will put into the hearts of those nation to turn against the a-c and his system. For so decrees The Almighty Father.

And after these things I saw another angel come down from heaven, having great power; and the earth was lightened with his glory (Rev. 18:1).

Notice all the angels we have read about have been male and they do not have wings. There are no babies or female angels. I know this is contrary to the painting by the great masters and human folklore, but it is true. Why? There is no need for them. Luke 20:34–38;

lets us know marriage is an earthly necessity for pro-creation and will be done away with when this world system is over. The Father made all the angels He needed, and since they cannot die, pro-creation is not necessary. "But we see Jesus, who was made a little lower than the angels for the suffering of death" (Hebrews 2:9). And nowhere in the Bible do we find humans becoming angels.

This angel has great power and his brightness lights up the entire earth. This is not Jesus Christ, nowhere is Jesus our Savior referred to as an angel. Watchtower, this means Jesus Christ is not Michael the arch-angel.

"And he cried mightily with a strong voice, saying, Babylon the great is fallen, is fallen, and is become the habitation of devils, and the hold of every foul spirit, and a cage of every unclean and hateful bird. For all nations have drunk of the wine of the wrath of her fornication, and the kings of the earth have committed fornication with her, and the merchants of the earth are waxed rich through the abundance of her delicacies. And I heard another voice from heaven, saying, come out of her, my people, that ye be not partakers of her sins, and that ye receive not of her plagues. For her sins have reached unto heaven, and God hath remembered her iniquities. Reward her even as she rewarded you, and double unto her double according to her works: in the cup which she hath filled fill to her double. How much she hath glorified herself, and lived deliciously, so much torment and sorrow give her: for she saith in her heart, I sit as a queen and am no widow, and shall see not sorrow (Rev. 18:2-7).

This is also a double prophecy; it concerns now as well as a time in the coming future. The saints of The Most High must depart from evil in all its glory and have no part in it. This book is a radical call for saints not to be part of the mystery of iniquity (sin). Billions of dollars have been made dabbling in sin. Many saints have gotten great wealth from sin and its related industries. We have saints who have large amounts of money invested by investment bankers into products with controlling interest in liquor, tobacco, pornography, and other evils.

The Father pulls no punches in describing evil; "is become the habitation of devils, and the hold of every foul spirit, and a cage of every unclean and hateful bird." I used to fish at the base of a dam near my house. The fishing there is pretty good. But it has one major drawback, Buzzards; they roost in the metal towers which support the electrical wires which carry electricity from the power station. To get to the dam, you must walk under the towers and through several inches of fecal matter from hundreds of buzzards. And because some of the buzzards are always roosting in the towers, you may end up having some of their fecal matter fall on you. Plus, the buzzards like to sit on cars park in the parking lot and drop their fecal matter, which smells terrible. Every time I read the above verse, I think of this spot.

Our Father is telling us to come out of this system now, while we have the chance. Sin has glorified itself and enriched those who drink of her cup. Those who part-take in and use mystery Babylon will be participants of her judgments. In Rev. 18:6, the angel asked The Father, to reward mystery Babylon just as mystery Babylon has rewarded Him. And to give her double, what she has given Him. The word double is used three times. Even the angels are ready to be rid of this evil. Many saints use all kinds of excuses to get as close to this world system as possible. But the closer we get, the greater the danger of assimilation.

We are too earth conscience, and not heavenly conscience. We have allowed the physical to control what we should desire in the spiritual. Most Christians would rather live here, than die and go to heaven (Philippians 1:21–26). They are like Lot's wife; she became what her life living should have been, salt.

"Ye adulterers and adulteresses, know ye not that the friendship of the world is enmity with God? Whosoever therefore will be a friend of the world is the enemy of God" (James 4:4). The Father includes both males and female in this. He is stressing a point. Be careful how you deal with the world. Many wealthy and intelligent people will not read this book, because they may think it is too simplistic and common. Their love for money will over ride all simple truths of The Father's word.

We have saints who love Hollywood and are doing their best to reform it, but they are only fooling themselves. They've gotten so close to Hollywood they do not see they have already been assimilated and conformed to Hollywood's evil standards. There was a Indonesian female dancer who would dance while holding defanged poisonous snakes. One day she danced while holding a King Cobra and she was unaware it had not been defanged until it bit her on the leg and she died. We have saints dancing with a Hollywood that has not been defanged and they have been bitten and are spiritually dead.

Those of you who are in the world of Hollywood, you are fooling yourselves as well as many others in the church. They may make a few films with some good values, because money is money. They want the saint's money just as bad as they want the world's money. Hollywood does not want to, nor will it be reformed to The Father's standard.

"Be ye not unequally yoked together with unbelievers: for what fellowship hath righteousness with unrighteousness? And what communion hath light with darkness? And what concord (agreement) hath Christ with Be-li-al? or what part hath he that believeth with an infidel (unsaved)? And what agreement hath the temple of God with idols? For ye are the temple of the living God; as God hath said, I will dwell in them, and walk in them; and I will be their God, and they shall be my people. Wherefore come out from among them, and be ye separate, saith the Lord, and touch not the unclean thing: and I will receive you" (2 Cor. 6:14–17).

We must ensure that any relationship we must enter into with non-believers, the saints must have as much control of that relationship as possible. If this is not possible we must be careful not to allow them to influence us to be partakers of their evil. And no saint should ever marry a non-believer.

Yes, we work for non-believers, but we do not have to lie because they lie or cheat because they cheat. "If one bear holy flesh in the skirt of his garment, and with his skirt do touch bread, or pottage, or wine, or oil or any meat, shall it be holy? And the priests answered and said, No. Then said Haggai, If one that is unclean by a dead body touch any of these, shall it be unclean? And the priests answered and said, it shall be unclean" (Haggai 2:12-13).

What does this mean? If someone who is holy (saved) touch or yoke up with someone unholy (unsaved), the holy person cannot make the unholy person clean before The Lord. But the holy person can become defiled or influence by being unequally yoked with an unclean (not saved) person. We are told; "Ye cannot drink the cup of the Lord, and the cup of devils: ye cannot be partakers of the Lord's table, and of the table of devils" (1Cor. 10:21). Jesus said; "No man can serve two masters: for either he will hate the one, and love the other; or else he will hold to the one, and despise the other, Ye cannot serve God and mammon (world)" (Matt. 6:24). We cannot serve two masters and there is no such thing as sitting on the fence between the two. Our Father has remembered her sins and all those who partake of those sins openly or secretly, He will reward.

Mystery Babylon, or may I say mystery of Iniquity (sin) thinks it has no payday. She has glorified herself and lived as she wants with people serving her every desire. She is calling out to all "come play with me" rich and poor. I stated earlier my wife and I was asked to go and speak at a correctional Officers convention in Los Vegas. While there my wife and I passed a six-foot tall TV screen with a woman wearing a tight and revealing evening grown and she was beckoning to all that passed the screen "come play with me." The mystery of iniquity is calling out to all "come play with me." But, The Father will not play nor has He forgotten this evil system. Payday is coming.

"Therefore shall her plagues come in one day, death, and mourning, and famine; and she shall be utterly burned with fire: for strong is the Lord God who judgeth her. And the kings of the earth, who have committed fornication and lived deliciously with her, shall bewail her, and lament for her, when they shall see the smoke of her burning. Standing afar off for the fear of her torment, saying, Alas, alas, that great city Babylon, that mighty city! for in one hour is thy judgment come. And the merchants of the earth shall weep and mourn over her; for no man buyeth their merchandise any more: The merchandise of gold, and silver, and precious stones, and of pearls, and fine linen, and purple, and silk, and scarlet, and all thyine wood, and all manner vessels of ivory, and all manner vessels of most precious wood, and of brass, and iron, and marble, And cinnamon, and odors, and ointments, and frankincense, and wine, and oil, and fine flour, and wheat, and beasts, and sheep, and horse, and chariots, and slaves, and souls of men. And the fruits that thy soul lusted after are departed from thee, and all things which were dainty and goodly are departed from thee, and thou shalt find them no more at all" (Rev. 18:8–14).

Our Father is giving us a concise description of the collapse and destruction of mystery Babylon. It says; "strong is the lord God who judgeth her." The Almighty has had enough of this world's evil system. We have a conundrum here: what exactly is this mystery Babylon? It seems to be a city, yet more than a mere city, but a great system of evil, and world-wide economic activity. There will be a headquarters somewhere for some part of this evil system. It may be wherever the a-c has his headquarters.

Notice the list in Rev. 18:12–14, it includes everything material which mankind holds precious, idolize, and has made money from: houses, cars, clothes, sex, precious metals and stones, ivory, rare woods, perfumes, spices, jewelry, liquor, drugs, food, animals, slavery, even those who process or control other's soul. All of this will be taken away from man. Money is the driver of everything mankind holds dear. This seems to be an indictment against the world's economic system and all its injustices.

Did you know there is still slavery going on in this world right now? In many Muslim countries both slavery and governmental enforced prostitution is an active institution. The leaders of the USA know this is going on. But they do not have the will or guts to try and stop it. There are sex slaves (women, young girls, and young boys) all over the world but nothing can be done; or should I say the will to do something is not there.

Maria Mercedes Lara/People Aug. 08, 2017 wrote the following; "The 20-year-old British model who was allegedly kidnapped to be sold in an online auction on the dark web. Chloe Ayling, A British glamour model who lives in London, revealed to British newspaper The Sun that she was the woman who was kidnapped during a fake modeling job in Millan and held captive in a small house where a group planned to sell her off online to the highest bidder."

Many foreign national leaders, which our government, call allies, are wicked and cruel despots over their people. We send billions to these crooks, who pocket the money, while their countrymen get little if any benefits from this largesse. And the USA gets nothing in return. You would think our leaders would see this, but there seems to be some disconnect once they get in power, which I think is caused by spiritual wickedness in high places. The Most High is calling unto us "come out of her, my people be not a partaker of her sins, because if you are a partaker of her sins you will be a partaker of her judgments."

"The merchants of these things, which were made rich by her shall stand afar off for the fear of her torment, weeping and wailing, And saying Alas, alas, that great city that was clothed in fine linen, and purple and scarlet, and decked with gold, and precious stones, and pearls! For in one hour so great riches is come to nought. And every shipmaster, and all the company in ships, and sailors and as many as trade by sea, stood afar off, And cried when they saw the smoke of her burning, saying, What city is like unto this great city! And they cast dust on their heads, and cried, weeping and wailing, saying Alas, alas, that great city, wherein were made rich all that had ships in the sea by reason of her costliness! For in one hour is she made desolate" (Rev. 18:15–19).

The wealthy who made their money sleeping with the whore will be devastated when she is destroyed. The more I read this, the more I think of America. Many people from all over the world have made and are making billions or should I say trillions from this land of the free. As I write this, much of the world is going through an economical slow down. But here in America, money is still being made every day. I am not saying this is America, but America is part of the system. I am not adding anything to the scripture. Who or whatever it is will be made desolate. Notice Rev. 18:16, the words "great city," but this is more than a city. No city is clothed in "fine linen, and purple and scarlet, and decked with gold, and precious stones, and pearls!" But money can get all those things mentioned.

"But they that will be rich fall into temptation and a snare, and into many foolish and hurtful lusts, which drown men in destruction and perdition. For the love of money is the root of all evil: which while some coveted after, they have erred from the faith, and pierced themselves through with many sorrows" (1 Timothy 6:9-10). Money is not the root of all evil, but the uncontrolled lust for money will cause you to do many wicked things and erred from the faith. Search your heart and see what is your relationship to your money? Do you rule it or does money rule you?

"Rejoice over her, thou heaven, and ye holy apostles and prophets; for God hath avenged you on her. And a mighty angel took up a stone like a great millstone, and cast it into the sea, saying, Thus with violence shall that great city Babylon be thrown down, and shall be found no more at all. And the voice of harpers, and musicians, and of pipers, and trumpeters, shall be heard no more at all in thee; and no craftsman, of whatsoever craft he be, shall be found any more in thee; and the sound of a millstone shall be heard no more at all in thee; And the light of a candle shall shine no more at all in thee; and the voice of the bridegroom and of the bride shall be heard no more at all in thee: for thy merchants were the great men of the earth; for by thy sorceries were all nations deceived. And in her was found the blood of prophets, and of saints, and of all that were slain upon the earth" (Rev. 18:20–24).

Read the following: "O Jerusalem, Jerusalem, which killest the prophets, and stonest them that are sent unto thee; how often would I have gathered thy children together, as a hen doth gather her brood under her wings, and ye would not" (Luke 13:34)! Now the city of Jerusalem did not kill anyone. The people of the city did the killing. The evil mindset of the people was the inciter for them to kill the prophets. This goes for mystery Babylon. A brick and mortar city cannot kill "all that were slain upon the earth." But an evil mindset would incite the occupants of the city or system to kill saints. Mystery Babylon is both a composite of a world-wide evil system and a city where the a-c will be headquartered. It may even be a spiritual city we cannot see, but we feel the effects.

The end of "Mystery Babylon" is approaching. It will be sudden and without mercy. Whether it is a city, country, financial system, evil world system, or religious system, our Father is going to bring it into righteous remembrance, with Holy indignation; "And a mighty angel took up a stone like a great millstone, and cast it into the sea" (Rev. 18:21). Just as a large rock when thrown into water will cause a violent upheaval. This too will be a violent event upon the world. Notice verse 24, "And in her was found the blood of prophets, and of saints, and of all that were slain upon the earth." This is the totality of evil upon the earth. Because no city has all "the blood of prophets, saints, and all that were slain upon the earth." "Wherefore I poured my fury upon them for the blood that they had shed upon the land, and for their idols wherewith they had polluted it" (Ezekiel 36:18). All the great partying, fornication, adultery, great works, witchcraft and killing of the saints will come to an end. "Come out of her, my people that ye be not partakers of her sins, and that ye receive not of her plagues."

THE RETURN OF JESUS, THE KINGDOM OF JESUS AND THE FINAL TEST

THE RETURN OF JESUS

"And after these things I heard a great voice of much people in heaven, saying, Alleluia; Salvation, and glory, and honor and power, unto the Lord our God: For true and righteous are his judgments; for he hath judged the great whore, which did corrupt the earth with her fornication, and hath avenged the blood of his servants at her hand. And again they said, Alleluia. And her smoke rose up for ever and ever. And the four and twenty elders and the four beasts fell down and worshiped God that sat on the throne, saying, A-men; Alleluia. And a voice came out of the throne, saying, praise our God, all ye his servants, and ye that fear him, both small and great" (Rev. 19:1–5).

A praise service is now going on. The Most High God has now judged mystery Babylon, found her guilty and condemned her. This confirms that mystery Babylon is a system of evil and we have just seen its total collapse. Notice verse 3: "And her smoke rose up for ever and ever." This is not a physical brick and mortar city being punished, but people who had the same evil mindset cast into in the lake of fire.

"And I fell at his feet to worship him, And he said unto me, See thou do it not: I am they fellow servant, and of thy brethren that have the testimony of Jesus: worship God: for the testimony of Jesus is the spirit of prophecy" (Rev. 19:10).

John fell at the feet of the angel to worship him, but the angel refused worship and told John to worship The Most High only. And the angel said "for the testimony of Jesus is the spirit of prophecy." Jesus was prophesied to come to this earth. There are well over two hundred prophecies concerning Jesus and His time on the earth and His soon return. So let no one tell you not to study prophecy. For prophecy speaks of Jesus Christ. And for those who have been fooled by evil spirits to worship angels, true angels refuse worship.

We must look at a parenthetical phase concerning the battle of Armageddon. This is the next to last great battle satan will have before he is cast into the lake of fire.

"And the sixth angel poured out his vial upon the great river Eu-phra-tes; and the water thereof was dried up, that the way of the kings of the east might be prepared. And I saw three unclean spirits like frogs come out of the mouth of the dragon, and out of the mouth of the beast, and out of the mouth of the false prophet. For they are the spirits of devils, working miracles, which go forth unto the kings of the earth and of the whole world, to gather them to the battle of that great day of God Almighty. Behold, I come as a thief. Blessed is he that watcheth, and keepeth his garments, lest he walk naked, and they see his shame. And he gathered them together into a place called in the Hebrew tongue Arma-ged-don. And the seventh angel poured out his vial into the air; and there came a great voice out of the temple of heaven, from the throne, saying, It is done" (Rev. 16:12–17).

The angel dried up the river Euphrates to enable all or some of those ten nations who are about to rebel against the a-c, to come on down. This may be Daniel 7:8: "Three of the first horns plucked up by the roots." The a-c may have attacked and conquered three of this ten nation confederacies. And the other seven may lead a rebellion against him. Whoever they are, these nations are moving toward Jerusalem to take care of the a-c and to finally put a stop (they think) to that pesky Jewish nation. In verse 14, we see the demonic trio calling all the nations to come and fight by using wicked spiritual frog-like creatures to lure them to battle. Remember evil forces do not get along with each other for very long. Our Father is also calling them to His wine press.

Read the following: "And another angel came out of the temple which is in heaven, he also having a sharp sickle. Another angel came out from the altar, which had power over fire; and cried with a loud cry to him that had the sharp sickle, saying, Thrust in the sharp sickle, and gather the cluster of the vine of the earth; for her grapes are fully ripe. And the angel thrust in his sickle into the earth, and gathered the vine of the earth, and cast it into the great wine press of the wrath of God. And the winepress was trodden without the city, and blood came out of the winepress, even unto the horse bridles, by the space of a thousand and six hundred furlongs" (Rev. 14:17–20). By thrusting in his sickle, the angel is spiritually calling the nations to this great battle. It is their destiny. This is the second reaping and it will be bloody. Notice the angle said in verse 18; "fully ripe." The Most High, has allowed the sins of the world to accumulate interest, and it is now time to pay dividends. The Rock is about to hit the statue and bring it down.

"Therefore wait ye upon me, saith the Lord, until the day that I rise up to the prey: for my determination is to gather the nations, that I may assemble the kingdoms, to pour upon them mine indignation, even all my fierce anger: for all the earth shall be devoured with the fire of my jealousy" (Zephaniah 3:8). The Most High God is determine to call the armies of these nations to their destruction.

The book of Joel also gives us insight into this great invitation. "I will also gather all nations, and will bring them down into the valley of Jehosh-a-phat, and will plead with them there for my people and for my heritage Israel, whom they have scattered among the nations, and parted my land. Proclaim ye this among the Gentiles; Prepare war, wake up the mighty men, let all the men of war draw near; let them come up: Beat your plowshares into swords and your pruning hooks into spears; let the weak say, I am strong. Assemble yourselves, and come, all ye heathen, and gather yourselves together round about: thither cause thy mighty ones to come down, O Lord. Let the heathen be wakened, and come up to the valley of Je-hosh-a-phat: for there will I sit to judge all the heathen round about. Put ye in the sickle, for the harvest is ripe: come, get you down: for the press is full, the vats overflow; for their wickedness is great. Multitudes, multitudes in the valley of decision: for the day of the Lord is near in the valley of decision" (Joel 3:2, 9-14).

Rev. and Joel use the same terminology: sickle, press, and harvest is ripe. This displays the continuity of The Word of God. These nations must come to the valley of Megiddo, Israel. It is also called "the valley of decision and valley of Jehoshaphat.

The Father is calling for the best fighting men with their latest weaponry, and bring their best battlefield tactics. There will be a great destruction of people and equipment as The Highest puts His end plan in motion. When Joel and others saw into the future they did not know what a tank, rifle, or airplane was. They put down what they knew which is horses, spears, and swords.

The nation of Israel is suffering because of their unbelief and the actions of the demonic trio: this is called Jacob's trouble. Other nations are full of the a-c and they think it is time to get rid of him. But they do not know they have an uninvited guest; who is He? Let me introduce Him; The Alpha and Omega, The Apostle of our profession, The Author and Finisher of our faith, The Bishop of souls, The Bread of life, The Branch, Captain of The Lord's Host, Chief Corner Stone, Chief Shepherd, Dayspring, Deliver, The I Am, The Door, The Hope of Israel, The Vine, Eternal, Faithful, Glorious, Great High Priest, Head of the body, Holy, Hope of Glory, Immanuel, Image of God, Horn of Salvation, The Just One, Judge, The Way, King Eternal, King of kings, Lamb of God, Light of the World. The Lord of lords, Messiah, Name above all names, Nazarene, Only Begotten Son, Savior, Redeemer, Omi-potent, Omniscience, Omnipresent, The Rock, The Rod, The Stem of Jesse and The Word of God.

He is also called; Wonderful, Counselor, The Mighty God, The Everlasting Father, and The Prince of Peace. He which is, which was, and which is to come. He who lived, was dead, and is now alive for evermore, The Amen. The Faithful Witness, The first Begotten of the dead. He who comes with eyes like a flame of fire. Out of His

THE SPIRIT OF THE ANTI-CHRIST

mouth goes a sharp two edge sword. His countenance shines as the sun. He has the seven Spirits of God.

He has the keys of hell and death; He is The Lion of the tribe of Judah. The Root of David. The Bright and Morning Star. He is The Lamb most-worthy. He is The Redeemer of men souls. He is The Mystery of The Father. He is The Man Child taken to heaven. He has shed His blood so we might overcome the devil. He treads the winepress of The Almighty; He is The Great Earth Quaker. He rides a great white horse; He is called Faithful and True. He is The King of saints, The Light of the New Jerusalem. He is The Resurrection and The Life. The First and Last. The Great I Am. Hallelujah!

No phony trials for Him this time, because He is The Judge on the great white throne. He is not coming as a lowly suffering servant, no Mary's baby, no manger, no Joseph's boy, no sweet little Jesus boy, no walking. No Man of sorrows, nor will He be acquainted with their grief. He is not the meek and mild Shepherd. No riding a donkey, there will be no attempt to stone Him or entangle Him in His words. No one will ask; are you The Messiah or That Prophet? No asking for a sign. No conspiracies, no plots or traps. The devil will not even think about tempting Him. No asking Him to leave your town, no attempt to stone Him, and you will not throw Him out of your town, because the whole earth will be full of His glory.

He will have a residence this time called the New Jerusalem. Fifteen hundred miles all around, streets of gold, twelve gates each made of a single pearl and garnished with all manner of precious stones. All this protected by heavenly fire. This same Jesus who fed five thousand, this same Jesus who open the eyes of the blind, this same Jesus who brought the dead back to life, this same Jesus who healed the sick, this same Jesus who cleanse those with leprosy, calmed the winds and the waters, is back.

He will not fret about some council to destroy Him. No one will ask by what or whose authority do you do these things? No betrayers, no lying witnesses, and there will be no sweat like great drops of blood. No one will ask are you a king? Nor will they say, "I could let you go free." No hitting or being attacked, no scourging with a flag rum, no wounding for the sins of others. No soldier will mock or make fun of Him. No one will take His garments. No carrying of sins this time. He will not be a lamb, to be slaughtered. He will not suffer this time. No stripes, no spitting in His face or slapping Him around. No cross to bear, no vinegar to drink. No thieves for pals, no one will revile Him about saving Himself. No nails, no spear in the side. No borrowed nothing, no stone to roll away. And intercession will cease.

Isaiah gives a command you need to heed: "The voice of him that crieth in the wilderness, Prepare ye the way of the Lord, make straight in the desert a highway for our God. Every valley shall be exalted, and every mountain and hill shall be made low: and the crooked shall be made straight, the rough places shall be made plain: And the glory of the Lord shall be revealed, and all flesh shall see it together: for the mouth of the Lord hath spoken it" (Isaiah 40:3–5). And if that is not enough; "Lift up your heads, o ye gates; and be ye lifted up, ye everlasting doors; and the King of glory shall come in. Who is this King of glory? The Lord strong and mighty, the Lord mighty in battle. Lift up your heads, O ye gates; even lift them up, ye everlasting doors; and the King of glory shall come in. Who is this King of glory? The Lord of host, he is the King of glory" (Psalm 24:7-10). HALLELUJAH!

The King of Glory Christ Jesus is now returning. The Mystery of The Father meets Mystery Babylon, mystery of iniquity, the a-c, and satan and only He will remain standing. "And the angel which I saw stand upon the sea and upon the earth lifted up his hand to heaven, And sware by him that liveth for ever and ever, who created heaven, and the things that therein are, and the earth, and the things which are therein, that there should be time no longer: But in the days of the voice of the seventh angel, when he shall begin to sound, the mystery of God should be finished, as he hath declared to his servants the prophets" (Rev. 10:5–7).

Those nations were coming to attack the a-c and Israel. But in the plain of Megiddo, The King of kings, The Mystery of God crashes the party and starts His song. They will look up and stop fighting each other for someone new is bursting through the clouds. Let me share what Jude says; "And E-noch also, the seventh from

Adam, prophesied of these, saying, Behold, the Lord cometh with ten thousands of his saints, To execute judgment upon all and to convince all that are ungodly among them of all their ungodly deeds which thy have ungodly committed, and of all their hard speeches which ungodly sinners have spoken against him" (Jude 14-15).

Jesus Christ said this concerning His coming: "Immediately after the tribulation of those days shall the sun be darkened, and the moon shall not give her light, and the stars shall fall from heaven, and the powers of the heavens shall be shaken: And then shall appear the sign of the Son of man in heaven: and then shall all the tribes of the earth mourn, and they shall see the Son of man coming in the clouds of heaven with power and great glory. And he shall send his angels with a great sound of a trumpet, and they shall gather together his elect from the four winds, from one end of heaven to the other" (Matt. 24:29-31). Let's read what was revealed to John by Jesus;

"And I saw heaven opened, and behold a white horse; and he that sat upon him was called Faithful and True, and in righteousness he doth judge and make war. His eyes were as a flame of fire, and on his head were many crowns; and he had a name written, that no man knew, but he himself. And he was clothed with a vesture dipped in blood: and his name is called The Word of God. And the armies which were in heaven followed him upon white horses, clothed in fine linen, white and clean. And out of his mouth goeth a sharp sword, that with it he should smite the nations: and he shall rule them with a rod of iron: and he treadeth the wine press of the fierceness and wrath of Almighty God. And he hath on his vesture and on his thigh a name written, KING OF KINGS AND LORD OF LORDS. And I saw an angel standing in the sun; and he cried with a loud voice, saying to all the fowls that fly in the midst of heaven, Come and gather yourselves together unto the supper of the great God; That ye may eat the flesh of kings, and the flesh of captains, and the flesh of mighty men, and the flesh of horses, and of them that sit on them, and the flesh of all, both free and bond, both small and great. And I saw the beast, and the kings of the earth, and their armies, gathered together to make war against him that sat on the horse, and against his army, And the beast was taken, and with him the false prophet that wrought miracles before him, with which he deceived them that had received the mark of the beast, and them that worshiped his image. These both were cast alive into a lake of fire burning with brimstone" (Rev. 19:11–20).

The King of kings and Lord of lords, The Rock has returned to dismantle and smash all earthly kingdoms, then establish His Righteous Kingdom. Notice He is wearing many crowns. All those imitation crowns the beast, the dragon, and those ten nations wore, are gone. The Righteous wearer is now wearing the real crowns. Jesus says of this time: "For these be the days of vengeance, that all thing which are written may be fulfilled" (Luke 21:22).

But first He must take care of a little house cleaning. The first task is to dispose of the a-c and his false prophet. Both are cast alive into the lake of fire burning with brimstone they bypass hell and are tossed straight into the lake of fire alive. The a-c may challenge Jesus; "He shall also stand up against the Prince of princes; but he shall be broken without hand" (Daniel 8:25). They do not have a trial, nor are they given a chance to explain themselves by saying "I was born this way, I couldn't help it." They are not killed but placed body, and soul into the lake of fire.

I must mention something here of which I am not sure of the meaning. Verse 20, says the a-c and the false prophet are cast alive into the lake of fire. Daniel wrote; "I beheld then because of the voice of the great words which the horn spake: I beheld even till the beast was slain, and his body destroyed, and given to the burning flame" (Daniel 7:11). Daniel says, "the beast is destroyed and given to the flame." Whereas Rev. says, "he is cast alive into a lake of fire." Is there a contradiction between the two verses? No! We do not understand what is meant. Because Rev. 20:10 says they will be tormented forever and ever. I can't explain this nor will I try any further. I will ask Jesus when I get to heaven.

"And the remnant were slain with the sword of him that sat upon the horse, which sword proceeded out of his mouth: and all the fowls were filled with their flesh" (Rev. 19:21).

Is there a literal sword coming out of Jesus' mouth? Let's see what Isaiah gives us: "But with righteousness shall he judge the poor, and reprove with equity for the meek of the earth: and he shall smite the earth with the rod of his mouth, and with the breath of his lips shall he slay the wicked" (Isaiah 11:4). Remember, "And then shall that Wicked be revealed, whom the Lord shall consume with the spirit of his mouth . . ." (2 Thess. 2:8). Christ Jesus who is God speaks the word and it is done.

In John 18:1–6, Jesus Christ said to those who came to arrest Him "I am He." the whole band went backward and fell to the ground. Jesus said, "It is the spirit that quickeneth; the flesh profiteth nothing: the words that I speak unto you, they are spirit, and they are life" (John 6:63). So no, there is no actual sword coming out of His mouth, but the force of His words will cut as a sword: "For the word of God is quick, and powerful, and sharper than any two edged sword, piercing even to the dividing asunder of soul and spirit, and of the joints and marrow, and is a discerner of the thoughts and intents of the heart" (Hebrews 4:12). There is dynamite in His every word: "And this shall be the plague wherewith the Lord will smite all the people that have fought against Jerusalem; Their flesh shall consume away while they stand upon their feet, and their eyes shall consume away in their holes, and their tongue shall consume away in their mouth" (Zechariah 14:12). The fowls are invited to eat what is left.

"The slain of the Lord shall be many" (Isaiah 66:16). All the armies of this satanic league, plus others are destroyed. "As concerning the rest of the beasts, they had their dominion taken away: yet their lives were prolonged for a season and time" (Daniel 7:12). Does this mean the leaders of those seven nations that were in league with the a-c are left alive? I am not sure so I shall leave it there.

We are not told what happened to those who took the mark of the beast but, "And the third angel followed them, saying with a loud voice, if any man worship the beast and his image, and receive his mark in the forehead, or his hand, The same shall drink of the wine of the wrath of God, which is poured out without mixture into the cup of his indignation; and he shall be tormented with fire and brimstone in the presence of the holy angels, and in the presence of the lamb: And the smoke of their torment ascendeth up for ever and ever: and they have no rest day nor night, who worship the beast and his image, and whosoever receiveth the mark of his name" (Rev. 14:9-11).

From reading this, all those who took the mark of the beast are consign to the lake of fire. When? We are not told, so I shall not speculate. However, I do know they would not enjoy living under the righteousness of Christ Jesus.

Back to the battle, The King of kings does all the fighting. The armies which accompany Him are just for show. He needs no back up, or emergency help. After finishing the battle, The King of kings comes back to the Mount of Olives. "And when he had spoken these things, while they beheld, he was taken up; and a cloud received him out of their sight. And while they looked steadfastly toward heaven as he went up, behold, two men stood by them in white apparel; Which also said, Ye men of Galilee, why stand ye gazing up into heaven? This same Jesus, which is taken up from you into heaven, shall so come in like manner as ye have seen him go into heaven. Then returned they unto Jerusalem from the mount called Olivet, which is from Jerusalem a Sabbath day's journey" (Acts 1:9-12). Jesus was taken up from the Mount of Olives into heaven and now He returns from heaven to the Mount of Olives.

"Behold, the day of the Lord cometh, and thy spoil shall be divided in the midst of thee. For I will gather all nations against Jerusalem to battle; and the city shall be taken, and the houses rifled, and the women ravished; and half of the city shall go forth into captivity, and the residue of the people shall not be cut off from the city. Then shall the Lord go forth, and fight against those nations, as when he fought in the day of battle. And his feet shall stand in the that day upon the mount of Olives, which is before Jerusalem on the east, and the mount of Olives shall cleave in the midst thereof toward the east and toward the west, and there shall be a very great valley; and half of the mountain shall remove toward the north, and half of it toward the south" (Zechariah. 14:1–4).

He will return with great power. His feet just touching the Mount of Olives will cause a major shift to the topography of the area.

"And I saw an angel come down from heaven, having the key of the bottomless pit and a great chain in his hand. And he laid hold on the dragon, that old serpent, which is the Devil, and Satan and bound him a thousand years, And cast him into the bottomless pit and shut him up, and set a seal upon him, that he should deceive the nations no more, till the thousand years should be fulfilled: and after that he must be loosed a little season" (Rev. 20:1–3).

An angel now has the enjoyable task of grabbing satan and binding him with a supernatural chain, placing a seal upon him and casting him into the bottomless pit for a thousand years. satan will be there with the rest of the evil angels who rebelled with him in heaven: "For if God spared not the angels that sinned, but cast them down to hell, and delivered them into chains of darkness, to be reserved unto judgment" (2 Peter 2:4).

satan becomes an inmate in the bottomless pit, and a seal is placed on him and he will not be able to deceive anyone. satan will not control anything in that pit, he will have no keys, no power, no kingdom, no subjects, and no rights, just darkness. This will be a most unbearable punishment for him. he had a few short years of worship, then nothing. No deceiving, killing, or destroying for a thousand years. At the end of the thousand years he will be loosed for a season to serve one last purpose which we will discuss later. We are not told what will happen to those others evil angels who were loose on the earth with satan. They may be locked up also, or sent on to the lake of fire.

The Kingdom of Christ Jesus

"And I saw thrones, and they sat upon them, and judgment was given unto them: and I saw the souls of them that were beheaded for the witness of Jesus, and for the word of God, and which had not worshiped the beast, neither his image, neither had received his mark upon their foreheads, or in their hands; and they lived and reigned with Christ a thousand years" (Rev. 20:4).

THE RETURN OF JESUS CHRIST

The righteous reign of our Savior is now starting upon the earth. It is a reign completely contrary to mankind's rule. Mankind governs by; favoritism, selfishness, lust of money, prejudice, lies, pride, and hatred. Christ Jesus rules in righteousness. He has no left or right leaning democratic or republican ideology, no hidden scandals or secrets, only righteousness. Who are some of the subjects of Christ Jesus Kingdom? Remember, there are natural people who did not take the mark of the a-c. And some were able to live through all the judgments of The Most High, the reign of the a-c, and the battle of Armageddon. Only the armies at the battle of Armageddon were destroyed. There are many natural people still around and they will have children during the thousand years of Christ reign.

Those raptured and tribulation saints returning with Christ will rule over parts of the earth. "And he that overcometh, and keepeth my works unto the end, to him will I give power over the nations: And he shall rule them with a rod of iron; as the vessels of a potter shall they be broken to shivers: even as I received of my Father" (Rev. 2:26–27). Also; "But the saints of the most High shall take the kingdom, and possess the kingdom forever, even for ever and ever. I beheld, and the same horn made war with the saints, and prevailed against them; Until the Ancient of days came, and judgment was given to the saints of the most High; and the time came that the saints possessed the kingdom. And the kingdom and dominion, and the greatness of the kingdom under the whole heaven, shall be given to the people of the saints of the most High, whose kingdom is an everlasting kingdom, and all dominions shall serve and obey him" (Daniel 7:18, 21-22, 27). For those "kingdom now" folks, this is where the saints of The Most High shall be given the kingdom. We will not take it and give it to Christ Jesus, He will take it and give it to us.

Since satan is locked up and can't deceived un-saved mankind to sin, why the rod of iron? "For out of the heart proceed evil thoughts, murders, adulteries, fornications, thefts, false witness, blasphemies: These are the things which defile a man" (Matt. 15:19–20). It is in the mind of unsaved mankind to do evil, it is their sinful nature. Remember, it is one area where the mystery of iniquity resides

(Romans 5:12–19). Mankind will not need satan to lead them into sin, it's in the unsaved mind. If a non-saved person kills, there will be no need for a trial because the rulers will know what happened, who did it, and why. Those who are bent on doing evil will have no place to hide, no high-price lawyers to confuse the jury, and no friendly judge to give them a second chance. They will not be able to say "the devil made me do it." This will cause many to stay away from evil, once they realize there is no hiding place for their sinful deeds.

There will be no need for 911, ambulances, EMS, doctors, hospitals, police, firemen, judges, supreme court, IRS, human government, gun stores, armies, navies, air forces, jails, lawyers, courthouses, bail bond men, or weapons of any kind. Some evil group maybe hiding behind closed doors and concocting some evil scheme, then a saint walks through the wall and bust them.

There is one other person ruling. "And David my servant shall be king over them: and they all shall have one shepherd: they shall also walk in judgments, and observe my statures, and do them" (Ezekiel 37:24). King David shall also rule. I do not know how this will be divided among the saints, but I do know it will be right because Jesus will do it.

How will all these people from all over the world communicate? "For then will I turn to the people a pure language, that they may all call upon the name of the Lord, to serve him with one consent" (Zephaniah 3:9). I believe Hebrew will be the worldwide language. I think this was the language everyone spoke before the tower of Babel. Now I have no scriptural reference for this, just my sanctified mind. This may have been the first language given by The Most High God.

The animals will now get along because the curse has been lifted. "And there shall come forth a rod out of the stem of Jesse, and a Branch shall grow out of his roots: And the spirit of the Lord shall rest upon him, the spirit of wisdom and understanding, the spirit of counsel and might, the spirit of knowledge and of the fear of the Lord; And shall make him of quick understanding in the fear of the Lord: and he shall not judge after the sight of his eyes, neither reprove after the hearing of his ears: But with righteousness shall he judge the poor, and reprove with equity for the meek of the earth:

and he shall smite the earth with the rod of his mouth, and the breath of his lips shall be slay the wicked. And righteousness shall be the girdle of his loins, and faithfulness the girdle of his reins. The wolf also shall dwell with the lamb, and the leopard shall lie down with the kid; and the calf and the young lion and the fatling together; and a little child shall lead them. And the cow and the bear shall feed; their young ones shall lie down together: and the lion shall eat straw like the ox. And the sucking child shall play on the hole of the asp, and the weaned child shall put his hand on the cockatrice den. They shall not hurt nor destroy in all my holy mountain: for the earth shall be full of the knowledge of the Lord as the waters cover the sea" (Isaiah 11:1–9). "And there shall be no more curse: but the throne of God and of the Lamb shall be in it; and his servants shall serve him" (Rev. 22:3).

With Adam's willful sin the earth lost "the full knowledge of the Lord." This Knowledge shall once again and forever more fill the earth. The little child will be able to play with the lion, the black mamba, even the spitting cobra. The little fat calf, will lay down with the lion. Real peace will be experience for the first time since the fall of Adam.

One other thing we must look at concerning this one thousand-year reign. We know everyone will not be willing subjects. What happens to those who refuse to come and worship?

"And it shall come to pass, that every one that is left of all the nations which came against Jerusalem shall even go up from year to year to worship the King, the Lord of hosts, and to keep the feast of tabernacles. And it shall be that whoso will not come up of all the families of the earth unto Jerusalem to worship the King, the Lord of host, even upon them shall be no rain. And if the family of Egypt go not up, and come not, that have no rain; there shall be the plague, wherewith the Lord will smite the heathen that come not up to the feast of tabernacles. This shall be the punishment of Egypt, and the punishment of all nations that come not up to keep the feast of tabernacles" (Zechariah 14:16–19).

All nations or representatives of each nation will be required to come to Jerusalem to worship and if they refuse they will be punished by drought or plague. Rebellion will not be tolerated. They will have no choice because this is the only power around. This tells me most non-saved, natural people will not be happy living in the kingdom of Christ. Even under His righteous rule. They see the animals are getting along, vipers are not biting, lambs napping alongside of lions and not inside of them. But seeing all this righteousness, the unsaved, will still act with their fleshly nature. "For out of the heart proceed evil thoughts, murders, adulteries, fornication, theft, false witness, blasphemies" (Matt. 15:19).

The Final Test

As I stated before, all throughout history, mankind has been tested to see who they will obey: The Father, satan or themselves. The angels and satan had a test. satan failed, along with a third of the angels. Adam had a test, he failed. All mankind has been given a test: Abraham, Moses, King David, Peter, Stephen. "For thou, O God, hast proved us: thou hast tried us, as silver is tried" (Psalm 66:10). Even Jesus had a test. "For in that he hath suffered being tempted, he is able to succor them that are tempted" (Hebrews 2:18). The word tempted means "to be tested." Salvation is a test. "And as it is appointed unto men once to die, but after this the judgment" (Hebrews 9:27). There is no reincarnation, you only get one shot at this test. Only The Most High can give a perfect test, because He is the perfect answer.

"The heart is deceitful above all things, and desperately wicked: who can know it? I the Lord search the heart, I try the reins, even to give every man according to his ways, and according to the fruit of his doings" (Jeremiah 17:9-10). This tells us The Father tries or tests the hearts of all mankind. We are now going to look at man's final test. satan was the leader of the first test and he will lead this last test. Only He who has all the correct answers can give a pass or fail score.

For one thousand years those unsaved people have been suffering from too much; too much goodness, too much righteousness, too much Jesus, too much holiness, too much Justice. Too much of going up to Jerusalem to honor The Most High. Too much of too much. The devil will give them a glimmer of hope.

"And when the thousand years are expired, Satan shall be loosed out of his prison, And shall go out to deceive the nations which are in the four quarters of the earth, Gog, and Ma-gog, togather them together to battle: the number of whom is as the sand of the sea, And they went up on the breadth of the earth, and compassed the camp of the saints about, and the beloved city: and fire came down from God out of heaven, and devoured them. And the devil that deceived them was cast into the lake of fire and brimstone, where the beast and the false prophet are, and shall be tormented day and night forever and ever" (Rev. 20:7–10).

This is it, the final test; satan is parole from his prison. The chain and seal are removed. The enemy of our soul is paroled, not for good behavior. But to give all unsaved people hope for all this too muchness. satan tells all natural un-saved people that there is a new leader in town. And if they follow him he will lead them to victory. We are not told how long satan will have to deceive un-saved mankind. Due to our new nature, those of us who are saved cannot be fooled this time by the tempter, all rebellion has been removed from us. "He that hath an ear, let him hear what the Spirit saith unto the churches; He that overcometh shall not be hurt of the second death" (Rev. 2:11).

satan is the ultimate egotist: every coup d'état he tried has failed, he will not stop. It is not in satan's nature to give up, he can't stop, he knows his fate, so he is grasping for straws. This is his last hurrah he will be stopped and put out of commission forever. Where will he get all these rebels from? Those un-saved people have been having babies for a thousand years. There are no abortions during Christ's reign. Thus, giving satan multitudes from all over the world. "The number of whom is as the sand of the sea" (Rev. 20:8).

They surround The new Jerusalem and what do they get for their efforts? Fire, Holy Fire! They are killed. Their leader, satan, is cast into the lake of fire and brimstone. There is no trial, no chance to explain his actions, just punishment. Christ Jesus said: "The prince of this world is judged" (John 16:11). Notice it says; "where the beast (a-c) and the false prophet are" (Rev. 20:10). The two of them have been there for a thousand years and have not burned up. The verse says "are" this means still there, tormented in the flames. Now satan, the last of their unholy trinity, joins them to "be tormented day and night for ever and ever." he is not there as ruler over a hellish kingdom, but as an inmate in a supernatural fire to be tormented forever!

The last thing satan or anyone else will do is; "Wherefore God also hath highly exalted him, and given him a name which is above every name: That at the name of Jesus every knee should bow, of things in heaven, and things in earth, and things under the earth" (Philippians 2:9–10). satan, and everyone who followed him, will bow the knee at the name of Jesus, then tossed into the lake of fire. GLORY!

THE GREAT WHITE THRONE JUDGEMENT

Let us now look at the second death or "eternal separation from God!"

"But the rest of the dead lived not again until the thousand years were finished. This is the first resurrection. Blessed and holy is he that hath part in the first resurrection: on such the second death hath no power, but they shall be priests of God and of Christ, and shall reign with him a thousand years" (Rev. 20:5-6).

All the saints who went to heaven in the rapture including the tribulation saints, are counted in the first resurrection. Christ Jesus called it: "The resurrection of life" (John 5:29). They are holy and are regarded as priests of God and cannot be influenced by satan, evil spirits or the flesh. At the great white throne judgment, all the unsaved living people will be there. The unsaved dead will be resurrected and prepared for "the second death." The term second death means "eternal" separation from The Most High God. Christ Jesus called it: "The resurrection of damnation" (John 5:29).

"I beheld till the thrones were cast down, and the Ancient of days did sit, whose garment was white as snow, and the hair of his head like the pure wool: his throne was like the fiery flame, and his wheels as burning fire. A fiery stream issued and came forth from before him: thousand thousands ministered unto him, and ten thousand times ten thousand stood before him: the judgment was set, and the books were opened" (Daniel 7:9–10).

Notice the following in the above verse. "Thousand thousands ministered unto him, and ten thousand times ten thousand stood before him." This is a spiritual picture of the great white throne judgment and it shows what Jesus said; "Enter ye in at the strait gate: for wide is the gate, and broad is the way, that leadeth to destruction, and many there be which go in thereat: Because strait is the gate, and narrow is the way, which leadeth unto life, and few there be that find it" (Matt. 7:13-14).

Daniel saw The Most High God sit on the judgment seat with thousand thousands ministering unto him. But ten thousand times ten thousand stand before Him to be judged. They have no mediator, no one to plead for mercy, no one to give their side of events, or to present mitigating circumstances. No advocate to tell of their rough childhood or how terrible their alcoholic or drugged parents were, or the abuse they suffered. It is too late for intercession. Jesus wants to be your advocate now. At the great white throne judgment, He is The Judge.

The wicked of the wicked shall be there. King Saul, King Omri, Hitler, Stalin, Lenin, and others the worst of the worst, highest of the highest, and the lowest of the lowest all who have rejected the salvation of Christ Jesus will be there. Will you?

The morally good person will be there. The billionaire philanthropists who gave millions to good causes will be there. Popes, bishops, rabbis, preachers, medical doctors, reverend doctors, arch-apostles, apostles, and evangelists. So called great healers, prophets and prophetesses will be there. Plain Jane, hip flip, evil Tyrone, Betty do-gooder, and many good philanthropists will be there. The beautiful and not so beautiful, the hot and the not so hot, both rich and poor will stand on equal ground. To all who consider themselves well off financially and trust in riches read this: "For what is a man profited, if he shall gain the whole world, and lose his own soul? Or what shall a man give in exchange for his soul?" (Matt. 16:26).

Those who profess salvation, but did not truly live it, they will be there. Read this indictment: "Enter ye in at the strait gate: for wide is the gate, and broad is the way, that leadeth to destruction, (hell) and many there be which go in thereat; Because strait (straight) is the gate, and narrow is the way, which leadeth unto life, and few there be that find it. Not everyone that saith unto me, Lord, Lord, shall enter into the kingdom of heaven; but he that doeth the will of my Father which is in heaven. Many will say to me in that day, Lord, Lord, have we not prophesied in thy name? And in thy name done many wonderful works. And then will I profess unto them, I never knew you: depart from me, ye that work iniquity" (Matt. 7:13–14, 21–23)).

Doing good works will not get you into heaven; being a healer will not get you into heaven. Attending church every-time the doors open will not get you into heaven. Trusting in a certain day or even preaching will not get you into heaven.

Getting baptized by itself may get your name in the preacher's book, but not in the books of Christ Jesus. The way to heaven is a straight and narrow way. It is not wide enough for your denominational creed. Nor is it broad enough for; buddha, hare Krishna, mohammed, scientology, christian scientist, jahovah's witnesses, nor mormons. Christ Jesus "The Narrow Way" will not listen to your saying three thousand hail Marys or notice how many thousands of eucharist ceremonies you may have participated in. Allowing yourself to be nailed to a cross will hurt and it may impress others, but the act will not impress "The Narrow Way." You can crawl on your knees three times around this world, but your bloody knees will do nothing to get you to "The Narrow Way." You may pass out a million watchtower tracts, but The Narrow Way will not be impressed.

Being a whirling dervish may impress others, but it does not impress "The Narrow Way." Walking on a hot bed of coals will impress others, but not "The Narrow Way". Christ Jesus; "The Narrow Way" has no fraternal orders, secret signs or oaths, none. You can stand before "The Narrow Way" and flash all the secret signals you know, but it will not benefit you. "The Narrow Way" will not listen to "the poor widow's son" call for help. "The Narrow Way" has no "worshipful master," for He is The Worshipful Master.

Trusting in a denominational or the apostolic creed will do nothing for you. Being Baptist, Lutheran, Methodist, Roman Catholic, Church of God, Church of God in Christ, Apostolic, Adventist, Anglican, Pentecostal, Presbyterian, Episcopal or Non-denominational in and of themselves will do nothing for you.

"The Narrow Way" says, you must come the way of the cross: "But what saith it? The word is nigh thee, even in thy mouth, and in thy heart; that is, the word of faith, which we preach. That if thou shalt confess with thy mouth the Lord Jesus, and shalt believe in thine heart that God hath raised him from the dead, thou shalt be saved. For with the heart man believeth unto righteousness; and with the mouth confession is made unto salvation" (Romans 10:8–10).

You must confess with your mouth. This means to speak a promise and acknowledge a covenant vow in which you will trust, obey and yield to Christ Jesus. You must believe Christ Jesus is God who came in the flesh to save you from your sins. Don't try to understand it just agree with The Father, He is right and you are wrong. "He that hath received his (Jesus) testimony hath set to his (you) seal that God is true" (John 3:33). Ask forgiveness of your sins now: "Neither is there salvation in any other: for there is none other name under heaven given among men, whereby we must be saved" (Acts 4:12).

The Bible says Jesus is the only name that will get you into heaven. This is a walk of faith: "For by grace are ye saved through faith; and that not of yourselves: it is the gift of God. Not of works, lest any man should boast" (Ephesians 2:8–9). We have millions of people bowing to cows, snakes, statues, men, and other foolishness. Forget that stuff and bow your knee to Christ Jesus, and say "Jesus is Lord."

Listen to what narrow minded Christ Jesus said; "Jesus saith unto him, I am the way, the truth, and the life: no man cometh unto the Father, but by me. If ye had known me, ye should have known my Father also: and from henceforth ye know him, and have seen him" (John 14:6-7). There is no other way to The Father. None. You must come the way of the cross.

"For the Father judgeth no man, but hath committed all judgment unto the Son: That all men should honor the Son, even as they honor the Father. He that honoreth not the Son honoreth not the Father which hath sent him" (John 5:22–23). Failure to honor Jesus is the same as failing to honor The Most High God. It does not matter what your so-called holy book says. You must honor Christ Jesus as God.

Are you are saved? If not, you are working on a death sentence and you are in the valley of decision, who will you serve? Serve The Most High God and let Him become your Father and advocate. Or will you serve satan, and join him in the lake of fire. You only have two choices, no middle ground. "The lord is not slack concerning his promise, as some men count slackness; but is long-suffering to us-ward, not willing that any should perish, but that all should come to repentance" (2 Peter 3:9). "For Christ also hath once suffered for sins. The just for the unjust, that he might bring us to God, being put to death in the flesh, but quickened by the Spirit" (1 Peter 3:18).

"How shall we escape, if we neglect so great salvation; which at the first began to be spoken by the Lord, and was confirmed unto us by them that heard him" (Hebrews 2:3). Neglect is the greatest sin you can commit. If you do not believe on The Lord Jesus Christ, you are already condemned. Jesus preached; "He that believeth on him (Jesus) is not condemned: but he that believeth not is condemned already, because he hath not believed in the name of the only begotten Son of God" (John 3:18).

No, you will not be perfect and if you worry about sinning after you are saved, the following was written for you: "If we say that we have no sin, we deceive ourselves, and the truth is not in us. If we confess our sins, he is faithful and just to forgive us our sins, and to cleanse us from all unrighteousness. If we say that we have not sinned, we make him a liar, and his word is not in us" (1 John 1:8-10). We are all sinners, but you must become a "sinner saved by grace."

To those who are self-righteous and say; "I believe in God." The Bible has this for you. "Thou believest that there is one God; thou doest well: the devils also believe, and tremble" (James 2:19). Saying I believe in God makes you no better than a devil. Why? devils believe and tremble, but they do not serve The Most High. They are evil angels who rebelled with satan.

"And I John saw these things, and heard them. And when I had heard and seen, I fell down to worship before the feet of the angel

THE SPIRIT OF THE ANTI-CHRIST

which showed me these things. Then saith he unto me, See thou do it not: for I am thy fellow servant, and of thy brethren the prophets, and of them which keep the sayings of this book: worship God" (Rev. 22:8-9). Righteous angels must also obey the teaching of the Bible.

Sinners who have not repented cannot receive The Most High's love. They get His mercy, but His love is in; "Nor height, nor depth, nor any other creature, shall be able to separate us from the love of God, which is in Christ Jesus our Lord" (Romans 8:39). The Love of The Most High God is in Christ Jesus and when you accept Christ Jesus as Lord and Savior, then, and only then, do you have The full Love of God. Until you do this you are only getting His mercy; "That ye may be the children of your Father which is in heaven: for he maketh his sun to rise on the evil and on the good, and sendeth rain on the just and on the unjust" (Matt. 5:45).

I have heard many Christian leaders say, "God loves everybody," or "God hates the sin, but loves the sinner." Read the following; "God judgeth the righteous, and God is angry with the wicked every day (Psalm 7:11). "There is no peace, saith the Lord, unto the wicked" (Isaiah 48:22). He that believeth on the Son hath everlasting life: and he that believeth not the Son shall not see life; but the wrath of God abideth on him" (John 3:36).

"Ye adulterers and adulteresses, know ye not that the friendship of the world is enmity with God? Whosoever therefore will be a friend of the world is the enemy of God" (James 4:4).

"For if, when we were enemies, we were reconciled to God by the death of his son, much more, being reconciled, we shall be saved by his life" (Romans 5:10).

"For many walk, of whom I have told you often, and now tell you even weeping, that they are the enemies of the cross of Christ: Whose end is destruction, whose God is their belly (flesh), and whose glory is in their shame, who mind earthly things" (Philippians 3:18-19).

And if that is not enough read the following; "That at that time ye were without Christ, being aliens from the common-wealth of Israel, and strangers from the covenants of promise, having no hope, and without God in the world:" (Ephesians 2:12).

"And you, that were sometime alienated and enemies in your mind by wicked works, yet now hath he reconciled" (Colossians 1:21).

"For to be carnally minded (un-saved) is death: but to be spiritually minded is life and peace. Because the carnal mind is enmity against God: for it is not subject to the law of God neither indeed can be" (Romans 8:6–7).

Enemy and enmity means the same thing you are oppose to God, and God is opposed to you. You can Greek this, Latin it, or get the Hebrew tense, if you are not saved and been reconciled to God by the blood of Jesus Christ, you are an enemy of The Most High and Holy Father! "He that believeth on the Son hath everlasting life: and he that believeth not the Son shall not see life; but the wrath of God abideth on him" (John 3:36).

The prayers of unbelievers are not even heard; "If I regard iniquity (sin) in my heart, the Lord will not hear me" (Psalm 66:18).

"Behold, the Lord's hand is not shortened, that it cannot save; neither his ear heavy, that it cannot hear: But your iniquities have separated between you and your God, and your sins have hid his face from you, that he will not hear" (Isaiah 59:1–2).

"Now we know that God heareth not sinners: but if any man be a worshiper of God, and doeth his will, him he heareth" (John 9:31).

"For the eyes of the Lord are over the righteous, and his ears are open unto their prayers: but the face of the Lord is against them that do evil" (1 Peter 3:12).

"For when we were yet without strength, in due time Christ died for the ungodly. For scarcely for a righteous man will one die: yet peradventure for a good man some would even dare to die. But God commendeth (sent) his love toward us, in that, while we were yet sinners, Christ died for us" (Romans 5:6-8). Christ died so that we could enter into the fullness of The Most High Father's love.

The first prayer He hears from sinners is when they admit they are wrong and The Most High is right. "But now in Christ Jesus ye who sometimes were far off made nigh (near) by the blood of Christ. For he is our peace" (Ephesians 2:12–14). The scriptures show the sinner only gets The Father's mercy. They do not get His full Love until they agree with Him and accept Jesus Christ as Savior.

Everlasting fire was not made for mankind. If you end up there, you will be there as an intruder. An intruder is someone occupying a place not belonging to them. "Then shall he say also unto them on the left hand, Depart from me, ye cursed, into everlasting fire prepared for the devil and his angels" (Matt. 25:41). This fire was made for satan and his crew, not for us. Hell and the lake of fire were not made for us but when you follow satan he becomes your father and you will follow your father into the lake of fire.

With so many people following satan, hell needed to do some remodeling; "Therefore hell hath enlarged herself, and opened her mouth without measure: and their glory, and their multitude, and their pomp, and he that rejoiceth, shall descend into it" (Isaiah 5:14). Hell had to begin a continuous enlarging program due to the multitudes blindly following satan and his mystery of iniquity. No preacher can preach you into heaven at your funeral. You cannot be prayed out of, nor can someone pay your way out of hell. Jesus has done it already in Romans 4:25, "Who was delivered for our offense, and was raised again for our justification."

Christ Jesus will have on His body the only man-made things allowed in heaven the scars from the cross: "And after eight days again his disciples were within, and Thomas with them: then came Jesus, the doors being shut, and stood in the midst, and, said, Peace be unto you. Then saith he to Thomas, Reach hither thy finger, and behold my hands; and reach hither thy hand and thrust it into my side: and be not faithless, but believing" (John 20:26–27). Accept those scars as payment for your sins now or you will pay for your own sins, but it will not get you into heaven.

Read this; "For then must he often have suffered since the foundation of the world: but now once in the end of the world hath he appeared to put away sins by the sacrifice of himself. As is appointed unto men once to die, but after this the judgment: So Christ was once offered to bear the sins of many; and unto them that look for him shall he appear the second time without sin unto salvation" (Hebrews 9:26-28). Did you notice the following words The Most High placed

THE GREAT WHITE THRONE JUDGEMENT

in verse 26: "Once in the end of the world." As far as He is concern we are in; "the end of the world." Christ Jesus actions brought us to; "the end of the world."

"And I saw a great white throne, and him that sat on it, from whose face the earth and heaven fled away; and there was found no place for them. And I saw the dead, small and great, stand before God; and the books were opened: and another book was opened, which is the book of life: and the dead were judged out of those things which were written in the books, according to their works. And the sea gave up the dead which were in it; and death and hell delivered up the dead which were in them: and they were judged every man according to their works. And death and hell were cast into the lake of fire. This is the second death. And whosoever was not found written in the book of life, was cast into the lake of fire" (Rev. 20:11–15).

Here is what is happening. The Most High God, who we know as Christ Jesus is on the great white throne to pronounce sentence on those who rejected His way. All unsaved people from Adam's day until He says; "it is done" (Rev. 16:17), must stand before Him; rich and poor alike, no difference. No one can go to the back of the courtroom and try to bribe someone, because there is no one to bribe. His power is so great the sky and the earth flee from before Him.

The books are open; all the books The Father used to record our actions are open. Within these books, everything you have ever done or said will be there. Even the secret places you went thinking no one saw you, and those secret acts you committed. "For God shall bring every work into judgment, with every secret thing, whether it be good, or whether it be evil" (Ecclesiastes 12:14).

"But I say unto you, That every idle word that men shall speak, they shall give account thereof in the day of judgment. For by thy words thou shalt be justified, and by thy words thou shalt be condemned" (Matt. 12:36–37). No judging on a curve, it will be straightforth. The most important book opened will be "The Book of Life."

The Most High God has a book with the name of everyone who are saved written in it. It is called "The Book of Life." At birth, your name is placed in the Book of Life. When you get to the age of accountability (this age is different for everyone due to your level of maturity) and are held accountable for your sins and refuse to get saved and confess your sins, your name is taken out of the book.

Let's look at this; "Yet now, if thou wilt forgive their sin; and if not, blot me, I pray thee, out of thy book which thou hast written, And the Lord said unto Moses, Whosoever hath sinned against me, him will I blot out of my book" (Exodus 32:32–33).

"Let them be blotted out of the book of the living, and not be written with the righteous" (Psalm 69:28).

"Whose names are in the book of life" (Philippians 4:3).

"He that overcometh, the same shall be clothed in white raiment; and I will not blot out his name out of the book of life, but I will confess his name before my Father, and before his angels" (Rev. 3:5).

"And all that dwell upon the earth shall worship him, whose names are not written in the book of life of the Lamb slain from the foundation of the world" (Rev. 13:8).

"The beast that thou sawest was, and is not; and shall ascend out of the bottomless pit, and go into perdition: and they that dwell on the earth shall wonder whose names were not written in the book of life from the foundation of the world, when they behold the beast that was, and is not, and yet is" (Rev. 17:8).

"And if any man shall take away from the words of the book of this prophecy, God shall take away his part out of the book of life, and out of the holy city, and from the things which are written in this book" (Rev. 22:19). When you agree with The Most High and get saved your name is returned to "The book of Life."

Paul tells us of this; "For I was alive without the law once: but when the commandment came, sin revived, and I died. And the commandment, which was ordained to life, I found to be unto death" (Romans 7:9-10). What does this mean? Paul is saying, when he was a child and had not reached the age of accountability. The law of sin and death did not have an impact on him. But once he reached the age of accountability, sin came alive and he was now held accountable for his sins. The Bible teaches; "Moreover your little ones, which ye said should be a prey, and your children, which in that day had no knowledge between good and evil, they shall go in thither, and unto them will I give it, and they shall possess" (Deuteronomy 1:39). The Blood of Christ Jesus is the only way for you to get your name back into His Book of Life.

Back to our scene. Every unsaved body in the grave will be brought back to life and united with its soul which has been in hell; to stand before Him. No one will be missed. All the bodies of those people who were vaporized during the bombing of Hiroshima and Nagasaki, He knows where every atom is located. From the dust of the earth, He will bring atom to atom, cell to cell, all back to flesh.

Those bodies long decayed at the bottom of all lakes and oceans. He will make them whole, to be united with their souls which have been in hell for all these many years. Those bodies left to rot on all battle fields will be brought together with their souls. He is The Most High God; He has the power to do this; "Behold I am the Lord, The God of all flesh: is there anything too hard for me" (Jeremiah 32:27).

Those Roman soldiers who slapped and beat Christ Jesus, will stand before Him. They will realize, if they have not already realized, that they slapped and beat The Most High God in human form. Those Scribes, Sadducees, Pharisees, Pilate, Herod and others will realize, if they have not already realized, Christ Jesus is The I Am. Hitler will realize if he has not already realized Christ Jesus is The only Savior. All cultist, agnostics, and atheist will realize if they have not already realized Christ Jesus is The Truth and The Only Way.

Everyone at this throne will be judged by their "works." This is in contrast to "faith." The word "faith" is not mention; it is too late for faith. "And you, that were sometime alienated and enemies in your mind by wicked works, yet now hath he reconciled" (Colossians 1:21). Without faith, your works are wicked no matter how well intentioned they were; "But without faith it is impossible to please him: for he that cometh to God must believe that he is, and that he is a rewarder of them that diligently seek him (Hebrews 11:6). "For whatsoever is not of faith is sin" (Romans 14:23).

And: "For by grace are ye saved through faith; and that not of yourselves: it is the gift of God: Not of works, lest any man should boast" (Ephesians 2:8-9). You will not be able to pat yourself on the shoulder and brag to The Most High about your good works. Works without faith will not get you into The Kingdom of The Most High God: "For the wages of sin is death: but the gift of God is eternal life through Jesus Christ our Lord" (Romans 6:23).

Once the sentence is pronounced, they are cast into the lake of fire, where satan, the a-c, and the false prophet are. All the evil angels who rebelled with satan are taken from the bottomless pit and cast into this lake; "For if God spared not the angels that sinned, but cast them down to hell and delivered them into chains of darkness, to be reserved unto judgment" (2 Peter 2:4).

There are no ceremonies, no good-byes, just into the lake of fire; "Be not deceived; God is not mocked: for whatsoever a man soweth, that shall he also reap. For he that soweth to his flesh shall of the flesh reap corruption; but he that soweth to the Spirit shall of the Spirit reap life everlasting" (Galatians 6:7-8). When you plant (sow), you harvest (reap) always more than you sowed.

"In flaming fire taking vengeance on them that know not God, and that obey not the Gospel of our Lord Jesus Christ. Who shall be punished with everlasting destruction from the presence of the Lord, and from the glory of his power" (2 Thess. 1:8–9).

Some of you know you are going to have a very large sin harvest and you are praying for crop failure. But that is a wasted prayer, instead you need to ask forgiveness of your sins and get saved. Once you are saved you automatically get crop insurance, because your sins are done away; "As far as the east is from the west, so far hath he removed our transgression from us" (Psalm 103:12). Look at a world globe, you can find the North pole and the South pole. But you can't find the East pole or the West pole. "For I will be merciful to their unrighteousness. And their sins and their iniquities will I remember no more" (Heb. 8:12).

You may ask why they are taken from hell to be cast into the lake of fire. You may think all fire is the same. Hell can be compared to the local or county jail. A person is held there until he or she is given a trial and once convicted they are sent to the state penitentiary to serve their sentence. Hell is the local jail with no bail, and the lake of fire is the penitentiary with no parole. And you will be there for

THE GREAT WHITE THRONE JUDGEMENT

more than a century. You will not burn up after a few years, you will burn forever, in a supernatural body, by supernatural fire. Jesus called it: "Cast into outer darkness: there shall be weeping and gnashing of teeth" (Matt. 8:12).

"Who shall be punished with everlasting destruction from the presence of the Lord, and from the glory of his power" (2 Thess. 1:9). It is the darkest, loneliest, and the hottest fire in the universe.

Even the spirit of death is placed there: "The last enemy that shall be destroyed is death" (1 Cor. 51:26). So; who all are incarcerated in this lake?"

"But the fearful, unbelieving, and the abominable, and murderers, and whoremongers, and sorcerers, and idolaters, and all lairs, shall have their part in the lake which burneth with fire and brimstone: which is the second death" (Rev. 21:8).

Read the following: "Know ye not that the unrighteous shall not inherit the kingdom of God? Be not deceived: neither fornicators, nor idolaters, nor adulterers, nor effeminate, nor abusers of themselves with mankind (LGBT), Nor thieves, nor covetous, nor drunkards, nor revilers, nor extortioners, shall inherit the kingdom of God. And such were some of you: but ye are washed, but ye are sanctified, but ye are justified in the name of the Lord Jesus and by the Spirit of our God" (1 Cor. 6:9–11).

"Now the works of the flesh are manifest, which are these; adultery, fornication, uncleanness, lasciviousness (indecent dress and acts), Idolatry, witchcraft, hatred, variance, emulations, wrath, strife, seditions, heresies, Envyings, murders, drunkenness, revellings, and such like: of the which I told you in time past, that they which do such things shall not inherit the kingdom of God" (Galatians 5:19–21).

Jesus spoke a lot about hell. He spoke more on hell than He did on heaven. So it must be a place to avoid and if hell is bad, then the lake of fire will be worse. The last thing each of them will do is at The Name of Christ Jesus, they will bow the knee before Him. "That at the name of Jesus every knee should bow, of things in heaven, and things in earth, and things under the earth; And that every tongue should confess that Jesus Christ is Lord, to the glory of God the Father" (Philippians 2:10–11).

And who will not be an inmate in this second death? "And he that sat upon the throne said, Behold, I make all things new. And he said unto me, Write: for these words are true and faithful. And he said unto me, It is done, I am Alpha and Omega, the beginning and the end. I will give unto him that is athirst of the fountain of the water of life freely. He that overcometh shall inherit all things; and I will be his God, and he shall be my son" (Rev. 21:5–7).

Mark 13:32–37 tells us to Watch and be ready for we know not when our master shall return. Luke 19:13 says "to occupy till He comes," this means we are to do His business until He comes back. Ezekiel 33:1–16 and 2 Peter 3:1–18 tells us what kind of business we must be about. We must grow in grace, faith and give warning to those who are not saved. "Nevertheless when the Son of man cometh, shall He find faith on the earth" (Luke 18:8). Forget all the religious books and gimmicks. Get in your Bible and live it.

"Seventy weeks are determined upon thy people and upon thy holy city, to finish the transgression, and make an end to sins. And to make reconciliation for iniquity, and to bring in everlasting righteousness, and to seal up the vision and prophecy, and to anoint the most Holy" (Daniel 9:24). As I have shown you, this verse will now be complete.

Some of you may be asking, "Preacher, do you believe all this you have written?" To which I say: "Yes, I do, with my whole spirit, soul, and body, I believe every word of it."

"For I am not ashamed of the gospel of Christ; for it is the power of God unto salvation to everyone that believeth; to the Jew first, and also to the Greek" (Romans 1:16). The Most High put it in His Holy Bible and I believe God. But the question is, do you believe The Most High God? Your very soul depends on your answer.

I want you to look up the following scriptures: Rev. 1:1, Rev. 12:12, Rev. 17:10, Rev. 22:6, Rev. 22:7, Rev. 22:12, Rev. 22:20. Notice the words; short, shortly or come quickly. Time is not on your side The Lord Christ Jesus could come any day. Or you could die any day. Death has no favorites, it is always prowling and peeping: "For death is come up into our windows, and is entered into our palaces, to cut off the children from without, and the young men from the streets" (Jeremiah 9:21).

Death is peeping in your window right now. Every missed heartbeat, every pain, every stiff joint, every gray hair, every accident, every birthday and each night you lay down death is peeping to see if you are next. And you can't stop it or shoo death away: "There is no man that hath power over the spirit to retain the spirit; neither hath he power in the day of death: and there is no discharge in that war; neither shall wickedness deliver those that are given to it" (Ecclesiastes 8:8). You can't escape death by running and hiding: "Whereas ye know not what shall be on the morrow. For what is your life? It is even a vapor, that appeareth for a little time, and then vanisheth away" (James 4:14). Death maybe peeping in your window right now or looking over your shoulder as you read this book.

The Most High God said: "And he that sat upon the throne said, Behold, I make all things new. And he said unto me, Write: for these words are true and faithful. And he said unto me, It is done. I am Alpha and Omega, the beginning and the end. I will give unto him that is a thirst of the fountain of the water of life freely. He that overcometh shall inherit all things; and I will be his God, and he shall be my son" (Rev. 21:5-7).

To those saints who are trying to eat at both tables: "Ye cannot drink the cup of the Lord, and the cup of devils: ye cannot be partaker of the Lord's table, and of the table of devils" (1 Cor. 10:21). This is what Lot tried to do. And when destruction was about to come his sons-in-law did the following: "And Lot went out, and spake unto his sons-in-law, which married his daughters, and said, Up, get you out of this place; for the Lord will destroy this city. But he seemed as one that mocked unto his sons-in-law" (Genesis 19:14). Lot did not live like someone serving The Most High God, so why should they have believed him. They did not take Lot serious. Would your family and friends take you serious?

If you are not saved Read on: "For the time is come that judgment must begin at the house of God: and if it first begin at us, what shall the end be of them that obey not the gospel of God? And if the righteous scarcely be saved, where shall the ungodly and the sinner appear" (1 Peter 4:17-18)? What does this verse means? If we the righteous ones saved by The Precious Blood of Christ Jesus scarcely or barely going to make it into His kingdom, what is the status of you who are unsaved? Hopelessness!

Your only hope; "I have heard thee in a time accepted and in the day of salvation have I succored thee behold, now is the accepted time; behold, Now is the day of salvation. Today if ye will hear this voice, harden not your hearts" (2 Cor. 6:2). Today is the day of salvation, not tomorrow, not when you get older, not after you get married, not after you sow a few wild oats; but today is the day of salvation. Please do not think of The Most High as the kindly old gray haired man upstairs who plans on allowing everyone in to His kingdom, no matter what kind of life they have lived. This is a lie from satan. You must be Saved.

Read the following: "God, who at sundry times and in divers manners spake in time past unto the fathers by the prophets, Hath in these last days spoken unto us by his Son, whom he hath appointed heir of all things, by whom also he made the worlds" (Heb. 1:1).

"Therefore we ought to give the more earnest heed to the things which we have heard, lest at any time we should let them slip" (Heb. 2:1). The wide road to hell is paved with the stones of good intentions and lines of neglect.

Look again at Hebrews 1:2: "Hath in these last days."

"Now once in the end of the world hath he appeared to put away sin by the sacrifice of himself" (Hebrews 9:26). The Most High considers these as the last days. Do you?

One last scripture for you who are not saved: "The Lord is not slack concerning his promise, as some men count slackness; but is long-suffering to us-ward, not willing that any should perish, but that all should come to repentance. But the day of the Lord will come as a thief in the night; in the which the heavens shall pass way with a great noise, and the elements shall melt with fervent heat, the earth also and the works that are therein shall be burned up. And account that the long-suffering of our Lord is salvation; even as our beloved brother Paul also according to the wisdom given unto him hath written unto you; As also in all his epistles, speaking in them of these things; in which are some things hard to be understood, which they that are unlearned and unstable wrest (wrestle), as they do also the other scriptures, unto their own destruction" (2 Peter 3:9–10, 15–16).

You have reached the age you are because The Most High is delaying your death. Stop wrestling with His word, just believe and be saved. The Most High, is giving you time to repent. Admit you are wrong and He is right. Daniel was told to seal some of the thing he wrote. But John was told: "I am Alpha and Omega the first and the last: and, What thou seest write in a book and send it to the seven churches... Write the things which thou hast seen, and the things which are, and the things which shall be hereafter:" (Rev.1:11,19).

To those saints who are discouraged and in despair, because mankind's wickedness seems to reach new heights and you wonder if The Father cares. Well, Rev. is here to let us know there will be an end to sin and you need to look up 'for your redemption draws near." Read the following; "We are bound to thank God always for you, brethren, as it is meet, because that your faith growth exceedingly, and the charity of every one of you all toward each other aboundeth; So that we ourselves glory in you in the churches of God for your patience and faith in all your persecutions and tribulations that ye endure: Which is a manifest token of the righteous judgement of God, that ye may be counted worthy of the kingdom of God, for which ye also suffer: Seeing it is a righteous thing with God to recompense tribulation to them that trouble you; **And to you who are troubled rest with us,** when the Lord Jesus shall be revealed from heaven with his mighty angels. In flaming fire taking vengeance on them that know not God, and that obey not the gospel of our Lord Jesus Christ: Who shall be punished with everlasting destruction from the presence of the Lord, and from the glory of his power" (2 Thess. 1:3-9). This life on earth is the worse you will ever get, in heaven you will never, never, ever have a bad day. Take a stand and stand with the full armor of God."

Thank you for allowing me to share this with you.

Now the blessing promised to us: "Blessed is he that readeth, and they that hear the words of this prophecy, and keep those things which are written therein: for the time is at hand" (Rev. 1:3).

"And he said unto me, These saying are faithful and true: and the Lord God of the holy prophets sent his angel to show unto his servants the things which must shortly be done. Behold I come quickly: blessed is he that keepeth the saying of the prophesy of this book. And he saith unto me, Seal not the sayings of the prophecy of this book: for the time is at hand. He that is unjust, let him be unjust still: and he which is filthy, let him be filthy still: and he that is righteous, let him be righteous still: and he that is holy let him be holy still. And, behold, I come quickly; and my reward is with me, to give every man according as his work shall be. I am Alpha and Omega, the beginning and the end, the first and the last. Blessed are they that do his commandments, that they may have right to the tree of life, and may enter in through the gates into the city. For without are dogs, sorcerers, and whoremongers, and murderers, and idolaters, and whosoever loveth and maketh a lie. I Jesus have sent mine angel to testify unto you these things in the churches. I am the root and the offspring of David, and the bright and morning star. And the Spirit and the bride say, Come. And let him that heareth say, Come, And let him that is athirst come. And whosoever will, let him take the water of life freely. For I testify unto every man that heareth the words of the prophecy of this book, if any man shall add unto these things, God shall add unto him the plagues that are written in this book: And if any man shall take away from the words of the book of this prophecy, God shall take away his part out of the book of life, and out of the holy city, and from the things which are written in this book. He which testifieth these things saith, Surely I come quickly. A-men Even so come, Lord Jesus. The grace of our Lord Jesus Christ be with you all. A-men" (Rev. 22:6-7, 10-21).

EVEN SO, COME, LORD JESUS. May the grace of our Lord Jesus Christ be with you all, AMEN. MARANATA (The Lord is coming).

GLOSSARY

Ancient of Days: An old Testament name for God. Used in the book of Daniel.

Anti-christ: Commonly refers to the man, satan will infuse with the spirit of the a-c in the coming last days. Along with the False prophet making an unholy trinity. Also called the beast, that Wicked, son of perdition, the evil one, man of sin, that wicked one, and king of fierce countenance.

Angels: Spiritual servants of God. There are also evil angels who rebelled with satan, commonly referred to as demons.

Eunuchs: Men or women who has given themselves to the service of a master and have forgone all sexual pleasures. They may be born eunuchs, surgically made eunuchs, or decide on their own they will live as eunuchs.

Falling Away: A time when mankind will turn from the truth of God's word. And follow their own mind or the teaching of satan. It is a sign of the coming of Our Father.

Great White Throne Judgment: The last judgment for all unsaved mankind.

Great Tribulation: A time when God's full wrath, satan wrath, and man's wrath is released upon the earth.

Hundred-Forty-Four-Thousand: Twelve thousand Jewish men chosen from each of the twelve tribes of Israel. They are all male virgins. There are no females in the group.

Mystery Babylon: A representation of the totality of an all-consuming, ever expanding evil upon the earth. Represented as a woman and works in conjunction with the mystery of iniquity.

Mystery of God: The Most High God's dealing with mankind throughout time. Culminating with the birth, life, death, resurrection, and return of Jesus Christ.

GLOSSARY

Mystery of Iniquity: Mankind's full evil rebellion, an ever expanding, all-consuming force of evil. Works in conjunction with Mystery Babylon.

Parenthetical Phrase: Background information the Bible gives when telling of certain events.

Rapture: The removing of the saints right before the coming of the a-c. It may be the catalyst for the infusing of the a-c by satan.

Reprobate: One whose mind disregards the working and commands of God.

Salt: The Bible uses this term to indicate Godly discipline in all saints.

satan: The leader of all rebellion on the earth. Also called Lucifer, great red dragon, serpent, enemy of our soul, god of this world, prince of the world, deceiver, father of lies and the devil.

Spiritual Adultery: Committed by anyone who places something or someone before The Most High God.

ABOUT THE AUTHOR

I have studied the Bible for the past thirty years with the goal; "Study to show thyself approved unto God, a workman that needeth not to be ashamed, rightly dividing the word of truth (1 Tim. 2:15). Thus enabling me to write the most comprehensive and compelling study on the anti-christ." It is not a rehash of other end-time books but a biblical look at scriptures interpreting scriptures without taking them out of context."

CPSIA information can be obtained
at www.ICGtesting.com
Printed in the USA
BVHW072048240123
656983BV00005B/155